THE DEMONISM of the AGES, SPIRIT OBSESSIONS so Common IN SPIRITISM, ORIENTAL and OCCIDENTAL OCCULTISM

By J. M. PEEBLES, M. D., A. M.

FOURTH EDITION

AUTHOR OF

The Seers of the Ages
What Is Spiritualism, and Who Are These Spiritualists?
Three Journeys Around the World
Immortality, and the Employment of Spirits
The Christ Question Settled
Death Defeated, or the Secret of Keeping Young
Reincarnation Discussed
Spiritualism vs. Materialism
Vaccination a Curse
Did Jesus Christ Exist? Etc., etc., etc.

INTRODUCTION.

A General Statement with Inquiries and Warnings.

I. Spirits, not necessarily gods or devils, are simply human beings released from their mortal bodies.

II. The event termed death neither spiritually exalts nor degrades a human being.

III. Spirits, conscious entities, to maintain their identities, must have taken with them consciousness, memory, disposition and tendencies.

IV. There are as many kinds, classes and castes of spirits in the spirit world, which lies over and all about us, as there are kinds and conditions of mortals on earth.

V. Hypnotism in this life, and hypnotic trance from the spirit spheres, being intimately allied, there are many phenomena connected with somnambulism and temporary loss of identity, clearly pointing to obsession as the only rational explanation. Many of the obsessed are utterly ignorant of the causes of their strange impressions and unaccountable doings.

VI. Persons that liked authority, position and the power to domineer over others in this life carry their monarchical traits into the invisible beyond, and naturally, for a time at least, become controlling, if not obsessing spirits.

VII. Sensitive individuals with negative temperaments coming within the radius of this class of spirits, become psychically influenced, and later obsessed without understanding the causes of their strange, restless, nervous conditions.

Introduction.

VIII. Earth-bound spirits are as naturally chained or held within the limits of the earth's atmosphere as lead is held to the surface of the earth by the fixed law of gravity.

IX. Different moral grades of spiritual beings can by their wills so impinge upon the auras of mortals and so hypnotically project their thoughts and their suggestions into the minds of those yet clothed in mortality, as to not only influence, not only co-ordinate the mentality, but to obsess them, and so in a measure sensuously re-live their lives on this earthly, fleshly plane.

X. Selfish, ignorant spirits thrust into spirit life by accident, or natural causes, soon seek their affinitizing associates over there, which, in regard to space, is logically here. They return to their old haunts; hence haunted houses. They also follow and if possible co-mingle their psychic emanations with certain mortals, and cling to them as fungus and moss to trees, thus vampire-like, absorbing their vitality. This is one of the worst forms of obsession.

XI. Hunters and vivisectionists, who torture animals, shoot innocent birds, attend prize fights, engage in maddened dueling, and rush fiercely into battle aflame with malice, to perish on the crimson warfields of slaughter, constitute many of the obsessional forces that blight humanity. These unredeemed personalities often incite mortals to the commission of crimes where no motive on this side of the great divide is discernible. Mrs. McKnight's case is an illustration. There was no appreciable malice—no motive for the killing of her husband, her sister and the children. She said she was sorry, but she could not help it — a clear case of obsession.

Introduction.

XII. Where, and who are the exorcists of these times competent to cast out demons as did the incarnate Christ of old, and so restore to health and harmony the afflicted? It is evident that the demon-infested cannot cast out demons.

XIII. Is it, or is it not, true that the demons of these demon-controlled mediums, being of necessity near the earth, near matter and material things, teach materialistic doctrines, rudest Darwinism, spontaneous generation, and the non-immortality of some human beings?

XIV. Are obsessions relievable? If so, by what methods,— Chinese, the Hindu or the Christian? Who have the power to bid these oppressed prisoners go free? Who are the wise, heaven-commissioned ones to transfer low, deceptive spirits into better conditioned fields with better facilities for moral growth?

XV. Can these ignorant, malicious or evil-disposed demon-spirits, often lying, pompous and pretentious, that benumb individuality, obsess, and if possible possess, be reached? Can their soul sympathies be touched by the fires of inspiration? Can their depraved natures be transformed, and so be prepared to ultimately enter into the higher Christ-spheres of the many-mansioned house of the Father?

All of these psychological questions, hypnotism, trance, witchcraft, monomania, motiveless crimes, obsessions by demoniac spirits, are discussed in this volume, solving the illustrious Blackstone's queries, found in the sixtieth article of the fourth book of "Blackstone's Commentaries." These were his words, "A sixth species of offense against God and religion, of which our ancient books are full, is a crime of which one knows not

Introduction.

what account to give. I mean the offense of witchcraft, enchantment and sorcery. To deny the possibility, nay, actual existence, of witchcraft and sorcery and demons, is at once flatly to contradict the revealed word of God in various passages of both the Old and New Testament, and the thing is itself a truth, to which every nation in the world hath borne testimony."

If a man lives hereafter,— and he *does*,— he is necessarily himself, and consciously knows himself. Individuality, God-implanted, is in its inmost, indestructible, and so identity defies the icy touch of death.

"Habits must necessarily cling to man," writes the eminent author, Dr. George A. Fuller, in his "Wisdom of the Ages" (pages 197, 198) "after the body physical has been thrown aside. No miracle occurs to transform a mortal in a moment's time from a demon to a saint. If his home has been in the realm of the carnal appetites and passions, death will not lift him out of that realm, for it can destroy only that through which these appetites and passions were gratified. Such spirits attach themselves as parasites to susceptible subjects, and through these usurped bodies seek to gratify their unhallowed desires. Inasmuch as there are malignant spirits encased in physical bodies, there are also malignant spirits denuded of physical habiliments, who disturb the equilibrium of everyday life, break down health and harass these physical bodies by sowing in them the seeds of disease. Much of the insanity of the world has been caused by unhappy suggestions and melancholy thoughts that emanate from these evil spirits that still hug the lower strata of physical life. Many times the holy sanctuary of life is not only invaded but also desecrated by these spirits. The rightful owner of the house, for the time being, is deposed and sometimes fairly driven away.

Introduction.

The most powerful adversaries man is called upon to meet are they of the invisible realms. Because of their invisibility they are the more dangerous. Their attacks are all carefully arranged and planned without our knowledge. The powers and principalities thou art called upon to wrestle with are not of this world of physical sensations, but of the great realm of the unseen, out of which everything that is proceeds.

"Not only are men directly controlled and influenced by these spirits, but the great social, political and religious worlds are invaded by them. Thus, ofttimes are they enabled to wield a powerful influence over the affairs as well as the lives of men. Here may be found in part the cause of the perversions in the great religions of the world. The social and political conditions that obtain in the world are also in a measure influenced by these denizens of the lower spheres.

"Ofttimes they invade the aura surrounding the sensitive and live on his very life. Through him they again live the old life, drink in once more its delights and revel in its associations.

"This species of vampirism is far more prevalent in the world today than many are willing to believe. The great body of men and women who are prone to investigate along the line of psychical phenomena are ever ready to hear of all that which is good and beautiful, while they turn away in disgust from him who would show them the darker side of human existence. Man cannot afford to wander longer in the realm of half-truths. In order that he may be well armed and fully equipped for the battles of life, he must know the whole truth. Therefore, he must be led to realize the dangers that confront him. Knowledge is one of the greatest sources of our strength and power. Ignorance makes

Introduction.

slaves of even the wisest of the earth. Ignorance draws dark curtains before the eyes of man, while spirit vampires creep upon him unawares. Knowledge lifts all curtains, dispels all fogs and clouds, revealing the enemy in his lair. When we know our enemy and the source of his strength, the battle is more than half won. Victory comes when we are led to realize our own strength and power.''

The observer of the times cannot doubt that we are in the closing years of a great cycle,—in the day of that great battle long prophesied between the demon hosts of a crude, selfish, atheistic spiritism, and the Christ-angel of Spiritualism,— in that period of competitions, wars and tribulations, when truth and error, whether lodged in the souls of mortals or spirits, must meet face to face for the final conflict.

The prophet is in the heavens, and this is the end of the world, age, or *aion,* the end of the world's great cycle and the opening of a new dispensation, when the "sea shall give up its dead.'' It is the day of resurrection, and the day of judgment, when every man's work must be tried by fire.

"Who is this that cometh from Edom with dyed garments from Bozrah. . . . I that speak in righteousness mighty to save. . . . I have put my spirit upon him; he shall bring forth judgment unto victory.''

Let old philosophies and' follies, truths and errors meet,— let old and modern necromancies, sorceries, magic white and black, theories good, bad and indifferent, come forth from their secret lurking places in the crypts of half-forgotten lore,— let them come forth and stand front to front with today inspirations, angel ministries and God's truth revealed in the divine book of nature.

SYNOPSIS OF CHAPTERS' CONTENTS.

		PAGE
I.	Evil Spirits and Their Influences	15
II.	Chinese Spiritism—A Demon in the Kwo Family	27
III.	Responses to the Nevius Circular Concerning the Works of Evil Spirits	37
IV.	More Demoniac possessions in China,—Responses to Circular of Inquiry	46
V.	Demoniac Possession in Japan and Korea	59
VI.	Demonical Obsessions and Possessions in India	64
VII.	More Stubborn Facts Concerning Demoniacal Possessions in Oriental Lands	68
VIII.	More Testimonies to Hindu Demonism, and the Casting Out of the Demons	79
IX.	The Demonism of the Ancient Greeks, and the Island Aborigines	89
X.	Judean Obsessions and the Actions of Demons in Jesus' Time	101
XI.	New Testament Demonism and Unclean Spirits	108
XII.	The Haunting Places of Demon Spirits	119
XIII.	Evil Spirit Obsessions Afar and Near in Our Seance Rooms	124
XIV.	Pitiful Letters from the Obsessed and Possessed	136
XV.	More Letters from Spiritist Mediums Relating to Their Obsessions	145
XVI.	Obsessions of the Early Methodists and Others	152
XVII.	Obsessions, Tobacco, Liquors and Haunted Gambling Dens	161
XVIII.	Obsessions and the False Names of Spirits.	174
XIX.	Obsessional History of a Cultured Woman	191
XX.	"Psychological Crimes" Instigated by Vicious Spirits	200
XXI.	Obsession, Witchcraft and Insanity. Is Spiritism Dangerous?	212
XXII.	Shall Men Pray for the Dead? Shall We Pray for Wicked, Obsessing Demons?	218
XXIII.	Do Demon Spirits First Hypnotize and then Obsess and Possess Mediumistic Subjects?	233
XXIV.	Can the Obsessed be Relieved, and How? Can Depraved, Obsessing Spirits Themselves be Saved?	243
XXV.	Probations and Dire, Delusive Obsessions. Their Causes	255
XXVI.	Swedenborg and His Obsessing Evil Spirits	266
XXVII.	Written Correspondence with Demons. They Here Speak for Themselves	278
XXVIII.	Internal Obsessions as Explained by a Discarnate Spirit. Further Experiences	302
XXIX.	An Obsessing Spirit Forced Away from His Victim. Spirit Imprisonments	309
XXX.	Spiritism and Demonism Versus Spiritualism and Angel Ministries	318
XXXI.	The Supernatural. The Christ. Religious Spiritualists. Obsessions	326
XXXII.	"Rescue Work on the Borderland of the Invisible World"	337
XXXIII.	Spiritualism as It Is, and the Message It Has for the World	369

PREFACE TO FOURTH EDITION

Of Demonism of the Ages and Spirit Obsessions

Some of the criticisms upon this book have been infinitely more amusing—pitiably more amusing than instructive, philosophical, or fraternal. Others from intellectual Spiritualists have been fair and manly.

The editor of the *Progressive Thinker*, Sept. 17, 1904, wrote thus:

"Dr. A. J. Davis's 'Diakka' and Dr. J. M. Peebles's great work on 'Spirit Obsessions,' are companion books; each one reflecting certain conditions existing in the spirit realms and each one should be carefully read and considered. The work of the 'Diakka,' veritable inhabitants of the spirit realms, is vividly portrayed by Dr. Davis, one of the greatest of living seers. Dr. Peebles, a scholar, a traveler, and a man of world-wide experience, presents a vast array of evidence in regard to evil spirits and their disastrous work among all classes."

Ella Wheeler Wilcox, cordially endorsing this book, wrote us as follows, from Connecticut, just before sailing for Europe:

"My Dear Doctor:
I have been reading your very valuable book and it is excellent—it is true and needed by the world. I congratulate you upon it. Oh, that the world could understand and believe—and take heed!"

Preface to Fourth Edition.

W. T. Stead wrote me thus:

"Thanks for your book on 'Spirit Obsessions.' I have read it with much interest and consider it well calculated to give more salutary warning to many who are disposed to display carelessness upon psychic subjects. . . ." In his "Review of Reviews," he said: "If any are inclined in a light, frivolous way, to dabble in Spiritualism, I would advise them to read this book on 'Spirit Obsessions' by Dr. Peebles. It is a popular survey of a difficult and dangerous subject. Its author is a veteran Spiritualist, and his testimony as to the perils surrounding the study of Spiritual phenomena is unimpeachable."

W. J. Colville, in reviewing this book upon "Obsessions," says:

"Spirits are helpers or hinderers, and it is useless to deny these multiplied testimonies that face us in this book, 'The Demonism of the Ages,' and also useless to attribute them exclusively to imperfect evidence and obscure nervous diseases after the manner of professed materialists. The facts confront us. . . . This is a book replete with such excellent counsel that it must have a noble mission to fulfill."

Dr. A. J. Davis wrote us these stirring words:

"I am downright glad and thankful that you have vigorously undertaken to 'give the devil his due,' because I believe that your 'danger signals,' when justly understood, will keep a large class of credulous and excessively impressible minds from running off the trunk-line of progression. . . . "

Dr. B. F. Austin, writing of these obsessing spirits, in his "Reason" of October, 1906, states that—

Preface to Fourth Edition.

"Multitudes in the spirit realms are still under the domination of the evil habits, passions, and appetites of their earth life. They seek to gratify these desires by controlling in part or wholly the organisms of sensitives and thus indulging again the passions of their earth lives. Sensitives have ever to wrestle against and actively oppose degrading alliances with undeveloped spirits; otherwise they become obsessed."

Reviewing this book upon "Obsessions," he further said:

"It should fill a place in every investigator's library."

Mary T. Longley wrote:

"I am convinced from my long experience with medical patients and with people who consulted my guides when I was the *Banner of Light* medium, as well as giving sittings in California, that obsessions have held many sensitives in direst bondage and that many so-called insane are actually obsessed by undeveloped spirits."

Startling Facts in Proof of Obsessions.

London Light, of March 8, 1884, has the following (much abbreviated) account regarding the long past obsession of the boy, J. Evans, ten years of age:

"A Mr. Heaton, living near by this family, frequently witnessed the boy's strange contortions and his efforts to destroy himself, also his whimsical pranks, piteous cries, and at times horrible shrieks. Mr. Heaton's prayers only enraged the boy. The doctors who attended him gave the case up as one that medicine could not reach. Finally they had recourse to solemn adjurations; during this religious ceremony, the boy's language could not be described, neither could his horrid distortions of countenance. He would spit upon every one who took active part, or pronounced the name of Jesus Christ. He was indeed possessed of an unclean, undeveloped spirit. After repeated adjurations and prayers at one time the boy rose up from a hellish rage and said, '*I am well now.*' . . .

"Within a week the unclean spirit controlled him again; growling, grinning, and biting furiously. Horrible suggestions were put into his mind by the controlling influences—unclean words issued from his mouth, and for three weeks more he wrestled with this demon. He was at length relieved through prayer and adjuration."

The truthfulness of the above account involving the desire to commit suicide was attested by several witnesses whose names in full were attached to the account. And this suicidal tendency reminds us of Hudson Tuttle who was obsessed to kill his father and also to commit suicide. As the love of life is natural, are not all suicides at least partially obsessed by either mortals or immortals?

Charles J. Anderson as an Obsessed Medium on the Pacific Coast.

Before me lies a pamphlet containing a speech delivered by Charles Anderson, at Ostrander, May 23, 1896, under the "spirit control of Abraham Lincoln." Among his first controls was a Bowery Theater actor who would dance and sing, calling for a banjo, etc. He was also purported to be entranced by Thomas Paine and other such notables according to Mr. James Jones and others who were present at the seances.

A few years ago at a campmeeting near Seattle, Wash., it was arranged for him and Mrs. Cooley to work together,

Preface to Fourth Edition.

she to give tests and he to lecture. Seances and tests were to be their system of work whilst traveling the country. Others, with Mr. G. C. Love, informed us that they often kept up their seances at this camp until one and two o'clock in the morning. About three o'oclock one morning Mr. Love was awakened in his tent and asked to hasten to young Anderson's tent, as he was entranced by a bad spirit—an obsessing spirit that would not leave—and who violently threatened to drown the medium. Hastily dressing Mr. Love, one of our solid, substantial men, found upon reaching the scene, one or two men, with Mrs. Cooley, holding this "boy medium" to prevent him from suiciding by drowning. Mr. Love, a lecturer and test-bearing medium, and gifted with an iron-like will, requested the parties present to promptly leave. This they did reluctantly. Then he took personal charge of this medium, demanding that he accompany him, which he so did. Under this new environment, Mr. Love began to talk firmly but kindly to the obsessing spirit. In substance Mr. Love now said: "You are in my charge—you must reckon with me—I am a spirit as well as yourself—the right must and shall be done—spirits are the subject of law as well as mortals. By what right are you entrancingly holding this young medium at this more than midnight hour? Why do you threaten to drown him? Do you not know that truth and goodness and right doing can only bring happiness?"

While finally sitting down by the wayside on a walk towards the seashore, this spirit was induced to tell the full story of his life. He was a suicide—he had drowned himself to get rid of life's miseries.

The Correct Account of Mr. Tuttle's Terrible Obsession from His Own Pen.

Here it is verbatim, so much of it as relates to evil spirits, appearing in the London *Medium and Daybreak*, of March

16, 1894: "The class of intelligences called by Andrew Jackson Davis 'Diakka' and by Dr. Peebles 'Gadarenes', have strong psychological power; being in close contact with earthly conditions, as is proven by the experience of all those who have investigated the subject experimentally. The result of obsession depends upon the character of the obsessing spirit. Whenever mediums surrender their will they are obsessed; that is, controlled by a will not their own, and placing their trust on an unknown power, they stand on dangerous ground. It may be that the controlling spirit is better and wiser than they, or it may be faithless and selfish.

Uncontrollable Desire to Kill.

"I was sitting with a circle of friends around a large walnut dining table, which was moving in response to questions. The intelligence claimed to be an Indian, and to the request said he would sketch his own portrait by my hand. I held a piece of chalk the size of a small marble, and automatically my hand drew a grotesque portrait. We all laughed, and my father, who had quitted the table and seated himself on the opposite side of the room, said, '*It looks like Satan.*' Instantly my mind, from light and pleasant thoughts, was changed to fierce and unutterable hatred. Anger turned the light to bloody redness, and *to kill was an uncontrollable desire, under which I threw the chalk, with the precision of a bullet, hitting the offender in the center of the forehead with a force which shivered the chalk to pieces.*

"Had it been larger, serious consequences would certainly have resulted. Of course the seance was at an end, but I could not escape that terrible influence for the evening. The study of this seance showed me the danger which menaced the sensitive, and gave the key to a class of crimes which hitherto had remained inexplicable.

"We often hear of those who have been trusted for years,

and models of honesty, fidelity, and moral uprightness, without warning, committing some heinous crime against property or person. They usually say they were seized by a sudden and uncontrollable impulse, and regretted their acts as soon as accomplished.

Suicidal Obsession.

"To apply this to the suicidal desire so prominent in the insane, I introduce another personal illustration. While sitting in a circle at the home of the venerable Dr. Underhill, I was for the time in an almost unconscious state, and recognized the presence of several Indian spirits. The roar of the Cayahoga river over the rapids could be heard in the still evening air, and to my sensitive ear was very distinct. Suddenly I was seized with a desire to rush away to the rapids and throw myself into the river. As I started up, someone caught hold of me and aroused me out of the impressible state I was in, so that I gained control of myself. Had the state been more profound and I had at once started, the end might have been different. The desire remained all the evening. I refer the immediate cause of the example to the pernicious influences of sitting in promiscuous circles.

The Treatment of Obsessions.

"A young man in the employ of a farmer became mediumistic and there was great excitement in the neighborhood, and night after night circles were held by the eager crowds. After a few days he found himself obsessed by a power which seemed determined upon his destruction. His language was dreadful to hear, and, if opposed, he became enraged, *foamed at the mouth, and sought to destroy those who spoke to him.* He would run across the fields and throw himself against the gate or fence, with a force which threatened serious injury. His friends brought him to me, hoping that they might learn how to overcome the fearful influence under which he had fallen. No sooner did he see me, nearly a fourth of a mile a way, than he rushed toward me like a wild beast, *cursing, raving, and foaming at the mouth.* At that time I did not know anything of the circumstances of the case, but as I could not escape I stood firm, and, catching his eye, held him at bay. I supposed him an escaped maniac, as I saw his friends coming in the distance; and as it had been my peculiar experience to invariably win the confidence of the insane with whom I have been brought in contact, I had no fears.

"When his friends came, they explained his case. There was only one remedy and that was for me to magnetize him and thus introduce my will in the place of that which held him. Filled with grief at his terrible condition, I exerted all my strength of purpose and after an hour found him obedient to my desires. I told his friends he was safe for two days, and then he must visit me. He became free from the influence and they neglected to return. On the evening he became again obsessed. The third day he became wilder and fiercer than at first, and barely did I succeed in controlling him. My spirit friends told them that he was in utmost danger, and if the obsession again occurred they could do no more; and, above all things, cautioned them against sitting in circles. That very evening, however, feeling fully restored and pressed to do so, he sat, and the obsession returned. This time I had not the least influence over him, and the obsessing spirit mocked my futile efforts. With brief intervals, this continued for some years until the death of the victim. It was the most decided case of obsession I ever witnessed. It would have passed for insanity, and I have no doubt that many cases which are treated as madness, would readily yield to magnetism, being strictly referable to obsession." (Hudson Tuttle.)

Hudson Tuttle as an Exorcist.

Could there be more direct evidence of evil spirits than the vicious firing of Mr. Tuttle's blood to murder his father?

Certainly he did not have in his heart an "uncontrollable desire to kill his father." And yet there are a few Spiritualists in this country and in England who deny the fact of both evil spirits and obsessions. These are speculating theorists. The late J. S. Loveland, of California, believed that all human passions and all tendencies to vice died with the body. And J. J. Morse, in the the *Two Worlds*, April 3, 1903, and Oct. 11, 1907, published the following:

> "The belief in evil spirits, human and other, has worked tremendous harm. Let us rise above it and look at the subject from the standpoint of science instead of still bowing under the influence of superstition. . . Bluntly put, if an evil spirit makes you do evil, it is because the active desire is in yourself; or otherwise you could not be made to do the evil."

In all my writings upon this important subject, I have taught that men may be obsessed by hypnotic empowered mortals as well as by immortals. I have used evil in the same one sense, whether in this, or the future word, and I have used the word salvation as meaning soul-growth; and I have used the word 'demon' as a selfish, undeveloped spirit; and the word 'death' as the mere severing of the earthly from the more refined and ethereal. And irrational and illogical asis churchianic salvation through the "atoning blood of the Lamb," I could just as readily believe it as I could believe in salvation or perfected happiness through death, coffins, and grave clothes.

Death does not clean the cranial slate of all earthly memories and earthland and relations; nor does it translate the riotous old debauchee in the twinkling of an eye into paradisaic blessedness; thus destroying conscious individuality.

The Fact of Spirit Obsessions Denied— Its Advocates should be Burned.

Doubtless nineteen twentieths of all intelligent Spiritualists believe in demoniacal obsessions; that is, psychic influences from evil-disposed spirits. And it is difficult to determine whether it is ignorance or a brazen-faced hardihood that denies the well-established fact of obsessions. Certain intolerant and bigoted spiritists, writing in Spiritualistic journals, devoid of all courtesy, blind to fraternity, and that heaven-inspired principle of brotherhood that characterises all great, generous souls, criticized and commented upon this book in the defunct *Light of Truth*, in the following style:

"I am a Spiritualist [rather a silly spiritist] and I wish that some grinning devil would impale the aforesaid Dr. Peebles on his red-hot pitchfork and dip him into the seething caldron of fear that he has prepared for so many others."

Olive Pennington, writing in the *Light of Truth*, Chicago, Sept. 17, 1906, said: "The publishing of such a book as 'Demonism of the Ages and Spirit Obsessions' is a crime; and I, for one, wish it were punishable by law. . . ."

Another writing in this same spiritistic journal used this language: "The idea of spirit obsession is a cruel, devilish, soul-wasting, demoralizing thing. It is something that should be publicly ignored."

The murderous-minded E. S. Chapman, writing for the Spiritualist press, "hoped that the demons which Dr. Peebles had roused up would sink the steamer which was to convey him to England."

Mrs. Eva Cassell, a Spiritualist writer, deliberately wrote in the *Progressive Thinker* that *"Both Dr. Peebles and his book ought to be burned in effigy. . . ."*

The fraternal, broad-minded J. R. Francis, of the *Thinker*, catching the idea of this persecuting "fire-burning" business, made and printed a cartoon in his Chicago *Thinker*. Here it is:

Dr. Peebles and His Book Mounted Upon This Pile of Leaping Fiery Flames—a Fair Exhibition of Irreligious, Materialistic Spiritism.

PREFACE.

If Kelper in studying the stars could "read the thoughts of God after him," so by candidly, conscientiously studying the manifestations of men in their normal and abnormal states, by studying the manifestations of spirits, and the various orders of invisible intelligences, can sensitive seers and savants measurably read their thoughts, grasp their aims, compass their purposes and decide upon their moral status, whether good or evil, angelic or demonic.

In the preparation of this volume, I have given more attention to the facts of trustworthy witnesses than to mere artistic expressions. It has been my sole aim to lift the mystic veil and sound the occult to its very depths; to ascertain by whom we are compassed about. Are they our loved relatives, or are they angels or devils?

The reader will observe that the pages are not filled with the mere records of investigators and the well-attested testimonies of psychic students and adepts, but they abound largely in what I have personally seen in the line of demon influences in China, India, Ceylon, Egypt, South Africa, the Pacific Islands, Asiatic Turkey, Mexico, in séances of materialistic spiritists, and in the unclean tents of crude, sectarian revivalists. Seeing is knowing.

Consciousness is a witness that cannot be silenced. Every sane man feels, knows himself to be a center of force and thought, and thought implies conscious existence, and self-consciousness is certainly the crown of individuality. To surrender it, to hypnotically, unwittingly merge it into other personalities, seen or unseen, is dangerous, if not suicidal. Self-control is doubly essential to moral growth, and to the deeper, wider dignity of humanity.

Is it safe to investigate the mist-shrouded occult? Is it wise to plunge into the unexplored realms of the invisible? If these unseen planes of being are peopled, by whom are they peopled? Are they saints, sylphs or demons? Can they affect mortals? Have they the power to hypnotize? Do they at times obsess and possess sensitive intermediaries? In exploring this vast territory, in entering this comparatively new harbor, what pilot is to be trusted?

Should one individuality ever be transferred or usurped by another? Should conscious, rational man ever be hypnotically controlled by unseen intelligences, incarnate or discarnate? Would not such a result be the merest, abject slavery? Is physical or mental slavery ever justifiable? Is the practice of promiscuous spiritism, which is only another name for necromancy, ever safe? Does it better the sensitive? Are well-balanced supersensitives, earnest saints and savants absolutely immune from evil influences? What the results of physical mediumship? Why not lift the veil?

Does converse with invisible entities conduce to the enlightenment, to the uplifting and moral betterment of its devoted patrons? Is not this a fair question? Do the Hindus and Chinese, who have believed in and practiced necromancy and spiritistic magic from time immemorial, excel all other nations in wisdom, virtue and the progressive enfoldment of all that constitutes goodness, purity and royal-souled greatness?

What does spiritism stand for? Is it demoniac? Is it only destructive and irreligious? Is its keynote iconoclasm? Is it anything more than necromancy—obsession, external, internal and infernal? If it has redeeming qualities, what are they? Are spiritism and Spiritualism synonyms? What is to be the final outcome of this movement that has stirred alike the thinking minds of the American materialist and religionist for the last half century?

This volume is designed so far as possible to answer these ever-recurring questions.

J. M. PEEBLES, M. D.

Battle Creek, Mich., Jan. 1, 1904.

CHAPTER I.

Evil Spirits and Their Influences.

ARE all men gentle, tender and angelic? Are the lives of any absolutely unselfish? Are their motives always pure? "If we say we have no sin," exclaimed the old apostle, "we deceive ourselves, and the truth is not in us."

Who has reached the towering height of altruism? Dare the wisest state that they have attained the sublime heights of all knowledge? Can the best and noblest conscientiously say, "I am perfect?" if not, then imperfect, undeveloped, sinful.

Examine the records of the last century—the last year; study today the moral status of the world. How many benevolent, self-sacrificing reformers do you find? How many saints, innocent of passion and all the enticing propensities that first dazzle then destroy? How many worthily crowned statesmen, honoring senate chambers, or parliamentary pantheons of justice, aflame with love and wisdom can be numbered? Think of the Japanese and Russian War now madly raging.

Take another view of the picture. There are some 400,000,000 almond-eyed, semi-enlightened Chinese; some 250,000,000 plague-stricken, polygamy-practicing, child-marrying, superstitious people of India; 200,000,000 ignorant, scantily-clad African negroes, with cannibal tribes in the central regions; millions of naked races in Southern Asia, tribes of mice, and vermin-feeding Bushmen of Australia; snake-eating Pacific islanders; scheming, gold-clutching millionaires of America; Whitechapel murderers of London, traveling road-side tramps and thieves; night-walking, outcast men and women that infest the cities; the liars, gamblers, unprincipled tricksters, slum-saloon patrons, wild, dazed, insane; criminals in jails and penitentiaries; intriguing, morally-perjured politicians;—these — *all these* are swept with the black, besom-wing of death into the spirit world! They are spirits — discarnate spirits now,— but are they pure,—are they good? If so, what has made them so? Was it the last death gasp? Is death a savior? Does dying inject, or transmit with a flash, beneficence and wisdom into a stupid African cannibal? Does death clean off the slate, making philosophers of idiots, and saints of savages? Are there no evil spirits just over the border? If not, then spirit identity is a fallacy, —a gigantic delusion.

The Diakka of Andrew Jackson Davis.

These countless millions above-named, divested of their mortal vestures, are now spirits, yet in tendency and sentiment, they are still of the earth, earthy. They are diakka. In his "Diakka and Their Victims," this seer, A. J. Davis, writes in substance thus: "The country of the diakka is where the morally deficient and the affectionately unclean enter upon a strange probation. . . . They are continually victimizing sensitive persons, making sport of them, and having a jolly laugh at the expense of really honest and sincere people. They (these demon-like spirits) teach that they would be elevated and made happy if only they could partake of whisky and tobacco, or gratify their burning free-love propensities. . . . Being unprincipled intellectualities, their play is nothing but pastime amusement at the expense of those beneath their influence. . . . Diakka are perfect in all sleight-of-hand performances. It adds nothing to a person's excellence because he happens to live in the parlor; neither does it necessarily exalt a person—at least not in my esteem—to tell me that he now resides in the spiritual world. . . . Death does not change the character of man, but simply strips off his masks and compels him to stand forth as he is, and he becomes after death the image of his own character."

How true this independent clairvoyant's words! "Death does not change the character." Are there no evil-minded, incorrigibly malignant persons in this world? Only the semi-brainless can rationally deny it. There must, therefore, be such undeveloped, conscienceless beings in the world of spirits. Getting unsheathed does not entitle one to an undeserved crown. Disrobing does not divest one of all unrighteous desires.

The human body is a tent, a temple, a shell that a death-spasm breaks, letting the imprisoned spirit free. The egg-shell that encloses the growing bird does not grow, but the germinal bird within does. This soon becoming compressed and cramped, breaks the barrier and bursts out into the sunlight; but the chick does not become by the hatching process an eagle; nor does the noisy, twittering wren become by the hatching process a musical mocking-bird, neither do morally stunted criminals that crowd the city prisons, become through death's unshelling, spirits of love or angels of peace. In reasoning, it is well to cling closely to both logic and nature.

The Make-up of the Spirit Body.

"How are the dead raised up, and with what bodies do they come?" was a question asked of old. We recognize our friends here by their bodies as well as their brains. Will it be different in those realms immortal? And yet, we have a class of metaphysical dreamers talking about the "thought-body." Just as well talk of a will-o'-the-wisp body, or a hope-body, as of an indefinable, shapeless thought-body. The real "spirit-body," sometimes unwisely termed the "astral," is a genuine, substantial body, constituted of the most delicate, imponderable auras, atomic emanations, etherealized fluids, and refined, invisible substances. It is from these infinitesimal elements and essences that the immortal principle, the divine ego constructs (by psycho-physiological laws, affinities, attractions and polarizations) for itself an enwrapping envelope,— an etheric soul-body, interpermeating the material body, and of course, of the same form.

At death, when the grosser, physical body, changing and disintegrating, is laid aside, the etheric or soul-body, rising from this decomposing mortal form, becomes what is known as the spiritual body. "There is," said Paul, "A natural (fleshy) body, and there is a spiritual body." And in dying, the potent, inmost spirit, acting as a psycho-magnet, holds to itself every spiritual element connected with and belonging to it. This emerging of the spiritual body from the earthly in dying is properly and logically a resurrection of the body,—the raising of it out of corruption into incorruption, out of mortality into immortality, into a higher spiritual state of existence.

Wherein Lies the Danger, the Evil of Obsessing Spirits?

It lies not in spirit,—"Spirit is God,"—"*Pneuma ho Theos.*" These were the alleged words of Christ. The spirit within man is a unit, is uncompounded, is an emanation, or a divine, ethereal filiation from and of the Infinite Spirit, God,—something as the tiny drop is of and from the ever-flowing crystal fountain.

The human spirit—the center of consciousness and life—is pure, is essentially, inherently divine. How, then, can it sin, or in any way become evil? is the inquiry. It cannot; and now comes the philosophy of how spirit acts on and through matter so as to produce evil, or permit the reign of evil spirits.

In considering this subject, let us go to the foundation. Did a hand after being amputated by a surgeon ever burn a building? Did a putrifying corpse ever disrobe itself of shroud and coffin and commit a bank robbery? But why not? Plainly, because the causative man, the real, conscious spiritual man had, at death, left the perishing, corpse-body, which was only a temporary appendage.

Rivet the fact in your mind as we proceed with the argument, that no act, good or bad, originated in the physical body. But the real man "over there," is still embodied, though the old mortal body has returned to dust. In the spirit world man is dual, but finite; and being finite, taking with him into the invisible world consciousness, emotion, desire, why should he not manifest from both the higher and lower states of his selfhood good and evil?

No solid thinker will affirm that the drunkard's craving is wholly of the material body; if so, the cadaver, while being dissected, might inquire why such unfeeling surgical slashings; and in consequence, might crave, if not demand alcoholic stimulants to better bear dissection. No, these desires were from the inwoven essences, elements, auras, blind forces and inter-related inharmonies pertaining to the soul-body, and *not* from or of the incorruptible spirit, which functions through the imperfect soul-organism.

This intermediate, particled organism existing between the conscious spirit and the material body may rightly be denominated the soul-body, or the soul, and is never in the Upanishads, in Vedic lore, in the Old or New Testament Scriptures, pronounced immortal; nor is it spoken of as returning to "God, who gave it." The martyr Stephen, it will be remembered, when dying, commended his spirit (not his soul) to God. This spirit so "commended" was a potentialized portion of God.

The phrase, "disembodied spirit," is a fiction. Spirits have cognizable forms. They are clothed, the quality of which corresponds to their conduct and aural associations on earth. Every molecule in the make-up of man has innate, inhering qualities all of its own. The soul-body, like the physical body, is particled, is afire with force. And this particled soul-body, constituted as aforesaid, in part at least, of the emanations from the atoms, the molecules, the electrical elements, the unseen aromas, the subtle, imponderable essences eliminated from the material body, is the vehicle, or etheric clothing of the inmost spirit. When the old tabernacle-body is cast off, this soul-body, with its qualities of good and evil, enters the world of spirits, which spirit world is here and now,— but not the spiritual world, nor the angelic world of purity and holiness. This being conceded, the

Evil Spirits and Their Influences. 21

conclusion is as irresistible as reasonable, that mortals passing the gateway of death, maintaining their personality (consciousness, memory and purpose), must continue to think and act right on, at least temporarily, in their old earth-accustomed ruts; must continue to experience the same or similar desires, propensities and tendencies, however base and wicked, that characterized them while dwelling in their terrestrial bodies.

Their thoughts and affections are of the earth. They are earth-bound. They are wandering, ghostly, spirit-tramps. They take on false names. They are restless demons roaming about seeking gratification and sensual pleasures by magnetically attaching themselves to sensitives. In their natures, they are Cimmerian demons obsessing and possessing mortals, and will so do until the grosser and more external, or earth-derived portions of their organisms shall have been expurgated of evil by such retributive, yet remedial, processes of purification as pertain to the next state of existence.

In the *Chicago Progressive Thinker,* Hudson Tuttle wrote a while since as follows:

"All spiritual beings were once human beings, and according to the fundamental principles of Spiritualism, by passing through the gateway of death have met with no change except such as they have gained by growth. Hence they are as good and as evil as they were here, no more, no less. Whenever they return and manifest their identity, we note the individual characteristics retained and carried into their spiritual lives. The lover of falsehood and deceit, the envious and hating, retain those qualities, until eradicated by years and ages of advancement.

"If there are evil persons in this life, there are in

the next, and if we open the way for their approach and allow them to influence us, we must expect them to manifest the qualities which distinguished them in earth-life."

Here is another paragraph from his pen:

"As the spirit enters the spirit world just as it leaves this, there must be an innumerable host of low, undeveloped, uneducated or in other words, evil spirits."

The brilliant Henry Ward Beecher, in commenting upon this apostolic passage: "For we wrestle not against flesh and blood, but against principalities, against powers, against rulers of the darkness of this world, against wicked spirits in high places" (the better translation), Eph. 6:11, 12, remarks:

"Look at the enumeration that the apostle makes. He begins by saying, 'Put on the whole armor of God;' as if he had said, 'There is occasion for every part of it.' And, as if they had looked around to see where the danger was, he says, "We wrestle not against flesh and blood.' In other words, 'it is not men, it is not armed hosts, it is not military force that you are most in danger of.' 'We wrestle,' he says, ' against'— and now comes the catalogue of spiritual forces—'principalities'—various sovereignties and dignities—'against powers, against the rulers of the darkness'—the ignorance—'of this world, against the spirits of wickedness in heavenly places'—for that is the exact, literal translation. Our version has, 'spiritual wickedness in high places,' but the original is, 'spirits of wickedness in heavenly places.'

"Our field of conflict is different from that on which men oppose each other. It comprises the whole unseen realm. All the secret roads, and paths and avenues, in which spirits dwell are filled with a great invisible host. These are our adversaries. And they are all the more dangerous because they are invisible. Subtle are they? We are unconscious of their presence. They come, they go; they assail, they retreat; they plan, they attack, they withdraw; they carry on all the processes by which they mean to suborn or destroy us, without the possibility of our seeing them. When, in physical warfare, the enemy that lies over against us establishes the line of a new redoubt, we can see that; and when a new battery is discovered, a battery may be planted opposite to it; but no engineering can trace these invisible engineers or their work. And there is something very august in the thought that the most transcendent powers in the universe, that fill time and space, are removed from the ordinary sight and inspection of men. It is a sublime and awful conception. It produces some such impression on my mind as is produced by the idea of haunted houses.

"Did you ever go into one alone? You are courageous. You do not believe in ghosts nor in spirits. You do not believe there is such a thing as a haunted house; yet entering one in the silent hour of dim hazy moonlight, listening to your echoing footsteps, you soon take discretion to the better part of valor, and retire without delay. You are conscious of a low order of invisible presences.

"There are many who do not believe that this world is the sphere of evil spirits. They do not believe that the overarching heaven just above is haunted; nor that the world beneath is haunted; nor that the laws and customs, and usages, and pleasures, and various pursuits are haunted. They do not believe in the doctrine of the possession of spirits. Nevertheless, I confess to you, there is something in my mind of profoundest conviction in the idea that the world is full of spirits, good and evil, that are pursuing their various errands, and that the little that we can see with these bat's eyes of ours, the little that we can decipher with these imperfect senses is not the whole of the reading of those vast pages of that great volume which God has written. There is in the lore of God and the realm invisible, more than our philosophy has ever dreamed of.

"Against this view of the peril of human life because it is girded on every side by multiplied powers, potential and sublime, that mean only evil—against this view it is argued, sometimes, that the benevolence of God would not permit disembodied spirits to work mischief among men on earth. In reply to that, I have only to say that he does, right before your eyes, permit *embodied* spirits to work mischief among men on earth; and that through long years. If devils are worse than some men, I am sorry for hell! If there is more malignity, more malice, more selfishness, more heartlessness, more cruelty in the other world than in this, I am mistaken.

"I do not conceive that a spirit is worse because it has lost its body. I hope it is better. We see embodied spirits that are bad enough, corrupt enough. And that is not all; not only do they love wrong, but they love those that do wrong, and hate those that do right, and seek to bring them down to their level. And is it inconsistent with the character of a benevolent God that the world should be full of wicked men? And if God will permit embodied spirits to do evil, how can you say that it is against the benevolence of God to permit disembodied spirits to do it? It is a thing which is beyond all controversy, that God does permit evil spirits to act in this world, with plenary power, so far as their own sphere of willing is concerned. Wicked men do have power, according to their education and experience, as well as good men; and they have the same opportunity for exercising their power that good men have. God makes his sun to rise on the evil and on the good alike, and sends his rain on the just and on the unjust alike. Wicked men in this world have a fair field and full sway. And why should you suppose that wicked spirits have not? I think modern mawkishness in this matter borders on the absurd. Men seem to be drifting away from their common sense on this subject.

"An evil spirit may be consummately refined, may be learned. Our first thought in contemplating this subject is, that an evil spirit must be a vulgar thing. Doubtless there are vulgar spirits; but it does not follow at all that spirits that are the most potential, and most to be feared, are vulgar. On the contrary, where spirits are embodied, it is supposed that those that are the most cultured are the most powerful for evil. The most exquisite artists, the most deft and subtle statesmen, the men that have the most conciliating and plausible ways, they who have such qualifications as corrupt lobby-plotters possess, are regarded as capable of doing the most mischief. And I can conceive that a spirit of evil, so far from being a grotesque Caliban, vulgar, debased, and representing the lowest passion, should be made up of intellect, yea, and of some degree of moral sense, with pride intense, vehement and cruel.

"The more knowledge a man has, unless it be governed by moral justice and true wisdom, the more wickedness he may do. Forgers are necessarily good penmen. Bank defaulters are excellent accountants. Thieves are expert mechanical lock-pickers. Dr. Webster, the Professor of Chemistry in Harvard University, murdered Dr. Parkman. Great, ambitious wargenerals that kill their thousands on crimson battlefields are intellectual men; and yet, men of war, men of blood; as such they die, and as such become the wicked spirits that obsess. Knowing these things, 'we contend not against flesh and blood, but against principalities, against powers, against the rulers of the darkness of this world, against spirits of wickedness in heavenly places.'

"There is no presumption, either, against the supposition that there are certain spirits whose office it is to assail particular faculties. I may say by way, not of analogy, but of illustration, that there is no leaf that grows that has not its parasite. The wheat and the tares grow together. While there are evil, obsessing spirits, there are also angels of light, spirits of the blessed, ministers of God. I believe, not only that they are our natural guardians, and friends, and teachers, and influences, but also that they are natural antagonists of evil spirits. In other words, I believe that the great realm of life goes on without the mortal body very much as it does with the body. And, as here the mother not only is the guardian of her children whom she loves, but foresees that bad associates and evil influences threaten them, and draws them back and shields them from the impending danger; so these ministers of God not only minister to us the divinest tendencies, the purest tastes, the noblest thoughts and feelings, but, perceiving our adversaries, caution us against them, and spiritually assail them, and drive them away from us. But they are not all-powerful. God alone is omnipotent.

"Our safety against these wicked spirits in high

places consists in living the life of the just and the upright, in clean, non-lascivious habits, in cultivating a calm religious spirit, in seeking good associations, in walling ourselves about with refined, social and harmonial environments, and ever invoking the presence of angel helpers, and putting an abiding trust in God.''

CHAPTER II.

Chinese Spiritism—A Demon in the Kwo Family.

KNOWLEDGE comes through the sense perceptions, in connection with intuition, reason and the higher judgment. I make no mention just yet of my psychic observations and experiences while a traveler and explorer in the Chinese Empire. English officials, American missionaries, mandarins and many of the Chinese literati (Confucians, Taoists and Buddhist believers alike) declare that spiritism in some form, and under some name, is the almost universal belief of China. It is generally denominated ''ancestral worship.'' ''There is no driving out of these Chinese,'' says Father Gonzalo, ''the cursed belief that the spirits of their ancestors are ever about them, availing themselves of every opportunity to give advice and counsel.''

''The medium consulted,'' remarks Dr. Doolittle, ''takes in the hand a stick of lighted incense to dispel all defiling influences, then prayers of some kind are repeated, the body becomes spasmodic, the medium's eyes are shut, and the form sways about, assuming the walk and peculiar attitude of the spirit when in the body. Then the communication from the divinity begins, which may be of a faultfinding or a flattering character. . . . Sometimes these Chinese mediums profess to be possessed by some specified historical god of great healing powers, and in this condition they prescribe for the sick. It is believed that the ghoul or spirit invoked actually casts himself into the medium, and dictates the medicine."

"Volumes might be written upon the gods, genii and familiar spirits supposed to be continually in communication with this people," writes Dr. John L. Nevius, in his works, "China and the Chinese." "The Chinese have a large number of books upon this subject, among the most noted of which is the 'Liau-chai-chei,' a large work of sixteen volumes. . . . Tu Sein signifies a spirit in the body, and there are a class of familiar spirits supposed to dwell in the bodies of certain Chinese who became the mediums of communication with the unseen world. Individuals said to be possessed by these spirits are visited by multitudes, particularly those who have lost recently relatives by death, and wish to converse with them. . . . Remarkable disclosures and revelations are believed to be made by the involuntary movements of a bamboo pencil, and through a similar method some claim to see in the dark. Persons considering themselves endowed with superior intelligence are firm believers in those and other modes of consulting spirits."

The Chinese are famous for gambling. It is their chief evening pastime, and one of their popular demons which they consult for luck is called the gambler's god. Before its image they bow, invoke and pray.

A Demon in the Kwo Family.

"In the spring of 1877," says Dr. Nevius, "I took part in the work of famine-relief, in central Shantung; and while visiting some enquirers at Twin Mountain Stream, I was told of a young man of the family named Kwo, living in the village of King-Kia, who was suffering all sorts of inflictions from an evil spirit. I desired to see the man, and it was arranged that we should pay him a visit. We found Mr. Kwo at work in the fields, where I had a conversation with him, which was as follows:

" 'I have heard that you were troubled with an evil spirit.'

"He replied, 'It is true, and most humiliating. That I, a man in the full vigor of health, should be a slave to this demon, is the trial of my life; but there is no help for it.'

" 'I assure you that there is help,' I said.

" 'What do you mean?' he asked.

" 'I will tell you,' I replied. 'I am associated with a foreign teacher of Christianity, who often visits the region east of you.' . . . In the meantime we had reached his house, and he pointed out to me the shrine where he worshiped the demon. I then told him that the first thing to do was to tear away this shrine. To this he readily consented. . . . On my way I learned further particulars of his previous life. He had never attended school, and until recently had been unable to read. Moreover (and this is very unusual in China) not a person in his village could read. He was a hardy mountaineer, thirty-eight years of age, bright and entertaining, with nothing in his appearance which could be regarded as unhealthy or abnormal. It was late in the afternoon when I reached his home. I was at once introduced into the reception room, which was the place where the evil spirit had formerly been worshiped. . . . I afterward had long conversations with his wife, and also conversed on the subject at length with his father. All the different accounts supplement and confirm his own, and agree in every important particular. I give these statements as I received them. I offer no opinion of my own respecting the phenomena presented. Of course, Mr. Kwo's statements respecting what he said and did when he was in a state of unconsciousness depend upon the testimony of those about him.''

Led by the Spirit to a Gambler's Den.

"The following story, in his own words, is as follows:
" 'Near the close of year before last (1875), I bought a number of pictures, including one of Wang-Mu-niang, the wife of Yu-hwang (the chief divinity in this part of China). For the goddess, Wang Mu-niang, I selected the most honorable position in the house; the others I pasted on the walls here and there as ornaments. On the second day of the first month, I proposed worshiping the goddess, but my wife objected. The next night a spirit came apparently in a dream, and said to me, ''I am Wang-Mu-niang, of Yuin-men San (the name of a neighboring mountain). I have taken up my abode in your house.'' It said this repeatedly, and I awakened and was conscious of the presence of the spirit. I knew it was a *shie-kwie* (evil spirit), and as such, I resisted it, and cursed it, saying: '' I will have nothing to do with you.'' This my wife heard and begged to know what it

meant, and I told her. After this all was quiet, and I was not disturbed for some days. About a week afterward, a feeling of uneasienss and restlessness came over me, which I could not control. At night I went to bed as usual, but grew more and more restless. At last, seized by an irresistible impulse, I arose from my bed and went straight to a gambler's den in Kao-Kia, where I lost at once 16,000 cash (sixteen dollars), a large sum for a peasant Chinaman. I started for home and lost my way; but when it grew light, I got back to my house. At that time I was conscious of what I was saying and doing, but I did things mechanically, and soon forgot what I had said. I did not care to eat and only so did when urged. After some days a gambler from Kao-Kia came and asked me to go with him, which I did, and this time I lost 25,000 cash. On the fifteenth and sixteenth of the first month, I went to Pe-ta, where there was a theater. The same night I again lost 13,000 cash in gambling. The next morning I returned hence, and just as I was entering my village, I fell down frothing at the mouth and unconscious; and was carried to my house. Medicine was given me which partially restored me to consciousness. The next day I dressed. The spirit came and attempted to run me away from home, but I soon found myself staggering; and everything grew dark, and I rushed back to my room. I soon became violent, attacking all who ventured near me. My father, hearing the state of things, hurried from his home to see me. As he entered, I seized a fowling-piece, which I had secreted under my bed, and fired it at him. Fortunately, the charge went over his head into the ceiling. With the help of the neighbors, my father bound me with chains, and took me to his home in Chang-yiu. A doctor was called, who, after giving me large doses of medicine without effect, left, refusing to have anything more to do with me. For five or six days I raved wildly, and my friends were in great distress. They proposed giving me more medicine, but the demon speaking through me, replied: "Any amount of medicine will be of no use." My mother then asked: "If medicine is of no use, what shall we do?".

Burning Incense to Expel the Demon.

" 'The demon replied: "Burn incense to me and submit yourself to me, and all will be well." My parents promised to do this, and knelt down and worshiped the demon, begging it to torment me no longer. Thus the matter was arranged, I all the time remaining in a state of unconsciousness. About midnight I attempted to leave the house. The attendants followed me and brought me back and bound me again. Then my parents a second time worshiped the demon, begging it to relieve me from my sufferings, and renewing their promise that I, myself, should hereafter worship and serve it. I then recovered consciousness, and my mother told me all that had happened, and of the promise they had made for me. On my refusing to consent to this, I again lost all consciousness. My mother besought the furor of the demon, renewing her promise to insist upon my obedience, and I again recovered consciousness. In their great distress, my father and mother implored me to fulfil their promise, and worship the evil spirit. At last, I reluctantly consented. The demon had directed that we call a certain woman in, Kao-chao, who was a spirit medium, to give us directions in putting in order our place for wor-

A Demon in the Kwo Family. 33

ship. So all was arranged, and on the first and fifteenth of each month we burned incense, offered food, and made the required prostrations before the shrine on which the picture of the goddess was placed. The spirit came at intervals, sometimes every few days, and sometimes after a period of a month or more, and gave directions which they afterward communicated to me, for though spoken by my own lips, I had been entirely unconscious of them. . . . The demon said he had many inferior spirits subject to him.'

"I would remark that Mr. Kwo's own account of Leng's visit exactly corresponded with that given above. Mr. Kwo, however, added the following: 'The death of our child,' said he, 'occurred a few days after we had torn down the spirit's shrine. My wife was much distressed, believing it was in consequence of my having offended the demon. She urged me to restore the shrine and resume the worship.' "

A Teacher's Testimony About These Evil Spirits.

The public teacher in Chen Sin Ling (W. J. Plumb) says: "In the district of Tu-ching, obsessions by evil spirits or demons are very common." He further writes that "there are very many cases also in Chang-lo." Again he says:

"When a man is thus afflicted, the spirit (*Kwei*) takes possession of his body without regard to his being strong or weak in health. It is not easy to resist the demon's power. Though without bodily ailments, possessed persons appear as if ill. When under the entrancing spell of the demon, they seem different from their ordinary selves.

"In most cases the spirit takes possession of a man's body contrary to his will, and he is helpless in the matter. The kwei has the power of driving out the man's spirit, as in sleep or dreams. When the subject awakes to consciousness, he has not the slightest knowledge of what has transpired.

"The actions of possessed persons vary exceedingly. They leap about and toss their arms, and then the demon tells them what particular spirit he is, often taking a false name, or deceitfully calling himself a god, or one of the genii come down to the abodes of mortals. Or, perhaps, it professes to be the spirit of a deceased husband or wife. There are also *kwei* of the quiet sort, who talk and laugh like other people, only that the voice is changed. Some have a voice like a bird. Some speak Mandarin—the language of Northern China—and some the local dialect; but though the speech proceeds from the mouth of the man, what is said does not appear to come from him. The outward appearance and manner is also changed.

"In Fu-show there is a class of persons who collect in large numbers and make use of incense, pictures, candles and lamps to establish what are called 'incense tables.' Taoist priests are engaged to attend the ceremonies, and they also make use of 'mediums.' The Taoist writes a charm for the medium, who, taking the incense stick in his hand, stands like a graven image, thus signifying his willingness to have the demon come and take possession of him. Afterward, the charm is burned and the demon-spirit is worshiped and invoked, the priest, in the meanwhile going on with his chanting. After a while, the medium begins to tremble, and then speaks and announces what spirit has descended, and asks what is wanted of him. Then, whoever has requests to make, takes incense sticks, makes prostrations, and asks a response respecting some disease, or for protection from calamity. In winter the same performances are carried on to a great extent by gambling companies. If some of the responses hit the mark, a large number of people are attracted. They establish a shrine and offer sacrifices, and appoint days, calling upon people from every quarter to come and consult the spirit respecting diseases. . . .

Temples for Spirit Revelations.

"There is also a class of men who establish what they call a 'Hall of Revelations.' At the present time there are many engaged in this practice. They are, for the most part, literary men of great ability. The people in large numbers apply to them for responses. The mediums spoken of above are also numerous. All of the above practices are not spirits seeking to possess men; but rather men seeking spirits to possess them, and allowing themselves to be voluntarily used as their instruments.

"As to the outward appearance of persons when possessed, of course, they are the same persons as to outward form as at ordinary times; but the color of the countenance may change. The demon may cause the subject to assume a threatening air, and a fierce, violent manner. The muscles often stand out on the face, the eyes are closed, or they protrude with a frightful stare. These demons sometimes prophesy.

"The words spoken certainly proceed from the mouths of the persons possessed; but what is said does not appear to come from their minds or wills, but rather from some other personality, often accompanied by a change of voice. Of this there can be no doubt. When the subject returns to consciousness, he invariably declares himself ignorant of what he has said.

"The Chinese make use of various methods to cast out demons. They are so troubled and vexed by inflictions affecting bodily health, or it may be throwing stones, moving furniture, or the moving about and destruction of family utensils, that they are driven to call in the services of some respected scholar or Taoist priest, to offer sacrifices, or chant sacred books, and pray for protection and exemption from suffering. Some make use of sacrifices and offerings of paper clothes and money in order to induce the demon to go back to the gloomy region of Yan-chow. . . . As to whether these methods have any effect, I do not know. As a rule, when demons are not very troublesome, the families afflicted by them generally think it best to hide their affliction, or to keep these wicked spirits quiet by sacrifices, and burning incense to them."

Obsession and Planchette Old in China.

The *London Daily News* of October 14 gives lengthy extracts from an address upon the Chinese by Mrs. Montague Beaucham, who had spent many years in China in educational work. Speaking of their religion, she said, "The latest London craze in using the planchette has been one of the recognized means in China of conversing with evil spirits from time immemorial." She had lived in one of the particular provinces known as demon land, where the natives were bound up in the belief and worship of spirits. "There is a real power," she added, " in this necromancy. They do healings and tell fortunes." She personally knew of one instance that the spirits through the planchette had foretold a great flood. The boxer rising was prophesied by the planchette. These spirits disturbed family relations, caused fits of frothing at the mouth, and made some of their victims insane. In closing she declared that "Chinese spiritism was from hell," the obsession baffling the power of both Christian missionaries and native Chinese priests.

CHAPTER III.

Responses to the Nevius Circular Concerning the Works of Evil Spirits.

THE following is an extract from Wang Wu-Fang's communication:

"Cases of demon possession abound among all classes. They are found among persons of robust health, as well as those who are weak and sickly. In many unquestionable cases of obsession, the unwilling subjects have resisted, but have been obliged to submit themselves to the control of the demon. . . .

"In a majority of cases of possession, the beginning of the malady is a fit of grief, anger or mourning. These conditions seem to open the door to the demons. The outward manifestations are apt to be fierce and violent. It may be that the subject alternately talks and laughs; he walks a while and then sits, or he rolls on the ground, or leaps about; or exhibits contortions of the body and twistings of the neck. . . . It was common among them to send for oxorcists, who made use of written charms, or chanted verses, or punctured the body with needles. These are among the Chinese methods of cure.

"Demons are of different kinds. There are those which clearly declare themselves; and then those who work in secret. There are those which are cast out with difficulty, and others with ease.

"In cases of possession by familiar demons, what is said by the subject certainly does not proceed from his own will. When the demon has gone out and the subject recovers consciousness, he has no recollection whatever of what he has said or done. This is true almost invariably.

"The methods by which the Chinese cast out demons are enticing them to leave by burning charms and paper money, or by begging and exhorting them, or by frightening them with magic spells and incantations, or driving them away by pricking with needles, or pinching with the fingers, in which case they cry out and promise to go.

"I was formerly accustomed to drive out demons by means of needles. At that time cases of possession by evil spirits were very common in our villages, and my services were in very frequent demand. . . .

A Demon Difficult to Expel.

"There was another case which I met with on the twenty-fifth day of the first month of the present year (1880). The subject, who was twenty-three years old, was the wife of the second son of Li Mao-lin. When under the influence of the demon, she was wild and unmanageable. This continued six days without intermission. The family applied to '*Wu-po*' (mediums,—literally, female magicians), and persons who effected cures by needles, but without success. They were at their wits' end, and, all other means having failed, a person named Li Tso-yuen came and applied to me. I declined going, but he urged me at least to go and look at her, which I consented to do. When we entered the house, she was surrounded by a crowd and her noisy demonstrations had not ceased. When they learned that we were approaching, the people present opened a way for us, and the possessed woman at once took a seat, began adjusting her hair, and wonderingly asked, 'Why are there so many people here?' Her husband told her what she had been doing for several days past. She exclaimed in a surprised way: 'I know nothing about it.' The people thought it very remarkable that she should be restored as soon as I entered the house; and I, of course, was very thankful for the result. . . .

"In our preaching, to be able to tell the people that in our holy religion there is the power to cast out demons and heal diseases, thus manifesting the love and mercy of God, is certainly a great help to the spread of the Gospel.

"In the village of Tu Wang-kia, there is a man named Wang Pan-hu, who was possessed of an evil spirit, but was entirely relieved after becoming a Christian. I know also of other similar cases, of which I cannot now make a full record. These have all come under my personal knowledge."

Translation of Extracts from a Communication of Wang Yung-ngeu, of Peking.

"It may be said in general of possessed persons, that sometimes people who cannot sing are able when possessed to do so; others who cannot ordinarily write verses, when possessed, compose in ryhme with ease. Northern men will speak languages, of the South; and those of the East, the languages of the West; and when they awake to consciousness they are utterly oblivious to what they have done.

"Cases of possession are less frequent in peaceful times, and more frequent in times of civil commotion: less frequent in prosperous families, and more so in unlucky, inharmonious ones; less frequent among educated people, and more so among the uncultivated.

" The varieties of outward manifestations of demons are very numerous, and their transformations are remarkable. The same demon will transform itself into any number of manifestations and personalities; so that it is very difficult to comprehend them. This is what they are specially noted for."

Translation of a Communication from Hsu Chung-ki, a Steady-going Man.

"Thirty-four *li* west of my house there is a small village called Ho Kia-chwang. In it lived a Mr. Chin, who was very wealthy and had a large family. He was also a noted scholar, and had many disciples. All at once his home became the scene of very strange manifestations. Doors would open of their own accord, suddenly, and shut suddenly. The rattling of plates and bowls was very annoying. Foot-falls were sometimes heard as of persons walking in the house, although no one could be seen. Often straw was found mixed with millet, and filth with the wheat. Plates, bowls and the teapot would suddenly rise from the table into the air; and the servants would stretch out their hands to catch them. These were constant occurrences. Various persons were called to the house to put an end to these disturbances. Efforts were made to propitiate the spirits by burning incense to them, and by vows and offerings. Mr. Chin entered a protest against the spirits in the Fung-Yoh Temple. All possible means were tried, but with no avail. This state of things continued for two years. The wealth of the family mysteriously disappeared. Mr. Chin died and now all his descendants are in extreme poverty."

The Rev. Timothy Richard, missionary, also writing in response to Dr. Nevius' circular, says:

"The Chinese orthodox definition of spirit is, ' the soul of the departed;' some of the best of whom are raised to the rank of gods. . . . There is no disease to which the Chinese are ordinarily subject that may not be caused by demons. In this case the mind is untouched. It is only the body that suffers; and the Chinese endeavor to get rid of the demon by vows and offerings to the gods. The subjection in this case is an involuntary one. . . .

The Class of Persons Most Controlled by Evil Spirits.

"Persons possessed range between fifteen and fifty years of age, quite irrespective of sex. This infliction comes on very suddenly, sometimes in the day, and sometimes in the night. The demoniac talks madly, smashes everything near him, acquires unusual strength, tears his clothes into rags, and rushes into the street, or to the mountains, or kills himself unless prevented. After this violent possession, the demoniac calms down and submits to his fate, but under the most heart-rending protests. These mad spells which are experienced on the demon's entrance return at intervals, and increase in frequency, and generally also in intensity, so that death at last ensues from their violence.

"A Chefoo boy of fifteen was going on an errand. His path led through fields where men were working at their crops. When he came up to the men and had exchanged a word or two with them, he suddenly began to rave wildly; his eyes rolled, then he made for a pond near by. Seeing this, the people ran up to him, stopped him from drowning himself and took him home to his parents. When he got home, he sprang up from the ground to such a height as manifested almost a superhuman strength. After a few days he calmed down and became unusually quiet and gentle; but his own consciousness was lost. The demon spoke of its friends in Nan-Kin. After six months this demon departed. He has been in the service of several foreigners in Cheefoo since. In this case no worship was offered to the demon.

"Now we proceed to those, who involuntarily possessed, yield to and worship the demon. The demon says he will cease tormenting the demoniac if he will worship him, and he will reward him by increasing his riches. But if not, he will punish his victim, make heavier his torments, and rob him of his property. People find that their food is cursed. They cannot prepare any, but filth and dirt comes down from the air to render it uneatable. Their wells are likewise cursed; their wardrobes are set on fire, and their money very mysteriously disappears. Hence arose the custom of cutting off the head of a string of cash, that it might not run away. . . . When all efforts to rid themselves of the demon fail, they yield to it, and say: 'Hold! Cease thy tormenting and we will worship thee!' A picture is pasted upon the wall, sometimes of a woman, and sometimes of a man, and incense is burned, and prostrations are made to it twice a month. Being thus reverenced, money now comes in mysteriously, instead of going out. Even mill-stones are made to move at the demon's orders, and the family becomes rich at once. But it is said that no luck attends such families, and they will eventually be reduced to poverty. Officials believe these things. Palaces are known to have been built by them for these demons, who, however, are obliged to be satisfied with humbler shrines from the poor. . . .

"Somewhat similar to the above class is another small one which has power to enter the lower regions. These are the opposite of necromancers, for instead of calling up the dead and learning of them about the future destiny of the individual in whose behalf they are engaged, they lie in a trance for two days, when their spirits are said to have gone to the Prince of Darkness, to inquire how long the sick person shall be left among the living. . . .

How Doctors Cast Out Demons.

"Let us now note the different methods adopted to cast out the evil spirits from the demoniacs. Doctors are called to do it. They use needles to puncture the tips of the fingers, the nose, the neck. They also use a certain pill, and apply it in the following manner: the thumbs of the two hands are tied tightly together, and the two big toes are tied together in the same manner. Then one pill is put on the two big toes at the root of the nail, and the other at the root of the thumb nails. At the same instant the two pills are set on fire, and they are kept until the flesh is burned. In the application of the pills, or in the piercing of the needle, the invariable cry is: 'I am going; I am going immediately. I will never dare to come back again. Oh, have mercy on me this once. I'll never return!'

"When the doctors fail, they call on people who practice spiritism. They themselves cannot drive the demon away, but they call another demon to do it. Both the Confucianists and Taoists practice this method. . . . Sometimes the spirits are very ungovernable. Tables are turned, chairs are rattled, and a general noise of smashing is heard, until the very mediums themselves tremble with fear. If the demon is of this dreadful character, they quickly write another charm with the name of the particular spirit whose quiet disposition is known to them. Lu-tsu is a favorite one of this kind. After the burning of the charm and incense, and when prostrations are made, a little frame is procured, to which a Chinese pencil is attached. Two men on each side hold it on a table spread with sand or millet. Sometimes a prescription is written, the pencil moving of its own accord. They buy the medicine prescribed and give it to the possessed. . . . Should they find that burning incense and offering sacrifices fails to liberate the poor victim, they may call in conjurors, such as the Taoists, who sit on mats and are carried by invisible power from place to place. They ascend to a height of twenty or fifty feet, and are carried to a distance of four or five *li* (about half a mile). Of this class are those, who in Manchuria call down fire from the sky in those funerals where the corpse is burned. . . .

"These exorcists may belong to any of the three religions in China. The dragon procession, on the fifteenth of the first month, is said by some to commemorate a Buddhist priest's victory over evil spirits. . . . They paste up charms on windows and doors, and on the body of the demoniac, and conjure the demon never to return. The evil spirit answers: 'I'll never return! You need not take the trouble of pasting all these charms upon the doors and windows.'

"Exorcists are specially hated by the evil spirits. Sometimes they feel themselves beaten fearfully; but no hand is seen. Bricks and stones may fall on them from the sky or housetops. On the road they may without any warning be plastered over from head to foot with mud or filth; or may be seized when approaching a river, and held under the water and drowned."

"In considering this subject," says James Gilmore, author of "Life in Mongolia" (page 74), "one feels himself transported back to the days of the apostles; and is compelled to believe that the dominion of Satan is by no means broken yet."

CHAPTER IV.

More Demoniac Obsessions in China—Responses to Circular of Inquiry.

"IN JUNE, 1876, the son's wife of Chang An-liang was seized with violent pains and contortions," writes William A. Willis, in a carefully prepared Chinese paper. "She soon seemingly swooned, and said her husband's first wife, long since dead, had come to take her and her husband away. The friends present were very much alarmed and promised the spirit that if it would leave the woman they would call six priests to chant the classics for three days. 'You can't get rid of me by this means,' said the spirit. Then a fishing net was spread over the woman, and the demon said: 'You can't catch me with this. I will stay. I will hold this medium.'" But when the Rev. Mr. Willis began to read the New Testament and pray, the evil spirit said, "Don't read; don't read. I will go." She went and the woman got up and attended to her duties.

H. V. Noyes says in a letter: "In the fourth month of the Chinese year, Hoko, I was in Fatshan giving an address. After the service a man came and asked Ho-Kao if he could cast out devils, stating that he had a son thus possessed. Ho-Kao replied that he could, and that Jesus of old could and did cast out demons. Ho-Kao then went with the man to his home in a village not far from Fatshan and found that his son, a grown-up man, had been obsessed for ten or more days, attacking people with knives, and making attempts to set fire to the house, so that he had to be chained to a tree. The demon seemed to know the past. He could read the people's minds. He told what was occurring far away, and the people were afraid of him. . . . An exorcist prayed for him. As soon as the prayer was finished, the chained man gave one or two leaps as high as he could, and then Ho-Kao said: 'Take off the chains!' They were all afraid to do this, and so Ho-Kao himself took them off, and led the man into the house. He was quiet and seemed much exhausted, and soon fell asleep. The family wished to burn incense, etc., but were told to do nothing of the kind. The father of the demoniac tore down everything pertaining to idol-worship in his house, and would have nothing more to do with it thereafter."

In July, 1880, Mr. Noyes wrote again as follows:

"There is a case of the supposed casting out of evil spirits which I have not mentioned. It happened ten years ago at Hin-Kong, in the Hai-Ping district. A returned Californian, named Chao Tsiming, prayed in the name of Jesus for a slave girl, who had been afflicted, as they said by an evil spirit for eight or nine years, and she recovered and has been well ever since."

Translation of Communication Relating to Demons from Ho Yuing-She.

"I was stationed in the city of Fu-san, and engaged in chapel preaching, when I was visited by a man from the neighborhood of Shin Tsuen, about twenty *li* distant. He said that his elder brother, Tsai Shi-hiang, had been for several months afflicted by an evil spirit; and they had made use of every kind of magic for expelling demons, and had exhausted all the forms of Chinese worship. The demon seemed to be malicious in the extreme. He delighted, not only in annoying, but in breaking things 'We had wasted the most of our substance on physicians without avail. Night and day we were borne down by this calamity, and had found ourselves absolutely powerless to drive this demoniac spirit away.' But Si-Hang, a Buddhist priest of great will power and force, commanded him to leave at once, and the man became himself again.''

In a letter dated February 1, I obtained the following communication, translated, from a very intelligent Chinese engaged in the tea trade:

"In the province of Shantung, in the village Yang Kia-lo, there is a family named Yang, in which a woman was grievously tormented by evil spirits, and had been for fifteen years. She formerly appeared on the streets declaring to the people that the teachings of the Christian religion came from heaven; and that men ought to believe and reverence this religion. She was asked, 'Has not the Mi-Mi religion (a local sect) power to cast you out?'

"She replied, 'The Mi-Mi Kia is a religion of demons; how could it cast me out? I am also a demon (Mo-Kwei).'

" Some of the native Christians heard this and said, 'When Jesus was in the world, he healed diseases and cast out demons. Why cannot we who believe in Christ do the same?' Whereupon those present, Yang Ching-Tsue, Yang Shing-Kung and Yang Shin-Ching, earnestly prayed for God's help in casting out this demon. After prayer, they proceeded to the afflicted woman's house. Before they reached it, the woman said, 'There are three believers in the heavenly doctrine coming.' On their arrival she called each one by name, and asked them to be seated. She then said, 'You are the disciples and the servants of the God whom I greatly fear.'

"They then asked, 'What is your name?'

"The answer was, 'My name is Kynin (legion).'

" The three men then charged the demon to leave the woman's body.

"The demon replied, 'I have helped this woman for fifteen years. She has not an ornament on her head or her feet which she has not obtained by my assistance.'

"After a violent fit of weeping, the demon promised to leave the woman on the tenth day of the first month; and on that day, agreeable to its promise, it left."

The following is from the weekly *Herald and Signs of the Times,* of Aug. 4, 1880; published in China:

"One Sunday morning, about a year ago, a woman with her husband and four children came to my house here, and asked to be taken in and taught Christianity, for the woman was possessed by an evil spirit, and had come a very long way at considerable expense, in obedience to a dream commanding her, if she would get rid of the evil spirit. . . .

"Some few days afterward, I was suddenly summoned by a message that the woman was in one of her fits, and I immediately went down with Dr. Taylor. We found her sitting on her bed, waving her arms about and talking in an excited manner. She evidently had no control over herself, and was not conscious of what she was saying. Dr. Taylor, in order to ascertain whether it was merely a hysterical fit, or something over which she had no control, called for a dinner knife, and baring his arm, laid the edge against the skin, as though he intended to cut; but the woman seemed to take no heed whatever. He then threw a cupful of water in her face; but she seemed to mind this as little as the knife; never for a moment stopping in her loud talk. . . .

"A few moments afterward, she shivered all over in a strange way. I caught her hands, thinking she was about to fall; but she seemed to get better, and lay quietly down on the bed. The next day or two she remained in bed, and on Saturday night following, she again had a vision. The evil spirit seemed to seize her by the neck, commanding her to leave Foo-chow at once, and return to her home, or it would kill her. However, instead of obeying, she ran by herself Sunday morning to the church, and while there, the pain she had been feeling all the morning in her neck left her, and she experienced a strangely happy sensation. Since that day she has had no return of those demon attacks which she had been subject to continually for three years previously, and to obtain a cure for which, she, poor woman, had presented many costly offerings to the idols."

A Familiar Spirit Ejected from the Yong Family.

Here is a verbal narrative by Miss A. M. Field:

"The first thing that I remember in my life is the distress of extreme poverty. . . . When I was fifteen years old, my mother was attacked by a demon and she could not drive it away. She was entirely unlike herself when controlled by this evil spirit. She had nervous twitchings, spasmodic contractions of the muscles and foaming at the mouth. Then she would speak whatever the demon told her to say. My father told her that it was very bad to be a spirit medium; but if she was determined to be one, she should take no more than fair pay for her services. She never took more than two or three cents from any one who came to her for a consultation with the demon. There were several spirit mediums in our village, but none were so popular as my mother became. When I was twenty-two, my father died and my brothers said that my mother's familiar spirit was a harmful one, and that they would no longer live in the house with it. My mother was greatly distressed with all this, and thought she would try and rid herself of her possessor; but the demon told her that if she tried to evict him, she would be the worse for it. She feared him and dared to do nothing. . . . But when she was released, as she afterward was, she went to live with her sons and myself. We have less money than we had when my mother was a spirit medium; but we have what is worth more than money."

A Moral Wreck by a Demon's Control.

In describing another case in her "Pagoda Shadows," Miss Field says: "An old woman named Lotus was made a terrible wreck by a demon's control. Her eyes had a wild appearance. She professed to see these spirits and foretell the future. Her hands shook so that she could scarcely hold a book; her head vibrated incessantly with a sort of nervous palsy; and her seemingly wild tongue, slashed often in her frenzies to draw blood for medicines, appeared like a strange one about to fly out of her mouth as she talked. Her mind was completely saturated with the demonism of idolatrous heathenism,—demon worship."

In a very able essay by Dr. Caldwell, long a resident

of China, the writer says: "I have examined many cases of the several phases of modern devil-worship, and must say that the subject is a very perplexing one. I dare say that I have seen almost as much of the cultus of evil spirits in the East as any living man has; and although I am far from being credulous, I should like to be convinced fully and finally of the unreality of these manifestations and strange phenomena. . . . I write of what I have seen, and I ask calmly and advisedly the startling question: Does demon-possession, in the sense in which it is referred to in the New Testament, exist at the present time? I have met many men of the widest learning and deepest experience who could not fully answer this question. No doubt the easiest way to dispose of this matter, is the Sadduceean method—that is by saying: 'there are no demons; there is no resurrection of the dead. There were in the past, and are today no demon possessions.' But this does not dispose of the facts. Strange phenomena occur in the present, and, as reported in the New Testament, they occurred in Palestine, in Greece and Rome. These demons had the power in apostolic times of inflicting bodily punishments. They rent some; others they made to gnash their teeth. They hurled living beings headlong to self-destruction. In a word, they appear to have a distinct spiritual personality. As I understand, it was not epilepsy, mania, raving madness, hysteria or dyspepsia that Jesus dispossessed; but he 'cast out evil spirits' which had taken possession of human beings. He addressed them as conscious personalities."

More Demoniac Obsessions in China.

Trance Mediums in China.

Most of the facts which I have quoted from Dr Nevius and other travelers in China are duplicated a thousandfold throughout that vast empire. In my own travels in that country, I have repeatedly witnessed nearly every phase of obsession detailed in Dr. Nevius' book. China is emphatically a nation of spiritists. From the highest to the lowest, the belief is far more general than it is in America; but in the lower classes it often develops into a gross form of superstition. There are vast numbers of trance mediums throughout China, mostly females, whose influences are regarded as from quite a different source from the major portion of those quoted above. These mediums generally use pointed pencil-like sticks, and a table sprinkled with white sand. They have all the phases of mediumship with which we are familiar in the West. They have their personating mediums, giving excellent tests; their seers who professedly reveal the future; and their clairvoyants, who, to express their meaning in English, "see in the dark." It may be affirmed without dispute, that spiritism in some form is an almost universal belief throughout the Chinese Empire.

How They Communicate with Demon Spirits.

In his "Social Life among the Chinese," Dr. Doolittle says: " They have invented several ways by which they find out the pleasure of gods and spirits. One of the most common of their utensils is the *Ka-pue,* a piece of bomboo root, bean-shaped, and divided in the center, to indicate the positive and the negative. The incense lighted, the *Ka-pue* properly manipulated before the symbol god, the pieces are tossed from the medium's hand, indicating the will of the spirit by the way they fall."

The following manifestation is more mental: "The professional takes in the hand a stick of lighted incense to expel all defiling influences; prayers of some sort are repeated, the fingers interlaced, and the medium's eyes are shut, giving unmistakable evidence of being possessed by some supernatural or spiritual power. The body sways back and forward; the incense falls, and the person begins to step about, assuming the walk and peculiar attitude of the spirit. This is considered as infallible proof that the divinity has entered the body of the medium. Sometimes the god, using the mouth of the medium, gives the supplicant a sound scolding for invoking his aid to obtain unlawful or unworthy ends. . . . Sometimes these mediums profess to be possessed by some specified god of great healing powers, and in this condition they prescribe for the sick. It is believed that the god, or spirit invoked, actually casts himself in some mysterious way, into the medium and dictates the medicine."

"The practice of divination," writes Sir John Burrows, "with many strange methods of summoning the dead to instruct the living and reveal the future, is of very ancient origin, as is proved by Chinese manuscripts antedating the revelations of the Jewish Scriptures."

An ancient Chinese book, called "Poh-shi-ching-tsung," consisting of six volumes on the "Source of True Divination," contains the following preface:

Fortune-telling Clairvoyants.

"The secret of augury consists in the study of the mysteries and in communications with gods and demons. The interpretations of the transformations are deep and mysterious. The theory of the science is most intricate, the practice of it most important. The sacred classic says: 'That which is true gives indications of the future.' To know the condition of the dead, and hold with them intelligent intercourse, as did the ancients, produces a most salutary influence upon the parties. . . . But when from intoxication or feasting, or licentious pleasures, they proceed to invoke the gods, what infatuation to suppose that their prayers will move them! Often when no response is given, or the interpretation is not verified, they lay the blame at the door of the augur, forgetting that their failure is due to their want of sincerity. . . . It is the great fault of augurs, too, that, from a desire of gain, they use the art of divination as a trap to ensnare the people."

Naturally undemonstrative and secretive, the higher classes of Chinese seek to conceal their full knowledge of spirit intercourse from foreigners, and from the inferior castes of their own countrymen, thinking them not sufficiently intelligent to rightly use it. The lower orders, superstitious and money-grasping, often prostitute their magic gifts to gain and fortune-telling. These clairvoyant fortune-tellers, surpassing wandering gypsies in "hitting" the past, infest the temples, streets and roadsides, promising to find lost property, discover precious metals and reveal the hidden future. What good thing is not abused? Liberty lives, though license prowls abroad in night time. Christianity wore the laurels it wove, though Peter denied and Judas betrayed. The great highway is open for the return of spirits to mortals, and that highway is traversed by the good and evil, the high and the low, the wise and the foolish. The tares grow plentifully in the grain-fields. But if we relate ourselves wisely, religiously, to this occult side of nature, it may not only become to us a mighty redemptive power, but a positive demonstration of a future existence.

Demons in Korea.

The Korean people, allied to both China and Japan, are superior in civilization to either of the above nations; and yet they have been abjectly at the mercy of China and Japan alternately, for centuries. And now Russia is politically struggling to seize and hold this lovely mountain peninsula. And so this war with Japan.

There are but two prominent beliefs in Korea. The one is materialism, and the other Oriental spiritism. The millions of this country never cherish a doubt of the fact that the blue above is filled with spiritual beings.

Dr. Landis, long a resident of Chemulpo, a populous Korean city, writes:

"Korea is the home of the most complex and all pervading witchcraft the world has ever seen. It is not cruel, like the fetichism of the Congo, but it is so servile and puerile that it has sapped the virility of a stalwart and attractive race.

"Obsession is common, and the Japanese methods of casting out these demons, though similar, is more severe than the Chinese.

"Parents are counted particularly lucky if they happen to have a son born blind. He can become a 'Pan Su,' or blind sorcerer, and is sure to be able to gain a handsome livelihood for the whole family. The 'Pan Su' are supposed to be gifted with supernatural instead of natural vision. The helpers of the male Shamans are the female sorcerers, who are everywhere in evidence. The function of these two classes of Shaman devotees is to propitiate the evil spirits which swarm in the air, three fourths of which demons being altogether malign. The 'Pan Su' and the 'Mutang' will not by any means exercise their spiritual gifts at a low figure. Their fees are most exorbitant, and it is computed that Shamanism costs the country not less than $500,000 annually!

"According to the popular creed, the selfish malign spirits fill largely every portion of space, anxious to manifest, or in some way seize upon the wretched citizen. Dr. Herbert Jones, having devoted much time and study to demonism in Japan, informs us that they consult their demon spirit attendants upon all important occasions.

"The 'Mutang,' or sorceress, is the most important sort of woman among the Koreans. She is everywhere in as much request as the blind 'Pan Su,' and as she can move about freely, not being blind as he is, she leads a much more active life. Yet, strange to say, this all-important personage is socially an outcast.

"If her prophecies fail, she is often punished. While the Koreans hold woman in lower esteem than any other civilized people, and the 'Mutang' is relegated to the lowest place of all, although she is the mediator between natural and supernatural agents.

" Children are sold to demons by very many families.

To sell a child to a spirit is reckoned by a Korean father to be the surest method of assuring its prosperity. The children thus consecrated still live with their parents, but they are considered to belong to the 'Mutang.'

"The late queen, a beautiful and talented woman, was a profound believer in Shamanism, spirit influences, and resorted continually to the demon oracles. But they could not save her from her cruel fate. She was foully murdered by Japanese assassins."

Meeting the Korean Ambassador.

It was my privilege while once crossing the ocean, to have the Korean ambassador to our country, for a cabin-mate. A perfect gentleman, he was educated in both Paris and London. He related to me by the hour the wonders, the manifestations and the obsessions that he had witnessed from his youth up, and he remarked rather facetiously that his country had been called "the land of devils," but he added, "I am skeptical on all matters pertaining to immortality."

What could be more consoling and uplifting than a knowledge that the spirits whom we had loved on earth, watched over us still? that affectionate, loving mothers kept vigil over us in the most trying hours of life? that the friends whose hands we had clasped so cordially, though "dead," still smiled unseen upon us? In the language of Washington Irving, "I think, it would be a new incentive to virtue, rendering us circumspect—even in our secret moments—from the idea that those we once loved and honored were invisible witnesses of all our actions."

CHAPTER V.

Demoniac Possession in Japan and Korea.

ALL close observers admit that rough, mountainous countries have produced the most seers and divinities, good and evil. Greece had its Socrates, Palestine its Nazarene, and Sweden its Swedenborg, who for many years held open converse with angels, spirits and demons of the underworld.

The Japanese islands, measurably rugged and mountainous, are haunted, it is said, by ugly ghosts and demons who afflict many of the people. The Bonzes (priests) are the exorcists. Their great book that treats of these occult phenomena is called "Baskwa-Shin-Eki." The demons that obsess so many of the people are called *Tengu*. They also have other names for evil spirits. All fortune-tellers are believed to be obsessed. A prominent fortune-teller is called *Shoko-Setsu*. These pass into dreamy, spasmodic states, when strange personalities speak through their lips. In this state of weird ecstasy they prophesy. The ignorant pronounce these ecstatic conditions, fits. The more intelligent pronounce these controls gods of the air, or demons of the dark regions, and priests are sent for to exorcise them.

The religious ceremonies of the Japanese Buddhists and the Roman Catholics are very similar. Catholic priests of the present day cast out these Tartarean demons. Pope Cornelius about the middle of the third century speaks of the exorcists as a special order of the clergy and the Council.

Laodicea forbid those who had not been ordained to exorcise either in the church or out. The so-called Fourth Council of Carthage prescribed a form for the ordination of exorcists, the same as that given in the Roman Pontifical, and used at this day! The bishop gives the book of exorcisms into the hand of the person to be ordained, and bids him to receive the power of laying his hands on these possessed by evil demons.

That excellent authority on Japan, Walter Dickson, informs us that "the demon spirits of Japan take a deep interest and perform an important part in the marriage of every pair. . . . The Mikado is allowed to have twelve wives; the Daimios eight, and the Shodaibu are allowed five. Evil spirits must obsess those that do not live together happily."

In this connection, we quote again from Dr. Nevius:

"In a visit to Japan in the summer of 1890, I found on inquiry that the beliefs and experiences of the natives of Japan in regard to demon-possession are not unlike those of the Chinese." I had a conversation and some correspondence with one of the professors in the Imperial University at Tokio, who is making a special investigation of this subject; and we may hope that the results of his inquiries will be made known to the public at no distant date. In the meantime, we have some very interesting statements relating to demonology in a recent work entitled, "Things Japanese," by Basil Hall Chamberlin, professor of Japanese and Philology in the Imperial University of Japan, published in 1890. Professor Chamberlin says:

"Chinese notions concerning the superhuman power of the fox, and in a lesser degree of the badger and of the dog, entered Japan during the early Middle Ages.

One or two mentions of the magic foxes occur in the 'Uji Jui,' a demon story of a long past century, and since that time the belief has spread and grown, till there is not an old woman in the land, or from the matter of that, not a man either—who has not a circumstantial fox-story to relate, as having happened to some one who is at least an 'acquaintance of an acquaintance.' . . . The names of such tales is legion, more curious and interesting is the power with which these demon foxes are credited in taking up their abode in human beings in a manner similar to the phenomena of possession by evil spirits so often referred to in the New Testament. Dr. Baelz, of the Imperial University of Japan, who has had special opportunities for studying these cases in the hospitals under his charge, has kindly communicated to Dr. Nevius some remarks, of which the following is a résumé:

"Possession by foxes (Kitsuni-tsuki) is a form of nervous disorder or delusion not uncommonly observed in Japan. Having entered the human being, sometimes through the breast, more often through the space between the finger nails and flesh, the fox lives a life of its own, apart from the proper self of the person who is harboring him. There thus results a sort of double entity, or double consciousness. The person possessed hears and understands everything that the fox inside says or thinks, and the two often engage in a loud and violent dispute, the fox speaking in a voice altogether different from that which is natural to the individual. The only difference between the cases of possession mentioned in the Bible, and those observed in Japan, is that it is almost exclusively women that are attacked, mostly women of the lower classes. Among the predisposing conditions may be mentioned a weak intellect, a superstitious turn of the mind, and such debilitating diseases, as for instance, typhoid fever. Possession never occurs except in such subjects as have heard of it already and believe in the reality of its existence.

"To mention one among several cases: I was once called in to a girl with typhoid fever. She recovered, but during her convalescence, she heard the women around her talk of another woman who had a fox, and who would doubtless do her best to pass it on to some one else in order to get rid of it. At that moment, the girl experienced an extraordinary sensation. The fox (a spirit) had taken possession of her. All her efforts to get rid of him were in vain. 'He is coming! He is coming!' she would cry, as a fit of the fox drew near. 'Oh, what shall I do! Here he is.' And then in a strange, dry, cracked voice, the fox would speak, and mock his unfortunate hostess. Thus matters continued for three weeks, till a priest of the Nichiren sect was sent for. The priest upbraided the fox sternly. The fox (always, of course, speaking through the girl's mouth) argued on the other side. At last he said, 'I am tired of her. I ask no better than to leave her. What will you give me for doing so?' The priest asked what he would take. The fox replied, naming certain cakes and other things, which he said must be placed before the altar of such and such a temple, at 4 P. M., on such a day. The girl was conscious of the words her lips were made to say, but was powerless to say anything in her own person. When the day and the hour arrived, the offerings bargained for were taken by her relatives to the place indicated, and the fox-demon quitted the girl at that very hour."

A scribe and literary assistant of Dr. J. B. McCarter, in Tokio, named Ga-ma-no-uchi described to Dr. Nevius a case which came under his own observation. He stated that he knew of no cases of demon obsession in Tokio, but that they were quite numerous in his home in Ki Shiu. He gave the case of a boy about fourteen years of age, named Mo-ri Sa-no Ki-Chi, possessed by a person calling himself a name which Mr. Ga-ma-no-uchi had forgotten, whose home was in Sendai: "I held long conversations with this new personality, who described accurately his former home in Sendai, which place the boy had never visited. The boy was sometimes his original self, and at other times the new personality spoke through him. There were not two co-existing personalities (the boy and the supposed spirit conversing together); but only one personality at a time. He was cured by priests who held a service over him, upbraiding the spirit and commanding it to leave. The spirit promised to leave on condition of certain offerings being made. When they were made, the boy was restored to consciousness, and by degrees gained his strength and became well again."

We are further assured by Dr. Nevius that Mr. Ga-ma-no-uchi is a man of literary culture, and by profession a physician. Dr. Nevius sums up his testimony on demonology in Japan in the following words:

"It is sufficient to state that the facts given in the above-mentioned volumes correspond throughout to those presented in the preceding chapters; showing the remarkable uniformity which, nowithstanding variations in minor particulars, resulting from race peculiarities and difference of culture, have characterized these manifestations always and everywhere."

CHAPTER VI.

Demoniacal Obsessions and Possessions in India.

IT WAS on the seventh day of that hot July month, 1878, that for the first time I reached the capital of India, Calcutta, the city of mingled poverty and palaces. The one prime object of this tour through the cities of India was to investigate the occult, to witness the much-lauded magic of the wonder-workers and to study Yogaism. Calling first upon our United States consul, I sought next morning the residence of Peary Chand Mittra, a commission merchant, writer and author; and with all the rest, a well-read psychic. And yet, though liberal, he was still a Brahmin of the Brahmins, and that Brahminical tinge permeating his higher religious convictions, had for me a thousand charms. He was for a time an automatic writing sensitive, but now his gifts pertained more to spiritual insight and inspiration. He assured me that his ascended wife was as a personality, as consciously present with him at times as though in her mortal body. He kindly gave me letters of introduction to prominent and distinguished people in several Hindu cities, which later I visited, witnessing magic performances, temple-girls dancing, automatic writing, white and black magic, demon obsessions, and several cases of the "casting out of demons" by the templed priests.

The oldest word for god in the *Veda*, is *deva*. The common name for fathers, or dead ancestors, was *pitris*. There are *Rig-Veda* prayers addressed to the gods which are known in other countries as ghosts, ancestral spirits, shades and manes. " The whole social fabric of India, with its laws of inheritance and marriage, rests upon a belief," says Max Muller, " in the *manes, pitris* and *pisachas.*" Manu, the ancient Hindu lawgiver, informs us that the "*devas* were born of the *pitris*, and the *pitris* of the *rishis.*"

The belief is universal among the various races and tribes of India that spirits, good and bad, especially the latter, have access to and the power to influence mortals. Among the hill-tribes, demoniacal obsession has become a sort of religion. To the same end, Dr. Caldwell, in the *Contemporary Review*, thus writes: "I contend that it appears that certain demonolators of the present day, as far as the outward evidence of their affliction goes, display as plain signs of demoniacal possession as ever were displayed eighteen hundred years ago in Palestine. I hold that as far as the senses can be trusted and history relied upon, several thousands could be produced tomorrow in southern India, who, as far as can be ascertained, are as truly possessed of evil demons as was the man who was forced by the fiends within him to howl that he was not himself, but that his name was Legion. Not a few of the persons I refer to are, on ordinary circumstances, calm and peaceful. They have their avocations and often pursue them diligently. Sometimes, they have their wives and children; they possess their inherited huts, small plantation gardens, wells, and scores of palmyras. But night draws near; the fire before the rustic devil-temple is lit; the crowd gathers;

the séance commences, waiting for the priest—medium. He is now here! His lethargy is thrown aside, the laugh of the fiend is in his mouth. He stands before the temple, the oracle of the demon, the devil-possessed! . . . He believes he is possessed of the local demon, whom he continually treats just as if it were a divinity; and the people believe in his obsessing hallucination. They shudder, they bow, they pray, they worship. The devil-actor is not drunk; he has eschewed arrack, and is not suffering from the effects of Ganja, abin-mayakham, as the Tamil poet calls it. He has not been seized with epilepsy, as the sequel shows. He is not attacked with a bit of hysteria, although within an hour after he has begun his weird performance, half of his audience are seemingly hysterical. He can scarcely be insane, for the moment the séance is over he speaks sanely, quietly and calmly. What is it, then? You ask him. He simply answers: 'Some devil seized me, sir.' You ask the bystanders. They simply answer: 'The demon must have seized him. He was possessed.' In this state he describes spirits and announces their names. What is the most reasonable inference to draw from all this? Of one thing I am assured—the devil-performer never 'shams' excitement. . . . Whether this be devil possession or not, I cannot help remarking that it appears to me that it would certainly have been regarded as such in New Testament times. It is an extremely difficult thing for a European to witness a devil scene of this kind and comprehend it. As a rule he must be disguised and be able to speak the language like a native, before he is likely to be admitted into the charmed circle of fascinated devotees, each eager to press near the possessed person to ask him questions about the future, while the divine afflatus is in its full force upon him."

A Demon Hard to Dislodge.

"In conversation with an intelligent Talu Khar, Abdul-Kurim by name, when I was magistrate in Oudh," writes W. Knighton in the *Nineteenth Century,* 1880, "I learned that this satanic or demoniacal possession was commonly believed in not only by the peasantry or Hindustan proper, but also by the higher classes, the nobility and learned proprietors. . . .

"Different exorcists have their own method of procedure, but violence and the infliction of pain to cast out the devils are the most common. When the cure is not effected, the devil is said to be vicious and obstinate. Then severe beating is resorted to, and in some instances cotton wicks soaked in oil are lighted and stuffed up the nostrils, etc. . . . Both Hindus and Mohammedans resort to the Dougah at Ghouspore, bringing with them their afflicted relations to be exorcised. . . . Faith in Ghouspore and its efficacy in the cure of the possessed with devils, is spread all over the adjoining country."

Mr. Knighton likewise gives an account of a woman named Melata, the wife of a man named Ahir. He saw the woman after the devil had been cast out: "A well-informed, active, intelligent woman, with large, lustrous black eyes." When her father and mother died, she sank into a mourning melancholy. Then it was that she became possessed. Neither she nor her husband had any doubt of the fact. . . .

"I conversed with several villagers on the subject. Possession by an evil spirit was plain to all of them, and the old hag, her enemy, who lived opposite to her, was accused as the cause.... She became morbid, sullen, taciturn. At length, her disease culminated in dumbness. The woman was taken to the shrine of Ghouspore, and treated at first by beating, questioning and enchantments; but all in vain. Then 'by the Ojah's command,' said Gemganarain, 'I tied her hands behind her. I tied her feet. Cotton wicks steeped in oil were prepared. They were lighted and stuffed up her nostrils and into her ears. It cured her. It drove out the devil. She shrieked and spoke. She was convulsed and became insensible. She is well now. The devil has left her. And it is true. In three days she returned with me; and the old hag died, and she has been well ever since. The darkness of hell was in our home before; now we have the light of heaven.' All the villagers confirm this; none more read" than Melata herself."

CHAPTER VII.

More Stubborn Facts Concerning Demoniacal Obsessions in India.

THE labors of psychic students in the line of demoniacal obsession have been in a sense duplicated by Colonel Olcott, of Adyar, India. Desiring to know directly from the Hindus themselves their beliefs concerning the conditions and the employments of their dead in the future world, he sent out a circular letter to Hindu theosophists, Hindu authors, and others all over India

Demoniacal Obsessions in India.

bearing upon spirit intercourse, demons, black magic, mediums, sorcery and soothsayers. The Colonel admits that the responses he received to this circular letter contained but a meager amount of information in consequence of "the Asiatic loathing for any meddling with the dead." But meager as it may be, it is perfectly satisfactory upon these points:

1. That the Hindu believes most sincerely in a future conscious existence.

2. That those existing or dwelling in the spirit world can and do hold intelligent intercourse with human beings. Spiritism in some form is a belief quite as universal in India as in China.

Incidentally, in passing, I remark that this New York-begotten, modern theosophical movement, so far as our progressive West is concerned, is a stupendous failure —a crab-like, backward movement toward the perishing superstitions of antiquity. Brahminism is a spent force. How absurd to seek the living among the dead. Northern India is the center of an effete civilization. The intellectual life once so potent on those high table-lands of Pamir is now transferred to the Western Hemisphere, and on Ganges' banks are old-style, plague-stricken cities, crumbling shrines, wasting desolation, moss-shingled ruins, and sepulchers that entomb a dead past. And yet, there is no death. The Aryan spirit can never die. Progress lies in the germ, not the shell. India, aroused from her lethargy by the heaven-descending inspirations of today, by science, and by an infusion of Western enterprise, will rise again, and a new India will blossom and bear golden fruitage.

With this digression from the main topic, I will here append a condensed portion of the responses to Colonel Olcott's circular:

Baroda-State Demonism.

"The space," says this Hindu writer, " they (the earth-bound) live in may be called Kama Loka, or the world of desire. Some of these souls may be so attracted to this earth by strong desires, that they may even remain in the regions inhabited by man. There are various narratives given in 'Yoga Vasishta' (a standard work on Yoga philosophy), of deceased persons with special attractions to the houses they had lived in, and some who had strong desires at the time of their death that they would be kings, etc., lingering in these very places; the consequence of which was that their souls, being cut off from the normal evolution from material existence toward the spiritual state, were tied, or tethered, so to say, to those places."

"Earth-bound souls can do us injury by sympathetically entering our auras, or possibly our visible physical bodies, giving them pain, and tormenting us even to death. It is thought that these borderland souls, the worst ones of them being called Bhutas or Pisachas, have very strong earthly desires for evil, but that they have not the physical instruments in themselves by which they can satisfy their desires, and so they enter the corporeal bodies of others to satisfy their desires."

"It is, in our estimation, a bad thing for mankind to encourage intercourse with their earth-bound, deceased friends or other persons; because these earth-confined souls, having become earth-imprisoned through strong worldly desires, cannot really give such instruction as will emancipate the soul of the living man, which is the highest goal that should be aimed at; and, secondly, because these earth-bound souls or demons are likely, by their intercourse, to inflame such desires in the living persons as will also make them earth-bound at their death."

"The lower spirits attach themselves to or possess certain persons whose nature and disposition are similar to theirs, or whose extreme passivity attracts their influence. Our firm conviction is that men attract to themselves such of these beings as are in sympathy with their habitual thoughts and predominant passions or tendencies."

Southern India Demonism.

"HYDERABAD.—The unsatisfied desire, the chief goal of a certain distinguished man's ambition to teach his grammatical lore to humanity, made him a denizen of Kama Loka. Ever after his death he used to haunt a tree in the back compound of his house, from whose top he used to recite verses for the edification of those pupils who were eager to profit by his instructions.

"It is said that the students who were allowed the privilege of hearing him were able afterward to rightly construe some of the doubtful passages of the Vedas. Of the pranks and mischief committed by the Kama Loka entities upon men of Tamo Guna there are hundreds of instances." (On my first visit to Madura, I spent several days with a Brahmin, demagnetizing or casting out demons.)

"During the Navaratri (Dasra) all persons, male and females, obsessed by ghosts resorted to the Madura pagoda. Every year the number amounts to nearly two hundred. Their wild contortions and their howlings, their superhuman actions in some cases, all make the pagoda a regular pandemonium during those nine days.

At San Kara Nainar Kovil, in Tinnevelly, this takes place all the year round. There is a small temple at Dattatraya, on the confluence of the Krishna and the Cunch Ganga. I saw several obsessed persons there when I visited it some fifteen years ago, several of whom were, as their relations told me (also Col. H. S. Olcott), in a fair way toward recovery. The place is very famous for curing people suffering from obsession. Priestcraft has not much scope there, because generally the obsessed person himself gets a dream or manifestation as to what he should do for the cure. Hundreds of cases are, it is said, cured there."

The Slaughtered Return to Obsess.

"Those in the Ramnad Chuttrum at Permagoody, Madura, were massacred to the last man. In consequence of this incident, the Chuttrum and the adjoining Brahmin quarters became haunted by the disembodied spirits of the dead. The poor people of the agraharam were tormented by these spirits; all sorts of howlings would be heard in and abount the Chuttrum; murderous sounds and groans would be loudly ringing in the haunted grounds.

"For one year the place about the Chuttrum presented a deserted appearance. About that time a Bairagi pilgrim from the North, who was on his way to Ramæsmaram, happened to break his journey at Permagoody, and put up in the haunted Chuttrum. The devils also tried their pranks upon him; but he was proof against soothsayers, sorcerers and demons.

"The injury they often do may be either physical or mental. The former is perceived by a gradual diminution of vital activity, culminating in death. This death sometimes takes place in a moment. But in either case, no trace will be perceptible of the manner of the wound or disease in causing death. No physical remedy will stand it; but any one accustomed to numerically manipulating these forces will be able to cure the malady.

"As for the mind, the man gradually develops disposition in one particular direction, and some tendency either for good or bad, which he had formerly, and which was not observed hitherto, begins to grow in intensity at the expense of all the rest. The man becomes nervous, irritable, a monomaniac, harmful or harmless according to the spirit that controls him. They attack men, women and children indiscriminately, producing fever, hysteria and many nervous complaints.

"I have also heard from a friend of mine the case of a Pariah, who was in communication with a spirit. He used to live in Sarum, a village about ten or twelve miles distant from Bulsar, in the Bombay presidency. This man had his séances every Tuesday and Sunday, and hundreds of men used to flock there, asking him numerous questions. These questions were not put verbally, but every man that had an inquiry to make put a pie and some rice upon a piece of wood before the Pariah. About a hundred such pies were placed in rows before he commenced work. In the beginning, he would untie his hair, take a brass plate and beat it vigorously, swinging his head to and fro. This process continued for about a half an hour, when all at once the brass plate would fall out of his hand, and the Pariah, continuing to swing his head as before, answered the questions put. My friend, who saw the man himself, said that questions were quickly, rightly answered, and almost all those who came to consult him went home satisfied with his answers.

"He ordered my nephew, a child of a year old, to be brought to him. The child was made to sit on the floor in front of us. He said he was going to show some wonder, and that I could ask any question of the child in any language I chose. He then covered himself with rettarium, and touched the child with a light rattan he had in his hand. The child immediately sat in a posture known as Virasanum, and gave me a learned discourse on Raja Yoga in beautiful Tamil verse. I was so struck with this wonder that I did not then avail myself of his permission to ask the child questions, but continued to be a passive hearer. While this was going on, I looked at the Yogi and found that his body was motionless and rigid. I thought he was in a trance and tried to wake him. His body was at first like a corpse; but in a few seconds he got up and at the same instant the child began to weep very loudly. His first words were, 'Take the child away and give it milk instantly.' This was done. It was exhausted by the invisible influences. . . .

"On another occasion he was talking of various things while on the river-bed, when we were performing japam, and all of a sudden he asked me to confess before him all the sins I had committed. I told him that I had nothing of importance to tell him. He then ordered me to bring 'olai' and an iron stylus. He then made me a seat of sand in a square shape, wrote on it some letters and asked me to sit upon it. After I had taken my seat he gave me a smart blow with a rod. I then suddenly began to write. I was conscious I was writing, but had no control over what I wrote. I could not of myself write; some mysterious force compelled me to do it. I yielded. I felt a sort of mild intoxication. About half an hour afterward, the Yogi snatched the 'olai' from my hands, splashed cold water over my face, and took me out for a walk. He then after some time, gave me the 'olai' to read. But what was my amazement, when in my own handwriting, I found a detailed and substantial account of all my peccadillos which I would not for the world have anybody know. There are different orders of these influencing demons. Some give such tests as finding lost property."

Mysor's Testimony about Spirits.

"Summoning and talking with spirits is a bad thing; no respectable family would encourage such intercourse; only sorcerers do so, and they always get punished for it. If they omit the least part of their magical ceremony, or in any way do anything to weaken their acquired will power over the 'spirits,' they are instantly killed by the latter. A sorcerer is said to have been thus destroyed a while since by fire in the streets of Calcutta. It is considered a wicked act of selfishness—an interference with the order of nature and the law of God to converse with demons.

"In relation to sex, women are more subject than men to their attacks, but only after attaining puberty. The victim, often losing health, appetite and interest in domestic affairs, constantly broods over the controlling Pisacha, and, when not controlled by it, seems stupid and absent-minded. She is often made to gratify his lust, but not through the marital act.

"Occasionally one hears that, through the intervention of a sorcerer, some one causes serious annoyance to his enemies by introducing unpleasant things (e. g., excrement) in the plate of rice (while being eaten or served), causing the fall of stones on house-tops and terrifying the people inside, etc. On the most vigilant search no human being would appear in the neighborhood. That these wild phenomena occur none deny.

"Both Brahma-pisachas and Pisachas obsess or take control of living persons; but the former are not malicious; persecutions and foolish phenomena are done by the latter. The 'bhuta' has some desire to satisfy, and if that is gratified, he will be released and go away. The Pisacha seems to take delight in causing confusion and trouble, inflicting pain, gratifying low appetites and taking life. A perfectly pure and good person, if of a religious mind, will not be attacked by an evil spirit; but any vicious habit attracts them. Ignorance of religious things, also, renders persons liable to their influence. Elementaries (Bhatas and Pretas) are generally considered to do injury to men that are evilly inclined."

Mantras and Demons.

"I am a pensioned rassalder (troop-leader) of the Mysore Horse, and my services took me into various districts, among other Shivamoogah, where it is a common thing for people to have intercourse with Pisachas.

"Some use mantras, or spells, by which they control the demons. (The word *mantra* may mean a hymn, a prayer or an invocation.) They demand, or compel them, at times, to guard their property. If a thief lay his hand upon any article in the house, or any fruit in the garden of a man so protected, he is unable to stir from the spot or withdraw his hand until the owner returns, and not even then until the spirit is ordered to set him free. A Pisacha so employed is called a 'chowdi;' by accepting this help for such a selfish purpose, the sorcerer gives him a stronger hold upon himself, and he has to exercise all the more caution, lest he fail for a moment to keep the control, and thus lose his life. Sorcerers can transfer the services of their chowdis, and it is a common thing for the purchaser of a garden to take from the seller the mantram by which the garden chowdi is controlled; otherwise, he would not be able to enjoy the fruits of the field or orchard. Pisachas sometimes take possession of a house, a well or a tree. They are driven away by a mantriki (one possessing knowledge of mantras), by reciting charms, suspending jantras (cabalistic signs inscribed upon sheet-copper plaques) on the walls, sides or branches, as the case may be, and other divices. Sometimes when the Pisacha (spirit-control) is expelled from a medium he is obsessing, the mantriki will cut a lock of her hair, wrap it about an iron nail and drive the nail into a tree; the Pisacha is then bound to the tree until the nail rusts away.

"There are various Sivaite and Vishnaite temples which are famed for relieving persons from obsessing Pisachas. I, myself, have seen the phenomenon a score of times at the Hanumanta, the Vishnu and the Durga temples in Bangalore. My wife has seen the same at the Minakshi temple, Madura. A Pisacha medium will not sit quiet to hear the Ranarana read; she will jump up and run away.

"A case happened in my own family in 1875-76, where the patient used to tell me (I was standing by and assisting the patient) that she could clairvoyantly see the devils (three in number) sitting by her and beside her,. as well as she could see myself. When the devil was to fall on her, she used to tell me: 'Now look here; the devil is preparing and girding up her loins to fall upon me. Be on the alert.' Immediately after that I used to notice the usual convulsions in the patient. The patient used to pre-announce the hours of attack by the devil, and she was so sure of it that she used to tell us, the assisting men, to go away. on our business, but be ready by the hour and minute predicted. I always found the prediction true. At last, the obsessing demon stated all the particulars of her unsatisfied desires to us through the lips of the patient, with the request that before driving her out by mantras we would satisfy them. The devil said, she (it was the spirit of a woman) died full of desires which were not yet satisfied. We complied with her wishes, and till this moment we have been free from further annoyance. The devil has kept its word. The man who subdued this spirit was a well-known 'white magician' who was respected by one and all of the community in which he lived. He was known to be an extraordinary good, pious, truth-seeking man.''

CHAPTER VIII.

More Testimonies to Hindu Demonism.

"MY MOTHER," said Prasad Chatterji, "used to tell me that her grandmother-in-law had become earth-bound, though she was a good-natured lady, through intense affection for her young children, whom she had left behind at her death. Her husband was an eminent magician, and she had constant opportunity of seeing obsessed persons, and it was believed that probably these scenes had something to do with her becoming earth-bound. Her medium was her daughter-in-law, that is, my mother's mother-in-law. Some members of the family did not believe in the truth of the manifestations, and regarded the medium as only pretending to be obsessed by her mother-in-law. One day her son became suddenly ill; all medicine failed, and it was thought he would die in a short time. Suddenly the medium became obsessed, and began to say that if any members of the family thought the obsession mere humbug, they might try all the medicines in the world and save her son if they had the power. The family members implored that the earth-bound soul which manifested itself through the medium, and was the guardian angel of the family, might save her son. The obsession ceased for a while, but reappeared soon afterward, and the medium began to say that she, the earth-bound soul, had to take very great trouble to drive off the earth-bound souls that had entered the house along with a certain idol that was brought into the family from a distant country, and that the idol should be at once removed and taken out of the house.

"This was done in the dead of night, and the medium scratched up a little earth from the ground and applied it to the forehead of her dying son, after which he at once got better and recovered. The medium used to become obsessed whenever there was great danger to any member of the family, and the earth-bound soul used to relate, through the mouth of the medium, that her strong desire for the children made her a Bhut, or Pisacha (earth-bound soul), and that that state of existence was not at all desirable. Mediumship with us is not considered a thing to be proud of, but rather the reverse."

Kathiawar and the Hindu's Warning Words.

"It is strange that in India mediumship, except in very rare instances, is looked upon by us as a great misfortune, while the Spiritualists of the West seem to encourage it as a means of communication between the living and the dead, or between men and the angels. It is sad to think what terrible misfortunes they are bringing upon their several communities by thus ignorantly breaking down the barriers erected by nature between the two worlds. Our knowledge has been bought by the miseries of ancestral experience, and perhaps the Western nations will have to journey the same road."

BHAVNAGER.—"As an unmistakable sign of these degenerate times in our country, we constantly hear much more of black magic than of white magic.

"I have a friend at R., a Parsee, a shop-keeper and merchant. He has a son P., about twenty years old, a nice young man, but physically weak, who was for nearly a year subject to wild ravings and fits, which his father, a man of common sense, at first attributed to hysteria. No medicine could cure him, and the boy became more and more violent, and his father assures us that in his fits he would talk a purer Hindustani than in his sober moments; that he was forced at length to suspect, against his will that there was something spiritually uncanny about it. He took him to his native place, E., not far from Surat. It is one of the most interesting features of this remarkable case that on the first occasion after the arrival of a Brahmin exorciser who was sent for from Surat in o violent fit, P., or rather his control, eyeing a pot of mesmerized water that the Brahmin had prepared beforehand, yelled in a highly excited manner and said that there was fire issuing from the pot, and the lambent flames were striking upon him with deadly effect. Evidently, he could see the antagonistic aura of the exorciser issuing from the pot. In accordance with the Brahmin's instructions, the father rubbed a small quantity of water on his chest, and P. got relief. This was continued as often as the boy got the fits or trances, but the control never left him for good. His father consulted many others known as exorcisers, but P. failed to get permanent relief from the vampire. At length, his father was advised to go to R. with his son, and consult a Sanyasi there. This holy man gave P. a string, evidently full of his pure magnetism, to be tied round his arm. By all accounts, as far as I know, P. is quite well now."

Bhavnager and Spirit Influences.

"Mediumistic phenomena are very common indeed in this part of India. Possessions and obsessions manifest themselves in tremors of the whole body. . . . The trembling medium, or rather the control, is compelled by the exorciser, by incantations or threats and objurgations, to declare who it is that possessed or obsessed the medium, and how it is to be pacified. These objurgations sometimes take days before any decisive issue is reached, during which time the exorciser frequently invokes his favorite Mata, by his own tremors, to compel the control, elemental or elementary, to leave the patient for good. The exorciser has, of course, the greatest reverence for his Mata; an image of her is religiously kept in a niche in his house, which he constantly honors and to which he offers his oblations and sacrifices.

"It is certainly considered by the intelligent classes that intercourse with deceased persons in highly dangerous."

Coromandel Coast and the Evidence of Demonism.

"There seems to be a wide-spread belief that intercourse with deceased persons should be avoided as much as possible. If the soul of the departed is invoked, it is only to find out the wishes and other particulars about the devil which possesses a man, whose cure is put in the hands of a 'mantrika' (one who knows about mantras) and, by satisfying those wishes or otherwise, to deliver the patient from the hold of the devil. Even this is not done by the mantrikas, who are supposed to be of the higher class. They only go through the man-

More Testimonies to Hindu Demonism. 83

tras and expel the devil, or Pisacha, without any invocation or any apparent intercourse with it.

"They are capable of doing us harm in a variety of ways; by depriving us of our 'means of subsistence,' by depriving us of our children and near relations; by bringing about sickness, madness, leprosy, etc., in the family; by the death of the medium or the exorcisers themselves; in short, by every ' imaginable means' that might bring about death and ruin in any of their forms.

"The black magicians make money by it. It is, even in these skeptical days, a lucrative trade. There are persons whose special subject is black magic, who are able to exorcise evil spirits from anybody, and take measures to prevent further visits from such unwholesome creatures. Such persons are to be found in the Coimbators and Malabar districts.

"They are supposed to injure us by possessing us, and thereby deranging our minds, and in various other ways. They phenomenally deposit rubbish in our boxes and rice-pots, tear our valuable clothes and such other things which involve the disintegration or destruction of tangible matter. In one instance, the 'devil,' or these demon spirits used to throw some babe in the house among thorns, where it was often found in the morning. This is an incident connected with the family of a relation of mine, and took place when I was a boy about ten years old. Many relations, who are still alive, can testify to the facts, as having seen them. Sometimes stones are pelted at men and into the houses. I know a case which was a matter of great notoriety in the town in which I am now living. There is a house which now belongs to a near relation of mine. During the time of its former owner, and for some time after it came into the hands of its present owner, one peculiar phenomenon was often witnessed by many men now living. This house stands close by a 'masjid' where there are some Mohammedan tombs. The masjid is supposed to be haunted, even up to this day. What occurred was, that huge stones would fall into this house and compound, from the side of the masjid. For some time it was supposed to be due to human agency, but all attempts to prove it so failed. The intelligences were invisible and dangerous."

Bengal and Black Magic.

"It is generally considered a calamity when a person is possessed by an elemental; but we find in some of the Tantric works how an elemental could be evoked and commanded to do the biddings of the human invoker; this is what is called the 'Black Art.' Those people who have control over the elementals do not command a very high respect, although they are dreaded. It is a common belief that it is not good to invoke elementals or to have anything to do with them. In many Hindu families the children wear maldoolies, or some other charms, to protect them from the elementals. The metal, iron, is used for the purpose. The customs regarding this protection are various. Injurious in all cases is this intercourse. None of the higher castes would attempt or seek to have intercourse with demons.

"When it is said that a woman is possessed by an elemental, she acts like a mad woman, and her health gradually decays and her whole appearance changes for the worst.

"Often I used to see in our village people being attacked by Dyeens, or witches, the symptoms being hysterical with twitchings and spasms; when persons who were experts in these matters used to come and utter certain incantations, the *djin* then left its medium.

"Any misfortunes, domestic calamity or peculiar phenomenon is attributed to the wrath of the Pitris, or the departed ancestors.

"No good can ever come of intercourse with the bad Pretas, who will only inflame the physical cravings of weak girls and men by 'possessing' them, and assist black magicians for the sake of offerings of drinks, flesh and lust. They are unknown as ' Chathans' on the Malabar coast, where Christians, Brahmins, and of course, also black magicians play the exorcists.

The Bhuwas, of whom a detailed account is given in Dalpatram's book, and who, as a rule are themselves mediums and induce mediumistic conditions in others, being an illiterate class, have no definite notion of the Kama Loka. Kama Loka, consider, signifies the dark spheres of desire, and Preta is the Sanskrit name for all disembodied souls. The devil-ridden only are put *en rapport* with weak mediums by the developing black magicians, but the deva-protected sometimes annoy their relatives and friends, just for prayers as helps to cross on to Devachan, or Swarga. The 'pitris' are the devas of dead worthies and ancestors.

"They may also do things which are impossible for man in his present state, by reason of their familiarity with certain laws which appertain to their existence. They are believed to be capable of assuming any animal form, and materializing, make themselves visible. But all these do not make them superior to men; but, on the contrary, they are absolute slaves of the spiritually-illumined adept who can control them completely and compel them to carry out his will. Such af these semi-human beings as are of mischievous tendencies can be coaxed into carrying out evil bequests by the black magicians.

"I have known a clairvoyant who used to hear (clairaudiently) the bemoaning cries of the creatures, at times innocent, at times mischievous, but always anxious to escape from the unenviable sphere.

"The residents of Kama Loka include entities that were once human gaints and demons (elementals) of terrible shapes, and Yama's messengers who are kind and gentle to pious souls, but extremely hard on the evil ones."

During all my journeyings in India, I do not recollect of ever conversing with an intelligent Hindu who had not a fixed belief that there were familiar spirits, demons and gods, inhabiting the unseen regions, all of which, if desiring, had access to the inhabitants of earth. A distinguished Brahmin informed me that there were ten classes of such beings, the first seven of which were created with the world, or by the thoughts and acts of the higher gods on whom they wait as servants, receiving some of their worship. But the last three classes were exclusively of human origin, being more or less ignorant, malignant, discontented beings, wandering in the invisible intermediate state, intent upon mirth, mischief and annoyance to mortals, chiefly by means of obsession, selfish possession, or wicked inspirations exemplifying the doctrine of "transferrence of thought and of transmigration and reincarnation."

The above three classes are known by the name of Bhuta, Preta and Pisacha, the first name being ordinarily applied to all three and sometimes to the seven superior classes. With others, they are used synonymously, sometimes as are demons and angels in Greek literature. But generally, the word Bhuta applies to evil, especially to the souls of those who have died untimely or violent deaths, or having been deformed or insane, or drunken, dissolute, or perversely wicked during life. Quite commonly the word Preta signifies the ghost of a child or one born deformed, imperfect or monstrous.

The "Pisacha," on the other hand, is derived from or refers more directly to mental characteristics, and is the strolling ghost of mad men, habitual drunkards, the lascivious, the treacherous and violently tempered, and in consonance with and realizing the idea that the evils which men do live after them and manifest as malicious spirits. Bhutas refer more directly to those who die by way of violence, die in war, died as suicides, or who have been robbers, notorious evil doers, and guilty of great cruelty. To this end, the eminent Mr. M. J. Walhouse, F. R. A. S., writing of devil-worship in India recently, said:

"The death of any well-known bad character is a source of terror to all his neighborhood, as he is sure to become a Bhuta or demon, as powerful and malignant as he was in life. Some of the Bhutas now most dreaded were celebrated personages of old days. All such persons on death are liable to become Bhutas, and attach themselves to any beings of the higher classes whom they first meet on entering the spirit-world, and derive from them power and assistance in tormenting and afflicting men and animals. As an example of how forcibly this idea possesses the popular mind, I will read an extract from a recent Indian newspaper: 'We learn from a correspondent at Cochin that, a couple of days before the Christmas holidays, a Nair of Chenganoor, in cold blood, murdered his paramour on suspicion of her infidelity. The noteworthy and strange feature of the case is, that when he was taken up and arraigned before the Sessions Court, he pleaded "guilty" to the charge, but earnestly implored that the extreme penalty of the law, which he admitted he fully deserved, might be carried out, not at the usual place of execution, but at the scene of his crime, in order that he might, according to his theory of the transmigration of the soul, assume the form and life of a "demon," and thereby have full scope for revenging himself on the man and his associates who were the cause of leading his unfortunate victim astray.' It is also held that by certain ceremonies and expiation, this form of existence can be dissolved, and the unquiet spirits remitted to regions of reward or punishment, according to their deserts on earth."

For thousands of years Brahmin priests ruled India with a rod of iron. Kings, or rather head-chiefs, were their agents. The masses maintained in consonance with caste, the upper classes in luxury. Their temples were store-houses for sacred relics, idols and sacerdotal treasures.

The Brahmins who officiated at the temples taught the people to read the first three books of the Vedas; taught them religious ceremonies, and how to perform sacrifices. The minor priests—the gurus—using the Atharva Veda, a great collection of magical conjurations, explained to the lower castes the nature of soothsaying, the evocation of spirits, the methods of exorcisms and all magical phenomena.

CHAPTER IX.

The Demonism of the Ancient Greeks and the Australian Aborigines.

NO STUDENT of history need be informed that Greece ever in her palmiest days, was aware of the well-attested fact that invisible agencies—demons— mingled with and influenced the people. These demons in Homer's, Hesiod's and Socrates' time did not necessarily signify evil spirits.

The term "demon" was used by Homer, who flourished about 1000 B. C., as a deity; hence, Minerva goes cheerfully to the palace of Zeus to meet "the other demons." Venus is described as a "demon" after her interview with Helen ("Iliad" iii: 420). "But the tendency was," says Dr. Alexander, "to apply the term to lesser personages." Hector threatening Diomede, exclaims with emphasis, "I will give thee to a demon ('Iliad' viii: 166)." Demons were said to suggest evil thoughts. A sick man pining away is "one upon whom a hateful demon has gazed." (" Odyssey " iii: 27.)

It may be said with safety that all the demons of the poet (see Hesiod, about 800 B. C.) were good intentioned; accordingly, he divides rational beings incarnate and discarnate, into gods, demons, heroes (demigods) and men. These demons were sometimes called the "guardians of men," and Zeus holds out the encouraging idea to some of his friends that they should sometime become "like demons" ("Works and Days," p. 314).

Empedocles taught that demons "were of a mixed and inconstant nature, and are subjected to a purgatorial process which may finally end in their ascension to higher abodes." And yet, he attributed to them nearly all the calamities, vexations and plagues incident to mankind. The great poet-philosopher, Plato, writes of demons, good and bad. He informs us that demons are tutelary officials to men, and that Zeus, the greatest sovereign of heaven, was followed by a "host of gods and demons." God, he assures us, "does not directly mingle with men, but uses demons as intermediates" (Sympos. 202: D). In referring to the Hesiodic demons, he informs us that these were the good and the noble of "the golden age." He used the phrase "divine demons," and at another time he tells of "fierce and fiery men who discharge the function of angels of punishment." Briefly stated, Plato's demons, mostly good, had a residuum of evil, that perplexed and obsessed mortals.

Aristotle, the son of a physician, less poetical and more metaphysical than Plato, especially concerning the material world, speaks directly of "demons influencing and inspiring the possessed."

Socrates (about 470 to 399 B. C.) claimed to continually have with him a conscious, speaking entity, a demon,—what would be denominated today, "a guardian spirit." One Meletus, a tragic poet of about 470 B. C., made himself conspicuous by hunting up and framing the charges that constituted the indictment against Socrates. Though licentious in his habits, and a moral profligate, he had considerable political influence for a

time. He was the chief accuser of Socrates, and these were among the accusations:
1. He did not believe in the gods accepted by the Grecian State.
2. He corrupted the Athenian youth by teaching them irreverence toward the gods, and encouraging strange divinities.
3. He professed to be attended by a good demon (spirit) whose advice he was wont to heed.

These were the words of a part of Meletus' deposition causing the indictment: "Socrates acts wickedly, and criminally curious in searching into things under the earth and in the heavens, and in making the worse appear the better cause in teaching these same things to others. . . . He pretends to obtain his wisdom by a certain natural inspiration and under the influence of enthusiasm, like prophets and seers." (Cary's translation, London.)

Socrates, in his apology or defense, while denying irreverence to the true God, thus admits his consulting oracles:

"I therefore asked myself in behalf of the oracle, whether I should prefer to continue as I am, possessing none either of their wisdom or their ignorance, or whether both as they have; I answered therefore, to myself and to the oracle, that it was better for me to continue as I am. . . . When the generals, Amphipolis, and others in command assigned me my post, I remained like any other person, where they posted me, encountering the dangers of death. But when the deity (a spirit) as I thought and believed, assigned it as my duty to pass my life in the study of philosophy, and in examining myself and others, should I on that occasion, through fear of death or anything else whatever, desert my post? O' Athenians, I honor and bow to you; but I shall obey God rather than you. . . . The cause of this is that which you have often and in many places heard me mention; because I am moved by a certain divine and spiritual influence which also Meletus, through mockery, has set out in the indictment. This began with me in childhood, being a kind of a voice which when present always diverts me from what I am about to do, but never urges me on."

Socrates, explaining to the youthful Alcibiades, said: "There is by a divine allotment, a certain demon that has attended me from my very childhood. It is a voice (that is, a warning voice) which when perceived, always signifies to me to relinquish what I am about to do; but it never at any time excites me on."

Apuleius gives a reason why the demon of Socrates was generally in the habit of forbidding him to do certain things, but never *exhorted* him to the performance of any act. Socrates, being of himself a man exceedingly perfect, and prompt to do whatever he ought, never stood in need of any one to exhort him, though he sometimes required to be forbidden, if danger happened to lurk in any of his undertakings. Being thus admonished, he was enabled to use due precaution, and desist for the present from his endeavor, either to resume it more safely at a future time, or enter it in some other way. It was usual for him to describe those warnings as a "voice proceeding from the demon"—in fact, his guardian spirit.

The lesson of the above is that the past recurs in the present. The indictment of Socrates on some vague charges, has, if not its counterpart today, its lesson of warning to official meddlers; for this Grecian Meletus, intriguing and ambitious as he was licentious, who got up the indictment against Socrates, was soon relieved of his political office and later was accused by the Athenians, who bitterly repenting their persecution of Socrates, put Meletus to death. How true, that those who "sow the wind, reap the whirlwind." And how true, too, the old prophet's words "God exerciseth justice and judgment in the earth." And how true, too, were these almost last words of Socrates:

"To me, then, O my judges,—and in calling you judges I call you rightly,—a strange thing has happened. For the wonted prophetic voice of my guardian deity, on every former occasion even in the most trifling affairs opposed me, if I were about to do anything wrong; but now, that has befallen me which ye yourselves behold, and which any one would think and which is supposed to be the extremity of evil, yet neither when I departed from home in the morning, did the warning of the god oppose me, nor when I came up here to the place of trial, nor in my address when I was about to say anything; yet on other occasions it has frequently restrained me in the midst of speaking. But now it has never throughout this proceeding opposed me, either in what I did or said. When then, do I suppose to be the cause of this? I will tell you: what has befallen me appears to be a blessing."

And so Socrates died to live in history immortal; while Meletus' name and indictment live, but live to be remembered in infamy.

The demon of the ancient Greeks and the lares and manes of the Romans had no reference to, nor were they in any way related to, that old theological dogma of "fallen angels," so beautifully, grimly versified by John Milton. A war in heaven with a crowd of Christ-conquered angels, thrust out, falling both hellward and earthward into an undiscovered Edenic garden, is only the gruesome fancy of a dreamy poet.

But all nations, from proud imperial Rome, down to the eucalyptus-shaded Australian Bushmen, have had their demons of darkness. Spending considerable time among these Bushmen during my different visits to Australia, I can write with authority in regard to their manners, customs, superstitions and beliefs in all kinds of spirit influences, celestial, terrestrial and infernal.

The great good spirit, whom they call Pirnmeheeal, is believed to be a gigantic spirit-man, living far above the clouds. He is only named with awe and respect. His voice is the thunders, and thunders prophesy of rains, which make the grass and roots grow for the benefit of man and beast. The stars are his eyes. The sun and moon his son and daughter. The great bad spirit they call Muuruup, sometimes, however, they call him Wambeen. He is the maker of bad-smelling smoke, causes droughts and floods and sickness. He flies through the air unseen. This evil demon and his imps, they greatly fear by night. He employs the owls and other night birds, they say, to watch them. When an owl is heard screeching, the children crawl under the grass. This Muuruup has multitudes of inferior spirits accompanying him. These incite people to be bad, to lie and steal. These demon or terrestrial spirits correspond among more enlightened nations to devils, wraiths and night-walking ghosts.

These demon spirits have the power to control persons. They entrance them, and then say wonderfully strange things. When under the spell they sometimes fall to the ground as though dead. They go wandering away in solitary gullies and desert places. They sometimes appear like madmen. At other times they just appear and then vanish from sight. It is a common saying when one dies, "He go down a black man, he come up a white man."

These aborigines believe that if an enemy gets possession of anything that once belonged to them, such as broken weapons, feathers, portions of dress, pieces of skin or refuse of any kind, he can employ it as a charm to produce sickness and even death to the person to whom they belonged. They are, therefore, very careful to burn up all rubbish upon leaving the camping-place. If an enemy can get hold of anything belonging to an unfriendly tribe, they use it as a charm to injure the enemy. While they make use of the charm-object, they chant imprecations on the enemy, and hurl poisoned spear-points and boomerangs in the direction where the enemy is supposed to be. They also throw hot ashes in the same direction, with hisses and curses. They seem to have discovered intuitively that bad thoughts may injure or kill.

They have among themselves what we should denominate sorcerers, or a low class of spirit mediums. These they believe to be possessed of supernatural powers. They fear them. They have the power to call good or bad spirits from the unseen depths, and they also have, they say, the power through concentration and mysterious charms, to produce what may be called the mystic sleep—a death-like entrancement. Then the controlling spirit foretells the future, fixes crimes upon those supposed to be guilty, tells where to find hidden treasures, cures the sick, or, if an enemy, causes his death.

If a chief's wife or one of superior rank is sick, the sorcerer-doctor, visiting the person at sunset, gives her herb-drinks, which, if it does not cure, he leaves his body and goes to the clouds and brings down ten spirits. These he places at a distance of some fifty yards from the sick person. He then holds a conversation with both his patient and the spirits whom he has summoned. He then breathes on the invalid, kneads, or massages, the seat of the disease, as the invisible agencies direct. Further, he warms his right hand at the fire and rubs it rapidly over the affected spot where the pain is, chanting at the same time some incantation. And while thus rubbing, he listens to what the invisibles say.

At their Korroboræs, they form during the time, a sort of rude circle, engage in weird dances, some of them falling into a seemingly death-like trance. These, they say, are obsessed by the spirits of their ancestors. They alternately smile, weep, howl, scream, climb trees and perform all sorts of unique and eccentric antics, sometimes exhibiting great physical strength, and then again violent anger toward an enemy. While in this obsessed state, these controlling demons have been known to give remarkable tests to those standing by, and to not only injure but to kill an enemy. These natives are exceedingly afraid of spirits, ghosts, demons and apparitions of any kind after dark. During the daylight they have but little fear. This rude form of weird spiritism, more properly demonism, is used among them mostly to injure enemies, or to avenge some real or imaginary wrong. They have, or had in their more prosperous days, an order of semi-chiefs corresponding somewhat to the priests of civilization.

Sometimes, when a Korroboræ has ended, the doctor

of the tribe calls on three or four female spirits to come down from the clouds, materialize and dance round the sacred priest-kindled fire; and, when accosted, each gives its name as that of a deceased member of the tribe. Any person may look at them, but none except the doctor, or ceremonial-dressed priest can speak to them, and nobody dares to run away.

The above occult happenings occurring among the lowest of the human species, may be termed 'nature demonism;' and yet, reduced to the last analysis, they correspond in principle somewhat to the higher phenomena, if not to the beliefs and mature admissions of the cultured races. Human nature is one and one because human.

Take as an example the following from that eminent scholar, editor and author, W. Stainton Moses (M. A. Oxon):

"Who are the spirits who return to earth? Of what class?

"Principally those who are nearest to the earth, in the three lower spheres or states of being. They converse most readily with you. They obsess. Of the higher spirits, those who are able to return are they who have what is analogous to mediumistic power on earth. We cannot tell you more than that we higher spirits find it very difficult to find a medium through whom we can communicate. Many spirits would gladly converse, but for the want of a suitable medium, and from their unwillingness to prolong their research for one, they will not risk the waste of time. Hence, too, communications vary much at times. Communications which you discover to be false are not always wilfully so. As time goes on, we shall know more of the conditions which affect communication.

"You have spoken of adversaries. Who are they?

"The antagonistic spirits who range themselves against our mission; who strive to mar its progress by counterfeiting our influence and work, and by setting men and other spirits against us and it. These are spirits who have chosen the evil, have put aside promptings and influences of good, and have banded themselves under the leadership of intelligences still more evil to malign us and hamper our work. Such are powerful for mischief, and their activity shows itself in evil passions, in imitating our work, and so gaining influence over the deluded, and most of all, in presenting to inquiring souls that which is mean and base, where we would tenderly lead to the noble and refined. They are the foes of God and man; enemies of goodness; ministers of evil. Against them we wage perpetual war.

"It is very startling to hear of such a powerful organization of evil. There are some, you know, who deny the existence of evil altogether and teach that all is good, though disguised.

"Alas! alas! most sad is the abandonment of good and choice of evil. You wonder that so many evil spirits obstruct. Friend, it is even so, and it is not astonishing. As the soul lives in the earth-life, so does it go to spirit-life. Its tastes, its predilections, its habits, its antipathies, they are with it still. It is not changed save in the accident of being freed from the body. The soul that on earth has been low in taste and impure in habit, does not change its nature by passing from the earth-sphere, any more than the soul that has been truthful, pure, and progressive, becomes base and bad by death. Wonderful that you do not recognize this truth! You would not fancy a pure, upright soul degenerating after it has passed from your gaze. Yet you fable a purification of that which has become by habit impure and unholy, hating God and goodness, and choosing sensuality and sin. The one is no more possible than the other. The soul's character has been a daily, hourly growth. It has not been an overlaying of the soul with that which can be thrown off. Rather it has been a weaving into the nature of the spirit that which becomes part of itself, identified with its nature, inseparable from its character. It is no more possible that that character should be undone, save by the slow process of obliteration, than that the woven fabric should be rudely cut and the threads remain intact. Nay more. The soul has cultivated habits that have become so engrained as to be essential parts of the individuality. The spirit that has yielded to the lusts of a sensual body becomes in the end their slave. It would not be happy in the midst of purity and refinement. It would sigh for its old haunts and habits. They are of its essence. So you see that the legions of the adversaries are simply the masses of unprogressed, undeveloped spirits, who have banded together from affinity against all that is pure and good. They can only progress by penitence, through the instruction of higher intelligences, and by gradual and laborious undoing of sin and sinful habit. There are many such, and they are the adversaries. . . .

"Many spirits are prematurely withdrawn from the body. They then pass before they are fit; and at the moment of departure they are in an evil state, angry blood-thirsty, filled with evil passion. They do mischief great and long in after life.

"Nothing is more dangerous than for souls to be rudely severed from their bodily habitation, and to be launched into spirit-life, with angry passions stirred, and revengeful feelings dominant. It is bad that any should be dismissed from earth-life suddenly, and before the bond is naturally severed. It is for this reason that all destruction of bodily life is foolish and rude: rude, as betokening a barbarous ignorance of the conditions of life and progress in the hereafter; foolish, as releasing an undeveloped, angry spirit from its trammels, and enduing it with extended capacity for mischief." ("Spirit Teachings," pp. 12, 13, 14, 17.)

The universe is a vast, echoing gallery of vibrations and expressions, many of which are inaudible to the material ear, yet not lost. A musical note may fade from your ear and mine into silence, but it goes on by the law of propulsion a ministering missionary of harmony, and will sweeten some life in realms visible or invisible. No thought dies. The ether wave it starts, propels, may affect minds in far-away climes. If buried for a time, some unlooked-for circumstance may revive it. Invisible agents, demons, spirits, angels, affect influence us, and we in turn may influence them. Catholic prayers for the dead are not useless. Good thoughts, noble aspirations are prayers. To this end Paul said, "Pray without ceasing."

CHAPTER X.

Judean Obsessions and the Actions of Demons.

IT WAS while spending a few months last year in London that I was privileged with hearing Professor Boscawen, a distinguished Egyptologist and Assyriologist, read Egyptian hieroglyphs, Assyrian inscriptions and old Chaldean magic formulas, chiseled in flinty rock-tombs, and upon the clay cylinders of Babylon. These readings and translations not merely delighted, they enthused me. Here was history, necromancy, magic, literally a resurrection of the ancient, or a recovery of the historical records and traditions of peoples living four and five thousand years before the Christian era.

The home of the Semites was doubtless originally in the high pasture lands of central Arabia. Being naturally a pastoral race, they were there attracted by the fertile plains of Shinar. The Hebrews were a branch of the Semitic family, and the Semitic tongue was a dialect of the Babylonian, as was the Hebrew of the Semitic. And Hebrew words relating to trade are found in the old commercial and religious texts as early as 4000 B. C., according to Prof. W. S. C. Boscawen. Baal and Set, and the Shepherd Kings, became, according to these unearthed records, the demons and obsessing spirits of the later races in Egypt and Israel. There is no proof that the Jews knew anything about evil spirits, wrote

Tholuck, a distinguished theologian and historian, till their captivity in Babylon.

Saul was "troubled with an evil spirit," and a cunning player on a harp was ordered to dispossess the demon (1 Sam. 16:16). Verse twenty-three reads, "And it came to pass when the evil spirit from God was upon Saul, that David took a harp and played with his hand; so Saul was refreshed and was well, and the evil spirit departed from him." Later, this evil spirit returned upon Saul, and he attempted to kill David. Theophrastus informs us that "music cures many disorders of the body and the mind, and dispels the demons that like both inharmony and darkness." Virgil represents the sibyl as foaming and raging and talking wildly of the gods; and Lucian represents the Pythian priestess as filled with fury, her hair standing on end, and her person foaming, twisting, and panting while delivering her oracle. Of these phenomena, Shakespeare writes:
"In the most high and palmy state of Rome,
A little ere the mightiest Julius fell,
The graves stood tenantless, and the sheeted dead
Did squeak and gibber in the Roman streets."

Grecian and Roman poets used the words demons, evil spirits, unclean spirits and familiar spirits as synonymous expresisons. Beelzebub, the god of Ekron, was considered the prince, or one of the most powerful of the influencing demons.

The Haunts and Doings of Demons.

The literature of the ages unites in declaring that demons have manifested in some form through all antiquity. A Chaldean magical formula runs thus:

"May the god of the house be installed in the house;
May the favorable demon, the favorable god enter the house.
The wicked demons, the wicked Alad, the wicked Gigim,
The wicked Telal, the wicked Maskim,
The phantom, the specter, the vampire,
O Spirit of the Heavens, conjure them,—
O, Spirit of the Heavens, conjure them, dispel them."

These demoniac spirits infest all places of filth. They cluster around and dwell in dark, foul caverns. They are at the elbows of dirty, filthy-mouthed people. They lurk in ill-ventilated cellars and underground caves. All places of uncleanness are highly congenial to this order of beings. Graveyards are their favorite resorts. They accompany grave-robbers. A certain class find desert lands an attractive place of abode. They may be allied to certain animals. They haunt ruined rock-baths and old damp vacant houses. They delight to dwell in liquor slums and dens of debauchery.

These earth-bound demons are the most active and effective in darkness. They shrink from the full blaze of noon-day brightness. They run from the golden sunshine as do worms, and hide in the ground when a piece of bark or a stone is lifted, letting in upon them a blaze of light. Some of these demons are malignant, and seek and delight in venting a malicious spite upon those whom they dislike, or use to gratify their carnal desires.

Ben Zacohai remarks, "Demons have the gift of speech, and they speak in behalf of themselves. They know the past and profess to know the future. They may be consulted in both respects; but questions about lost treasures had better not be directed to them. . . . They dwell in dark places. They infest the ill-tempered in dingy hovels. They produce convulsive ailments in children. They impose upon their subjects slavish restrictions. . . . They haunt butcher-shops, where lie the carcasses of slain goats. They like sacrifices of blood (Targum, Onk. Lev. 17). It was Egyptian demons that withstood Moses.''

The demon Asmodemus of the Book of Tobit was malignant and viciously wicked. The demons of this class lodge in deep, unclean wells. Demons, declared the Grecian poets, cause epilepsy. In India, suicide is a recognized mode of becoming an evil spirit in pursuit of ghostly vengeance. A British officer mortally wounded, a Travancore, and a notorious criminal at Trichnopoly entered at once, said the neighboring Hindus, into a state of demonism, obsessing their enemies. Scores of people declared that they saw and felt the presence of this criminal after his death. He so materialized that they could describe his approach. Milton put one of this class of facts in verse:

"As they please,
They limb themselves, and color, shape or size,
Assume as likes them best, condense or rare.''

The Ancient Oracles.

There is little doubt but that the Sibylline oracles of Greece were what this age would call writing-mediums. They may have been automatic. Some of the prophecies uttered possibly came true; but very many of them were only the wild imaginations of the demon-inspired. And yet, the cultured Greeks and Romans would not have consulted the oracles if they did not utter some truths. The higher classes discriminated between gods

Actions of Demons.

and demons, and even invented tests. Crœsus, King of Lydia, before consulting the oracle at Delphi, sent messengers to inquire at a specified day and hour what the king of Lydia was doing. At that time, the king proceeded to boil in a brazen cauldron, with a brazen lid, the flesh of a lamb with the flesh of a tortoise. It is said that the oracle, at the time the king was thus engaged, minutely described this event to his messengers.

The Emperor Trajan made a like demand of the oracle of Heliopolis by sending a sealed letter to which he required an answer. The oracle replied by sending to the emperor a bit of blank paper nicely folded and sealed. Trajan was amazed to find the answer in perfect harmony with the letter sent, which contained nothing but a blank paper."

When at Madura, India, I received the following from a Brahmin, a cultured gentleman, speaking excellent English. "My son fifteen years old was studying under the guardianship of an intimate friend of the famliy. Though seemingly healthy, he would have strange spells. He suffered no pain at these times. The spells increased in frequency, and when in them he would talk in another voice; after a few months, in several voices, and one tongue was wild gibberish. Some thought him insane; but when not under this psychological influence he was himself in every particular, except more sensitive, nervous and suspicious.

"Things went on getting worse, till the priest of the temple assured us that he was obsessed by an invisible, haunting demon. The statement shocked us; and yet, some of our sacred books are crammed with these Pisacha influences, wrecking health and happiness.

"As time advanced, he showed, at times, great moral

recklessness, losing his moral balance. In these 'fits' he ran away from home, returning sometimes in the night-time besmeared with filth. The whole tendency of his past happy life was reversed. He demanded stimulants—became revengeful, defying all authority. At length, when seeming to be himself in part, he was *not* himself, but another personality. Finally he became cunning, subtle, insolent and obstinately violent, vulgar in speech, and absolutely uncontrollable, attempting at one time to commit suicide.''

What was the matter? Originally, this boy was quiet, obedient, dignified for one of his years, and very anxious to excel in his studies. He was now considered insane by many; and yet, in his rational hours when no ''spells'' were upon him, he thought and acted like his real self, declaring repeatedly that he could tell when the worst seizures were coming on, because he could see an apparition, a huge figure of a dark-faced hairy man, with red, piercing eyes peering out from under black, tangled hair, falling loosely over his shoulders and face. As he looked at him, a fainting-like giddiness, then darkness came over him, and with the fading out of the last ray of light, he would lose consciousness.

The boy was losing flesh. His nervous system was becoming shattered, his eyes losing their luster. The family now sent for a very noted exorcist—a Mantrika. He came, and going through with some Pujah exercises, or priestly genuflexions, he stepped to the bed, and putting his hand upon the boy's head, breathed out a prayer to the gods in some unknown tongue. The boy cowered, trembled and sat down. Then some circular lines were drawn upon the floor, and the lad was placed within the charmed circle. Then incense was burned, and dried herbs, in which were mingled particles of camphor, set on fire. While this was burning the Mantrika was chanting tantrams. Soon the exorcist, straightening up as though he might weigh a ton, rushed toward the boy, and throwing a handful of holy ashes upon the subject's head, shouted, "Begone! begone, you demon of black magic!"

The demon spoke in grim, gutteral tones through the lad's lips,—"Why do you do these things to me?"

"Because you have no business here—you are ruining this young man. Tell me who you are and why you are here unwanted,—tell me at once, or I will chain you to a rock, or to a dying charm-cursed cocoanut tree."

"I was a Tamil in the body, and was commanded by a magician to obsess this boy to punish the family for slandering a relative, marrying into another caste. I like to get into or around this person, because I can enjoy my bodily life again, measurably gratify my desires, and gain power."

"Now from this moment do you leave this boy, leave this family,—leave him forever!"

The boy was himself—actually himself, weak, but pleasant and happy. He was then bathed, given a new suit of garments, and given a charm to wear attached to the sacred, three-stranded Janeo cord. This was the end of the obsession. The young man pursued his studies, becoming a "pleader."

CHAPTER XI.

New Testament Demonism and Unclean Spirits.

AND he came down to Capernaum, a city of Galilee. And he was teaching them on the Sabbath day; and they were astonished at his teaching; for his word was with authority. And in the synagogue there was a man who had a spirit of an unclean demon and he cried out with a loud voice, Ah! what have we to do with thee, thou Jesus of Nazareth? Art thou come to destroy us? I know thee who thou art, the Holy One of God. And Jesus rebuked him, saying, Hold thy peace and come out of him. And when the demon had thrown him down in the midst, he came out of him; having done him no hurt. And amazement came upon all, and they spake together, one with another, saying, What is this word, for with authority and power he commandeth the unclean spirits, and they come out? And there went forth a rumor concerning him into every place of the region round about. Luke 4: 31-37.

And they arrived at the country of the Gerasenes, which is over against Galilee. And when he was come forth upon the land, there met him a certain man out of the city, who had demons; and for a long time he had worn no clothes, and abode not in any house, but in the tombs. And when he saw Jesus he cried out, and fell down before him, and with a loud voice said, What have I to do with thee, Jesus, thou Son of the Most High God?

Demonism and Unclean Spirits.

I beseech thee, torment me not. For he commanded the unclean spirit to come out of the man. For often it had seized him: and he was kept under guard, and bound with chains and fetters; and breaking the bands asunder he was driven of the demon into the deserts. And Jesus asked him, What is thy name? And he said Legion; for many demons were entered into him. And they entreated him that he would not command them to depart into the abyss. Luke 8: 26-30.

When they came to the disciples, they saw a great multitude about them, and scribes questioning with them. And straightway, all the multitude, when they saw him, were greatly amazed, and running to him, saluted him. And he asked them, What question ye with them? And one of the multitude answered him, Master, I brought unto thee my son, who hath a dumb spirit; and whithersoever it taketh him, it dasheth him down; and he foameth and grindeth his teeth, and pineth away; and I spake to thy disciples that they should cast it out; and they were not able. And he answered them and said, O faithless generation, how long shall I be with you? How long shall I bear with you? Bring him unto me. And they brought him unto him; and when he saw him, straightway the spirit tare him grievously; and he fell on the ground and wallowed foaming. And he asked his father, How long time is it since this hath come to him? And he said, From a child. And ofttimes it hath cast him both into the fire and into the waters to destroy him; but if thou canst do anything, have compassion on us, and help us. And Jesus said unto him, If thou canst! All things are possible to him that believeth. Straightway, the father of the child cried out, and said, I believe; help thou mine unbelief. And when Jesus saw that a multitude came running together, he rebuked the unclean spirit, saying unto him, Thou dumb and deaf spirit, I command thee, come out of him, and enter no more into him. And having cried out, and torn him much, he came out: and the child became as one dead; insomuch that the more part said, He is dead. But Jesus took him by the hand and raised him up, and he arose. And when he was come into the house, his disciples asked him privately, saying, We could not cast it out? And he said unto them, This kind can come out by nothing, save by prayer. Mark 9:14-29.

Jesus went out thence and withdrew into the parts of Tyre and Sidon. And behold, a Canaanitish woman came out from those borders and cried, saying, Have mercy on me, O Lord, thou son of David; my daughter is grievously vexed with a demon. Jesus answered and said unto her, O woman, great is thy faith, be it unto thee, even as thou wilt. And her daughter was healed from that hour. Matt. 15:21, 22, 28.

With him were certain women who had been healed of evil spirits and infirmities,—Mary that was called the Magdalene, from whom seven demons had gone forth. Luke 8:2.

And it came to pass that as we were going to the place of prayer, a certain maid, having a spirit, a Python, met us, who brought her masters much gain by soothsaying. The same following after Paul and us, cried out saying, These men are servants of the Most High God who proclaim to you a way of salvation. And this she did for many days. But Paul being sore troubled, turned and said to the spirit, I charge thee in the name of Jesus

Demonism and Unclean Spirits. 111

Christ to come out of her. And it came out that very hour. Acts 16: 16–18.

And God wrought special miracles by the hand of Paul: insomuch that unto the sick were carried from his body handkerchiefs or aprons, and the diseases departed from them, and the evil spirits went forth. But certain also of the strolling Jews, exorcists, took upon them to name over them that had evil spirits, the name of the Lord Jesus, saying, I adjure you by Jesus whom Paul preacheth! . . . Acts 19:11–16.

When the even was come, they brought unto him many that were demonized, and he cast out the spirits with a word, and all that were ill he healed. Matt. 8: 16.

Jesus was going about in the whole of Galilee, teaching in their synagogues and preaching the good news of the kingdom, and healing every disease, and every infirmity among the people. Preaching and casting out demons. Mark 1: 39.

He called unto him his twelve disciples, and gave them authority over unclean spirits, to cast them out, and to heal every disease and every infirmity. Jesus commanded them, saying, Heal the sick, cleanse the lepers, raise the dead, cast out demons. Matt. 10: 1, 5, 8.

Go ye and tell that fox, Behold I cast out demons today and tomorrow. Luke 13: 32.

Heal the sick and say unto them. The kingdom of God is come night unto thee. The Seventy returned with joy, saying, Lord even the demons are subject to us, in thy name. Luke 10: 9, 17.

These passages clearly, definitely state that there were "evil spirits," "unclean spirits," "demon obsessions." in Jesus' time, and that himself, the twelve and the seventy, demagnetizing the troubled parties, "cast them out." Making no special mention just here of the New Testament demon obsessions, this belief, according to Josephus and Greek writers of that period, was common. None except Sadduceean materialists disputed the fact.

In considering this important matter, it must be kept well in mind that devil and demon are not convertible terms. They are never used by the ancient writers synonymously. Our best scholars admit that the original Greek is much plainer than the long authorized version of King James, which sometimes translates *diabolus, daimonion,* and *daimon,* by the word "devil," or devils, and also demons. This was so incorrect that the revised version translates *diabolus* "Devil," and the other two, *daimonion,* demons, and *daimon,* demon. *Diabolus* means "slanderer," a "false accuser;" see the following passages:

"Their wives must not be devils." I Tim. 3:11.

"In the last days men will be devils." 2 Tim. 3:3.

"The aged women should not be devils." Titus 2:3.

"Have I not chosen twelve and one of you is a devil." John 6:70.

The Devil vs. Demons.

The words *daimon* and *daimonion* (demons) are frequently used in the New Testament both in the singular and plural; but never as the exact synonym of *diabolus* (devil). This word *diabolus* occurs in the New Testament some thirty-six times.

Demonism and Unclean Spirits.

There is, then, in the Scriptures, but one devil, and he not a fallen angel; while the number of demons is "legion" and more. Beelzebub was not the devil, but the prince, the leader of the demons. There have been and are many such leaders in the hells. They organize, wrangle, dispute and disorganize.

The word "demon" is used in the "Septuagent Seventy" to denote the spirits of the dead; and Josephus says that demons are the spirits of wicked men. But the phrase, "familiar spirits," is not found in the New Testament. There is not a scintilla of proof that Babylonians or Jews, or Greeks, believed that demons were fallen angels, who "kept not their first estate." This strange theory is but a myth,—a wild dream of theological poesy.

Demons, evil spirits and unclean spirits are convertible expressions. Plato speaks of the "sepulchers of demons." The Gentiles "sacrificed to demons," said the apostle. Hesiod said, "After this generation were dead, they were by the will of Jupiter, demons, keepers of mortal men, clothed in air, and always walking about the earth." Xenocrates taught that the "heavens are divine, and the stars the abodes of the celestial gods, and that besides these, there are terrestrial demons, a middle order between gods and man, that are like human beings, capable of passions, inferior and dangerous to mortals."

Herodotus gives a thrilling account of the demon possession and the barbaric mutilation of one Cleomenes.

Plato in his "Republic," not only speaks of demons of various grades, but mentions a method of treating and providing for those obsessed by them.

Plutarch, in his excellent work, "The Failure of the Oracles," describes the case of the Pythoness of Delphi, who got obsessed in the discharge of her manifestations, "being seized," writes W. Menzies Alexander, "with a speechless and evil spirit," and dying shortly afterward. Both Sophocles and Euripides describe in thrilling language, cases of demon influences, and the eccentricities of the possessed. The Roman Horace and Celsus, who so scathingly criticised the Christians (see Origen's exhaustive reply), describe an obsessed actor, who, becoming spasmodic and demonized, tore his garments and went screaming through the streets.

Human nature in all nations is similar, and so were demon influences, whether abounding in Semitic, Grecian or Roman times, or in the various enlightened nations of today. It was and is, among dull, stupid conservatives, fashionable to pronounce the obsessed, insane. Those versed in psychoses know better. Physicians in lunatic asylums should be thoroughly schooled in phrenology, physiognomy, psychology, mesmerism, suggestion and auto-suggestion; but, sad to say, they are not. They are back chapters in psychology.

The agents and subjects of obsessions and possessions are variously designated in the New Testament. The following are samples: "spirit of an unclean demon," "whom a spirit seizes" (Luke 9:39), "whom a spirit assails" (Mark 9:18), "whom a foul spirit enters" (Matt. 12:45), "being a foul spirit" (Mark 1:23), "having a foul spirit" (Mark 3:30), "vexed with unclean spirits" (Acts 5:16), "they are the spirits of demons working miracles" (Rev. 16:14), "annoyed by spirits" (Luke 6:18), "and the man on whom the evil spirit was, leaped on them and overcame them" (Luke 19:16).

Here is testimony amounting almost to superogation,

from Jews, Greeks, Romans and New Testament writers, to facts,— such positive facts as the following:

1. That the word demon, with very few exceptions, in past literature, secular and religious, referred to the spirits of undeveloped wicked human beings.

2. That these demoniacs—these wicked spirits—had the power to influence, affect, to injuriously obsess; and further, to so selfishly, maliciously possess mortals as to measurably re-live their earthly lives in their auras, and so again revel in the gratification of selfish, sordid and sensual propensities.

3. That there were those so full-orbed and royally organized by nature, and so psychically gifted that, aided by unseen, heavenly helpers, they could and did "cast out"—that is, demagnetize and liberate those obsessed and possessed by vexing, lying demons.

The noted Dr. Tyler in his "Primitive Culture," says with becoming frankness, "It is not too much to assert that the doctrine of demoniacal possession is kept up, substantially the same theory to account for substantially the same facts, by half the human race, who thus stand as consistent representatives of their forefathers back in the primitive antiquity."

And yet, with these admissions of rationalists, with the unqualified statements and testimonies from Babylonia, Egypt and India, from Jewish and classical writers illustrious for observation, research and wisdom, there is a class of modern Sadducees, agnostics, materialistic inclined pathologists, who with more modern audacity than adept knowledge, declare that these demon obsessions were and are nothing but physical and mental diseases; such as lunacy, insanity, "maniacal mad-fits," "lycanthropic transformations," "eccentric insanity," "oracular inversions," hysteria, epilepsy and various nervo-derangements. Suppose, then, in consonance with this strained, irrational interpretation of clearly related facts, we insert disease of some kind into certain New Testament passages, and see how it sounds to rational thinkers. Take the eighth chapter of Luke, where a man came from the city obsessed with "demons," that is, epilepsy. This man for a time had worn no clothing, and had lived in the tombs. And further, epilepsy had driven him at times "into the desert," and when Jesus saw him, he "asked him"— epilepsy — "what is thy name?" And epilepsy said, "Legion." And these "epilepsies" entreated Jesus that he "would not command them to depart into the abyss." How do you fancy putting disease for demons?

Consider the gospel by Mark, ninth chapter, where a man brought his son to Jesus, obsessed with "a dumb spirit"—hysterics—and the hysterics "tear him," and "cause him to gnash his teeth and foam," and the disciples could not cast him (hysterics) out. And they brought him to Jesus, . . . and straightway the spirit (hysterics) tore him and he fell to the ground and wallowed, foaming. And when Jesus saw the people come running together, he rebuked the foul spirit (hysterics), saying unto him, Thou deaf and dumb spirit (hysterics), I charge thee, come out of him. And the spirit (hysterics) cried and rent him sore, and came out of him."

Take as another example the fourth chapter of Luke, where in the synagogue there was a "man which had a spirit of an unclean devil (epilepsy, insanity, leprosy, hallucination or some other mental disease), who cried out with a loud voice (mark well, *a loud voice*) saying, Let us alone. What have we to do with thee, thou Jesus of Nazareth? And Jesus rebuked him (the leprosy or dropsy), saying (epilepsy or dropsy), Hold thy peace. And when the demon (epilepsy, dropsy or the hallucination) had thrown him in the midst, he (epilepsy) came out of him." But enough—this, if possible, is more than pitiably absurd. It degenerates into contempt.

The student of psychoses can readily understand that a "spirit of infirmity, bound by Satan fourteen years," was possessed that length of time by a controlling demon, and that Paul's "thorn in the flesh," the messenger of Satan, was doubtless the demon obsession that so troubled him; for often, when he would do good, he says, "evil was present with me."

There is generally a slight paroxysm for a time in passing from the normal condition to the abnormal, whether the influence be demon or angel. This was the case with Dr. Dunn, who was with me much of the time for fourteen years. Remember that devil (diabolos) and satan, following the old translations, are often used synonomously. This occurs in the thirteenth chapter of John. The devil had already "put it into the heart of Judas to betray Jesus," that is, the demon had impressed him, and in the twenty-seventh verse of the same chapter, it is said, "Then entered Satan into him," that is, fully influenced or possessed him.

If kindness is commendable, a determined will is indispensable in dealing with these obsessional cases. These are the Nazarene's steel-pointed words, "Hold thy peace, and come out of him." "I charge thee, come out of him." Such was the firm, positive language of the Christ, who "rebuked" the devils, and "suffered them not to speak." In the Nazarene's time there was no doubt, among Pharisees, or the thinking, as to the nature of lunacy. To wit, Matt. 17:14:

"Lord, have mercy on my son: for he is lunatic, and sore vexed, for ofttimes he falleth into the fire, and oft into the water."

In this instance the disciples had failed to exorcise the evil spirit, or demon, "because of their unbelief," and they were reminded that "this kind goeth not out but by prayer and fasting."

In Luke 10:20, we read: "Rejoice not *that the spirits are subject to you*, but rather rejoice because your names are written in heaven."

The Rev. Charles Beecher, when reporting officially upon Spiritualism, said, "It is not enough that a theory can, by great effort, embrace the phenomena of clairvoyance, rhabdomancy, apparitions, oracles, haunted houses, rappings, etc.; it must also take in the facts of the Bible. It must give to the Bible its natural meaning; not explaining away, by false accommodation-principles, its demoniac possessions, its pythonesses, its laws, its history of the evoking of Samuel and of the false prophets. Whatever physiological law accounts for odylic phenomena in all ages, will, in the end, inevitably carry itself through the whole Bible. . . . If a theory be adopted everywhere else but in the Bible, excluding spiritual intervention by odylic channels *in toto*, and accounting for everything physically, then will the covers of the Bible prove but pasteboard barriers. Such a theory will sweep its way through the Bible and its authority. . . . Belief in the immortality of the soul has been no more persistent during all the elder ages than has the belief in unseen evil agencies. These, since the Christian era, had uniformly antagonized Christ. They were 'wicked spirits in high places,' using the correct translation of the apostle's words. Accordingly," he continues, "if the theory of spiritual intervention, through odylic channels, be accepted in the Bible, it cannot be shut up there."

This is sound philosophy. The theory of "spiritual intervention," through odylic or psychic channels, pertains to all Bibles, Vedic and Buddhistic, Jewish and Christian,—and so does the theory and the undeniable fact of obsessions.

CHAPTER XII.

The Haunting Places of Demon Spirits.

IT IS no more natural for water to seek a level, or for the vibrating needle to point northward, than it is for men in the flesh and spiritual beings out of it, to gravitate toward the state, or moral condition to which they correspond by the law of adaptation. The feather floats, lead sinks, while the balloon filled with hydrogen gas rapidly ascends. So evil-minded, demoniac spirits, earthly and selfish, naturally descend, dwelling not only within the atmosphere of the earth, but in the filthy and foulest places of city slums and hovels. All history confirms this.

In the book of Enoch we are told that those who "worship foul spirits and demons, are drawn down to low places to abide with them."

In the Sibylline oracles it is written, "Ye shall have the reward of your evil counsel; ye have made your sacrifices to demons in Hades, and ye shall dwell with them."

"The air above and the earth beneath pulsates with the Mazziquin, the hurtful ones. They seek the low places." Pes. 54 d.

"The appearance of demons is mostly human, but they assume various forms at will. Their reflection is different from that of man. Those associated with dirty places appear in clouds of smoke." Kidd, 72 a.

"When conjured up by wish or will, they appear sometimes suddenly. They infest all ill-aired places. The atmosphere of dark swamps and garbage deposits is charged with them." Abaji, 7 a.

"Shadows cast by the moon, certain trees mossy by sluggish streams, and dark vaults are natural lurking places for demons." Ber. 51.

"All places of uncleanness are congenial to them. Graveyards are their favorite resorts. Old ruined bathing places invite them." Nidd. 17 a.

"The demons sometimes attach themselves to certain animals. . . . Ruins should be avoided on account of these unseen foes. 'The searcher after the dead,' said Adjorum, 'remained fasting on a grave to get into touch with an unclean spirit. He came and held him to injure his foe.'" Shab. 151 b.

Dr. W. Menzies Alexander, in his elaborate work, "Demonic Possession," assures us that "the demons form themselves into bands—'the society of the angels of destruction' (Ber. 51 a). According to the same passage, a whole legion lies in wait for a person to fall into their hands on the commission of some fault. Their action is thus a kind of obsession, which may really pass into possession. . . . Under cover of darkness, demons surround houses and injure them that fall into their hands. This is especially the case if there be unclean places. . . . Demons are more active in darkness than in the light. At cock-crow their power begins to weaken. The Shabriri was always a menace to those who drink water from stagnant pools."

This author further says, " Demons have the gift of speech; and Rabbi Ben Zacchai knew their language. These demons know the future and the past, so that they may be consulted in both respects, but questions about lost property had not better be directed to them on the Sabbath." Sarh 101 a.

A prominent "demoness of sickness is Bath-Chorin. She touches the hands and lower limbs by night. Many diseases are caused by demons."

"To demons may be ascribed leprosy, rabies, asthma, cardiac diseases, nervous diseases, which latter are the specialty of evil demons, such as epilepsy." Shab. Rab. 67 a, Jos. Ant vi-8, viii-5.

This author further says, "Bodily diseases affect the mind, and the mind affects the body, and evil demons affect the mind by putting into it bad thoughts. 'Shibta causes convulsive ailments among children especially at night. Obsessing spirits are always busy. Among the humbler functions of the Shedim was the sending of evil dreams, . . . or causing a religious crank to afflict himself with fasting.'" Bab Taanith, 22 b.

Rabbinical demonology prevailing during and for two or three centuries after Jesus' time, would have been intolerable if the undeveloped spirits had had everything their own way. But all finite things and forces have their limitations. So these demoniac influences were restricted by environments. The partial loss of the divine image through wilful perversions, rendered succeeding mortals more subject to these nefarious agencies.

Perasee Lendenta, a highly intelligent individuality in supernal life, once said to me, "Master mind, and you have mastered the universe." It is certain that mind, thought, purpose and suggestion pertain to all civilizations and to all states of existence, incarnate and discarnate, in earth life and spirit life. The process of suggestion through etheric vibration is natural: the agents are fallible and the authors may be good and wise, or wicked. The telegraphic wire may be instrumental in conveying communications both true and false. So long as no thought is given to habits, so long as no moral qualifications are considered essential, so long as moral freedom remains an attribute of the soul, and so long as both savants and savages—the latter largely in the majority—pass into spirit life, just so long by parity of reasoning, must we conclude that undeveloped spirits will be free to use the spirit telegraph, and sufficiently incarnate themselves into the auras of mortals to obsess them, and so by proxy partially continue their hold upon the fleshly life. And just as such great souls as Pythagoras, Socrates, Jesus, Joan of Arc and Swedenborg were born in mountainous countries, where the scenery was grand and the air pure, so these demoniac-obsessing spirits, begotten parentally in lust, were in their mortal bodies the frequenters of, if not dwellers in foggy boglands, and caves for concealment from the good and regal-souled—frequenters of dingy gambling dens, liquor slums and brothels, the patrons of which were inflamed with passions infernal, choosing darkness rather than "light, because their deeds were evil."

These poor human beings, though deprived of their physical organizations, are not dead—are not annihilated. They retain their identity. They are conscious.

The Haunting Places of Demon Spirits.

They have taken with them to this other state of existence memory and are often malicious as well as ignorant of matters moral and spiritual. Their thoughts, their purposes and wills, turn toward the flesh—toward sordid earthly affairs, and they just as naturally seek, cling to mortals magnetically, good and bad, as poison ivy clings to the sturdy oak or the sun-kissed rock. It is said that this position violates the immutable law that like attracts like? There is no such immutable law. A characteristic fact under similar conditions is not an immutable law or a fixed principle. Electricity is in proof. Thus, positives repel rather than attract. A lady teacher, symbol of refinement and purity, in passing through a grove is attacked, assaulted by a lecherous tramp. In this case where was the "law" that like attracts like? These were both human beings.

Here is a good industrious man's house by the wayside. Because of honest, arduous toil, he is a man of thrift. A band of robbers breaks in, gag and ruthlessly rob the residents and then to hide the crime, burn the residence. This has been done repeatedly. Was there any attraction here between the peaceful toilers in the home and these, red-handed murderers? So in the next stage of being these murderous monsters of earth-life, now demons may—*do* at different times, through will-power stimulated by selfishness, break into the aural, or odylic environments of mortals, and thus obsessing play the deceiver, the psychic robber, the villainous vampire.

It is an old adage that "fools rush in where angels fear to tread." There may be well-disposed, yet ignorant spirits—more emotional and egotistic than wise—who psychically influence and use a human organism till it is unbalanced and shattered if not ruined. The remedy for these obsessions will appear later.

CHAPTER XIII.

Evil Spirit Obsessions Afar and Near.

IT MAKES a vast difference in mathematical value upon which side of the unit the cipher is placed. It is the small sands constituting rock and strata that make up the mountain. Prefixes and suffixes are proportionally small, yet often they are mighty in meaning. No philologist, or even ordinary scholar, would use synonymously spirit and spiritual. Spirit, in its broadest and highest sense, implies Absolute Being. Spiritual, according to all philologists of standing, implies and refers to beings—beings conscious, rational and measurably conscientious. The *ual* of spiritual is a suffix implying and indicating moral quality. A spirit-man, earthly embodied, compounded, particled and physically vestured, may be a thief or a murderer; but a moral, spiritual or spiritually-minded man keeps the righteous commandments of the higher life, doing right for the love of right, and walking worthy of that high vocation which constitutes the harmonial man, the companion of the altruistic good, and of angels even, while clothed in mortality. So, from the above may be seen the vast, the almost infinite difference between Chinese juggling, Hindu magic, low, selfish spirits obsessing mortals for gratification, and the pure-minded, loving, soul-inspiring angels, who, peopling the Christ-heavens, project their thoughts, or wend their shining way earthward, in the attitude of ministering angels of mercy.

It was perfectly reasonable that the communing with perverse, obsessing spirits of old should be denounced. Voluntary communications with evil-disposed spirits whether in the body or out, is to be deprecated. Those nowadays who seek such communications are the patrons of necromancy and sorcery as much as those in Babylonian and Old Testament times. No change of law or condition can make evil communications for evil purposes any less than evil. True, there is a little knot of egotistic, sophistic spiritists in the world who deny the existence of a vestige of evil in the universe. Everything is lovely. A pig-stye is just as sweet as a rose garden. They cannot comprehend that the qualities of good and evil are just as opposite as are the properties of heat and cold in physics. Briefly put, to these unfledged pedagogues, vice and virtue are when "properly understood," synonyms. Rape is just as divine as religion; hell just as holy as heaven, and concentrated malice and murder are but the expressions of "undeveloped good." Whether this class of sophists is nearest to senility or insanity, it is difficult to decide. But when practically brought face to face with their pet dogma, and forced to take their own medicine, these quasi-optimistic sophists excel in faultfinding, criticising and gruesome grumbling at the ever-recurring ills of life.

When in China, spending hours at different times in and about the great Chinese Temple and the adjoining group of temples of the five hundred genii, my eyes tired of seeing, and my ears tired of hearing the vocal jargon. Entering the courtyard of the "Temple of Horrors," one may see the Buddhist pictures of hell and its vicious demons, compared with which John Calvin's hell would be quite comfortable, if not paradisaical.

Here are painted exhibitions of the wicked wriggling in boiling oil; here the process of flaying alive; here the pounding of some wretches in mortars; here sawing them in twain; here frying them on gridirons; here slashing and beheading them! and further on in a rude painting may be observed the process of transmigrating souls back into the lowest brutes, and fish with horns and scales. And still further along in a sort of an indescribable booth, I saw a literal sample of sorcery spiritism. The implements in use were round tables thinly covered with white sand, and obsessed women with hawk-bill shaped sticks writing comunications; here again were two half-bits of wood kidney-shaped when united. These were tossed into the air, and the way they fell meant yes or no; and here was a dragon-shaped piece of metal suspended by a string, and some spirit-god being invoked, the image moved pointing to some Chinese characters upon the wall. These communications were taken down by attending scribes. In these rude séance assemblies, gods and various grades of spirits are invoked to aid in gambling, in speculating, in love-making, in money-getting and in the commission of criminal offenses. At times, the spasmodic tumblings, the facial contortions and wild spirit chatterings through these obsessed, Chinese sensitives could only be compared to the demon-dances described in Dante's "Inferno."

Somewhat in line with the above is the following description of a most painful case of obsession published in London *Light,* from the pen of Rosina Bernardy, of Florence, Italy:

"On the Tirrenian seashore, between Varreggio and Massa di Carrara, in a small summer resort called Forte dei Marini, I know of a 'demon-possessed woman' who during the past thirty-two years has done many strange and astonishing things.

"For instance, once she remained open-mouthed under a fountain during two hours to receive into her body much of the water flowing from it, and then she went to an inn near by and ate a big piece of salted meat, a large loaf of bread of more than seven pounds' weight, drank wine and coffee and still screamed for more. Afterward she went up an olive tree, crowed as a cock, came down with her hands bleeding, walked bare-footed upon a hedge, without the hedge bending under her weight, and finally went miles and miles at night, screaming desperately.

"Knowing by experience the sufferings of the poor possessed, I took an interest in the wretched woman, and, helped by a lady, treated her according to the new method taught us by the good spirits, i. e., moralizing the low spirit abiding in her, by magnetizing and addressing him directly.

"After much talk and great patience, we secured a little rest for the poor woman.

"The spirit became less greedy also in his need to eat, and less arrogant with her, leaving her will more free from time to time.

"Although the woman is uneducated, I compelled her to write, which she, under my order, did and then translated into the Italian language. I have now such psychic power over the spirit that he trembles at my presence, and surrenders to my will, except to finally leave the woman, which he says he cannot do.

"Lately I heard her bark like a dog, mew as a cat, and scream as a savage, in a country church before the image of the 'Holy Virgin,' and then I saw her crawl on all fours as a beast all along the church.

"When thus obsessed, she speaks an impossible dialect, but now I can force her to speak Italian, keeping up conversation with the spirit for hours and hours. So I heard this story, by which I came to understand that I have to deal with a poor spirit, almost still in the elemental state, who cannot yet remain out of matter nor live a true spiritual life.

"We hope that by and by we shall bring him to understand himself better, and help him to enter upon a new phase of existence.

" Touched by the pains of the poor tormented women, whose number is very great in Italy, I join my earnest wishes to those of your Indian correspondent, that some healers, or exorcists, should come to Italy, too, in order to deliver humanity from such devil spirits.

"ROSINA BERNARDY,
"Florence, June 19, 1902."

It is appropos that I here state that I knew a family residing in Kalamazoo, Mich., a number of years ago, noted for wealth and social influence. They were also substantial, outspoken spiritists. They held frequent séances in their sunny homes, but never permitted any of their servants to attend them. One of these servants, by the way, was a pleasant, sensitive young woman of unimpeachable character.

Suddenly and unexpectedly this young woman became a medium, spasmodically and unconsciously entranced, speaking rapidly in some unknown tongue. At length she was controlled by an Indian spirit, using some English words. This delighted the family for a few months. But all at once, after having some difficulty with another household woman, she was seized by some low, unseen intelligence, which proved to be an "outcast Indian squaw." She talked gibberish, intermixed with some profane words, to the horror of all present. She was completely obsessed. Occasionally the spirit would throw this young woman on the floor, pull her hair down loosely over her shoulders and draw the corners of her mouth down till her features resembled those of a basket-making Indian squaw.

Matters became worse. This uninvited influencing demon-spirit would call, beg—plead for tobacco and firewater. At one time they gave her a plug of chewing tobacco, and she actually, through her entranced instrument, chewed over half of it during the hour's sitting. At another time she asked for whisky, "fire-water," as she called it. They secured, and by way of experiment, gave her a pint bottle of whisky, and she drank it all in less than half an hour. Sensing the exhilarating stimulus, this spirit became unruly, used vulgar language, and with seemingly Samson-like strength, she grasped bits of wood back of the stove, and began beating the inmates. It took three persons to hold this rather delicate woman; and while thus holding her, a mediumistic lady was impressed to place the right hand upon the back of this obsessed woman's neck, and the left hand upon the forehead, at the same time stamping the foot and exclaiming, " Go! go! go! you Indian squaw," and she left.

The medium becoming conscious, was a little nervous, showing some fatigue, but not the least effect of any inebriation.

This was a very clear case of temporary obsession. Her relatives hearing of the matter, removed her to another locality, where with new environments and beautiful social surroundings, there was no more obsessional trouble.

Saved from Obsessing Demons.

The following letter from Mr. Johnstone, of Greenock, Scotland, a gentleman both intelligent and reliable, appeared in London *Light,* April, 1903. It is similar to hundreds that I have received from this and different countries within a few years:

"SIR: During a good portion of my life I was a worshiper of God according to orthodox ways, being a member of the Presbyterian Church of Scotland, and I was happy enough until a little more than two years ago, when my body and mind began to give way under some mysterious force and I found myself, to my utter astonishment, quite overpowered by evil influences. I was alarmed at my singular misfortunes, and naturally applied for help to the pastor of a church here, but all he could do for me was to advise me to rely upon Christ, read the Bible and all would come well. But that was exactly what I could not do, for evil spirits defied me, in words that I distinctly heard, either to enter a place of worship or go near a street preacher, or listen to any spiritual teaching whatsoever.

"However, I went on with the struggle myself, unaided for a time and gave myself constantly to prayer, and on one occasion I strayed about the roads for six days and five nights and tasted nothing but water, praying and waiting on God, but all to no purpose.

"I was in despair, and longed for death, for the sufferings I endured were beyond the conception of human beings. It will hardly be believed, but it is a positive fact, that evil spirits forced me to do things against my own common sense and judgment. I was so afflicted that I thought perhaps by giving way to my tormentors a little, I might possibly obtain some relief, for I had got thoroughly worn out by resisting them; but as soon as I began to obey them, they showed me not the least mercy.

"My friends ridiculed the notion of spirits and advised me to go to a doctor, which I did, but I found the doctors as ignorant as the parsons; four of them certified that I was physically sound enough except that I suffered a little from indigestion, which would pass over in time, but they could not account for the mental tortures I complained of, and which were so absolutely real to me.

"I suffered inconceivable misery; and although I had ministers and pastors and people of all religions praying with me, and also evangelists, I could get no relief. The Spiritualists here, too, told me that they could do nothing for me as my obsession was so very serious that they were afraid of getting obsessed themselves, and people were warned against sitting in séances with me. But I met among them about this time a friend of Mr. Clement Harding, 20 Harbledown Rd., Munster Park, Fulham, S. W., and I immediately wrote that gentleman and begged him for God's sake to ask his spirit friends to come to me and save my life. He kindly sent me a letter at once, and as I was reading it, I felt conscious of the presence of powerful spirits moving about me, and some sort of healing powers darted through me and I began to feel like a new man. The voices of the evil spirits also began to grow fainter and fainter, and I commenced to grow stronger and more courageous. I kept myself *en rapport* with Mr. Harding by reading his letter two or three times a day, and then I and a few friends sat under his direction, and it was not till then that my enemies were thoroughly vanquished.

5 Lyndock St., Greenock.

"DAVID JOHNSTONE."

Obsession Near Home.

It is known to thousands that Dr. E. C. Dunn, of Rockford, Ill., a wealthy, influential citizen, member of the city council, accompanied me on my first journey around the world.

This young man, when about sixteen years of age, lived in Battle Creek, Mich., uneducated and busily engaged in "sowing wild oats;" about this time he went up on to Prof. I. Sterns' platform one evening, where he was giving public exhibitions in hypnotism. Young Dunn went up as a sport to expose the tricks of the professor; but instead of doing this, he became hypnotized, making an excellent subject. The professor put him through strange gymnastic antics several evenings, exhibiting the power of the will, and at the same time amusing large audiences.

A few evenings later, while in the hypnotic state with others, he became singularly nervous, and then the arms and even the body became spasmodic. The professor stepping promptly to him, exclaimed, "All right, all right!" But he was not all right, that is, consciously normal. The hypnotist stepping close to him, and reversing the passes, exclaimed still louder, "All right, open your eyes!"

The audience beginning to show considerable anxiety, a Mrs. Whitney, an excellent clairvoyant, still residing in Battle Creek, partly rising to her feet, said, "Pardon me sir, but I see several strong positive spirits around that young lad, and I get the impression that they want to write."

Paper and pencil were procured, put before him on a table, when his spasmodically excited and perturbed system calmed down, and this superior hypnotizing intelligence wrote several lines through his hand backward and bottom upward, relating to a railroad wreck in Canada, which was described at length the next morning in the Detroit papers. The test was really wonderful, and none were more astonished than the professor, who smilingly said, "I am beaten—badly beaten this time." This was the entering wedge to his acceptance of the spiritual philosophy.

This Dr. E. C. Dunn was with me much of the time for fourteen years, and nearly a dozen phases of mediumship were manifest through him. The two most interesting to me were his leviations and unconscious trances. His leading controlling intelligence, Aaron Knight, informed me several times that dark spirits, unprincipled selfish spirits, and wilful demon spirits accompanied him and us, and whenever the medium got into a lower stratum of aural influence, whether in hotel, theater or circus, these undeveloped spirits sought to magnetically seize him, using him for their gratification or for the execution of some scheme.

During our voyage around the world, we had a sitting regularly every Thursday afternoon, and sometimes twice a week. Leaving New Zealand for China, we took aboard one hundred and seventeen Chinese returning miners. There were two lots of them, using largely different dialects. And when about two weeks at sea, these different Chinese clans got into a fight among themselves, using marling-pins as well as their fists.

The captain seeing the fighting, called upon the shipmates and some of the sailors to go down and stop the fight. In their well-meant efforts to still the Chinese combatants, the captain and shipmates had to fight the combined forces of the Chinese. At this status of the melée, Dr. Dunn rushed down and joined in the struggle. The mad affray quieted,—the doctor returned to the deck another man—changed, transfigured, entranced by a strange, positive invisible control as unlike any of his former encircling intelligences as the hells are unlike the heavens.

When stepping into our cabin-room, I took hold of one of the sensitive's hands and inquired, "Who are you?"

"He turned his glassy eyes at me, tossed up the medium's head and exclaimed through a sardonic smile,— "Ha, ha; I've got him—I've got him, and I'll hold him!"

"Did you," I asked, "get the consent of the medium's circle of guiding spirits to entrance this sensitive?"

"Ha, ha! That's my business. I've got him. I've long sought the opportunity. I've got him, and I'll do my work through him."

"What is your special work that you propose to accomplish?"

"Ha! that's my business. I was a French philosopher. I studied nature in all her elementary processes, up to the controlling of kings and the balancing of empires."

This was Monday, and for three days this pretentious, pompous and positive demon held his trance-influence over Dr. Dunn, who, by the way, was no more Dunn, to all appearances, than he was the captain of the ship. He wandered about, eyes glaring, eating little, sleeping little, talking seemingly into the air, excitable, irritable, defiant. It was a clear case of obsession. I was puzzled. The medium's identity was gone. He was to me as a stranger.

I went into our room—into the silence of silent prayer. This was Thursday—the day for our séance. Accordingly, I prepared for the moral battle by having the steward thoroughly clean the cabin, change the bedding, open the port-holes; and then, I sprinkled salt in the corners of the room, and cologne upon the walls. Exalted spirits must have a pure, sweet atmosphere.

At the hour for our séance, two o'clock, I said to Dr. Dunn, or rather to the obsessing intelligence,—"Come, this is the day for our séance—come, let us go to our room."

The prompt, stern reply was, "You will forego your séance today. I have this young man in charge. I am going to hold him and do a great work through him in my way—*away with you, sir!*" were his defiant words.

Regardless of this demon influence that had taken complete control during the Chinese fight, I took the young man by the coat collar, saying firmly, "Come on;" and with something of a struggle, observed by others, I drew him into our room and quickly locked the door. I then grasped both his hands firmly in mine, exclaiming, "Come, angel guides; come, Aaron Knight; come, Powhattan,—come all, and dislodge this demon,—come and assert your well-deserved rights!"

The young man's form soon began to tremble, shake, stiffen, and then he slid from his seat on to the floor, becoming stiff and rigid as a bar of steel. His face flushed to crimson, and his eyes rolled back in their sockets, becoming blood-shotten. It was a fearful moment! I thought he might die, and I actually preferred to have him die to remaining thus insanely obsessed.

Tightening my grasp, and silently praying, soon his muscles began to relax, his joints limbered, his eyes closed tightly,—when with an Indian war-whoop and a bound, he sprang up, and standing upon his feet, exclaimed, "Me got him—*me got him!*" words in the cheery, well-known voice of his Indian influence. The demon was dethroned, the victory won.

His higher, invisible helpers then controlling him, explained the causes of this temporary obsession, and harmonized as best they could his nervously unstrung system; and then psychically left him to become normal, yet increasing the protecting spirit-guards about him. He had not, nor has he to this day, the least objective memory of those three dark days of obsession. They were a seeming blank. It was weeks before he fully recovered from the abnormal nervous strain.

CHAPTER XIV.

Pitiful Letters from the Obsessed.

UNDER the above heading the first three letters are from the facile pen of J. W. Dennis, Buffalo, N. Y., a gentleman of position in society, a thoroughgoing, successful business man, an excellent presiding officer in camps and other public meetings, and an old-time, substantial Spiritualist, still residing near one of the beautiful parks that dot and brighten the city of Buffalo.

It must not be conceived that I endorse everything as absolutely true in this series of letters, although I do in the main. Obsession is far more common than is supposed by the ordinary observer. In many households it is as carefully concealed as is the leprosy in the first families of the Orient.

Only culled portions of the letters upon this subject are here presented. Some of these required a partial rewriting to make them grammatically readable, but the ideas have been carefully retained.

"BUFFALO, N. Y., Dec. 7, 1899.

"DR. PEEBLES:

"In answer to your request I will write you some of my experiences:

"Several years ago a worthy business man came to me and asked me if I could aid him in getting rid of a spirit that controlled his hand and wrote such abominable obscenity that he would let no one see it. In a few moments I clairvoyantly saw standing beside him a most beautiful nun, apparently. This person, he said, was none other than his afflicting 'Sally Brown.' After this interview, I went home, and the next sitting we held this nun came, and my spirit wife urged me to allow her, the obsessing spirit, to attend our circles, for the purpose of trying to reform her. I allowed her to enter the psychic aura of our band, and at the end of six months I drove her away, as she was slyly trying all this time to magnetically get hold of me, and I did not want her to obsess or annoy me as she had done the business man. Then she confessed that priests had in earth life used her for wicked purposes, and were yet using her for similar purposes in the dark spheres of spirit life. It is not all purity or bliss after the event called death.

"Once, when I was unwell, and quite weak, I became conscious that a vampire sort of a spirit had gotten into the habit of visiting me every night and drawing away and absorbing my vitality. At last I got rid of him by sleeping under a bright gas light for two years.

"About two years ago a maiden lady who was sitting for mediumship called at my home. She said she was under the continual influence of an ignorant Irish spirit. During the conversation with this spirit-control, I said, 'Pat, why don't you leave this medium, and not torment her with your continued presence, influencing her all the time?' He replied, 'I do not know how. Where shall I go, sir?' 'Go up higher—take a step up into a higher life.' He replied, 'I do not know how, sir.' I said, 'Then come to me, and give that poor woman a rest.' I did not get up the next morning until nine or ten o'clock, and then I did not recognize my room or any of my surroundings. I took a cup of coffee and said nothing to any one. I had forgotten the invitation that I had given to the obsessing spirit the night before, and I went out into the street not caring where I went, and finally came to a wooded park not far from my home. Two policemen came along that I knew, and they spoke to me, but I felt 'a fear'—an unusual fear at the sight of them. All at once I thought of Pat, and how I had invited him to come to me, and at once with strong will-power, I drove him from me. He at once returned to the woman, and she is now in the State Hospital for the Insane. The M. D.'s can do her no good.

"Some time ago an acquaintance of mine, an unusually bigoted Scotch Presbyterian, lost his wife, and I called on him while her body lay in the casket in the home. I saw her spirit, and it was in a dark, blind, dazed condition, and I could hear her beg of me to tell her husband that she was not dead, but was alive and with him now. When I left for home, she sympathetically and psychically attached herself to me, and I at once proceeded to hold a séance, and purposely put her into the hands of spirits of a higher realm than earth. She reluctantly left me, and I have never heard from her since.

"At Lilly Dale Camp a few years ago, I found an old lady whom an ignorant Indian spirit had obsessionally held for about six months, and Mother Stearns, with my aid, deposed the Indian spirit, and put her loving spirit mother in charge of her, and all has been well with the old lady since.

"About a month ago I met a young German woman at a friend's house, who complained that she had sat for mediumship for two months, and at times a lying spirit got hold of her that nearly scared her to death. I tried to tell her how to get rid of him, and said that 'he could come to me for a while.'

"He immediately came to me, and attached himself magnetically, good and strong. He did not control me as he did the girl, but he hung right around me somewhere all the time. He troubled me. When we had our regular séance, I learned that this spirit had been a member of the German Lutheran Church, and was totally ignorant of anything in the mesmeric or spiritual line, and actually did not know how to leave me, or know what was the matter with him. With the aid of a higher control, and an educated German woman present, we put him under the care of an old German spirit and so he left us. I have found in all cases that it is best to make a positive arrangement with the obsessing spirit and some other brighter spirit who will take charge of the poor darkened mind that you wish to send on to a higher plane.

"A few years ago a friend of mine left the earth-life suddenly, and the night after his death he came and psychically attached himself to me. I felt that I did not wish to forcibly send him away, for I knew him to be a very bright young fellow, and he ought to go on to a higher state of existence. I sat down and wrote to an older medium than myself asking for advice. Before I had finished the letter, the spirit left me, and yet has been a regular visitant to our circles since, and he will kindly go at my request anywhere in earth-life. I do not wish any spirit that I send on and up higher to leave me altogether, but to again and again allow me and my spirit guides to do what I can do for them.

"Obsession and the control of mediums is but little understood among the mass of Spiritualists, and I fear that under the present condition of things, it will not be soon understood. While I am writing, my German spirit-friend has called on me, and I have allowed him to make a visit, but he understands that he cannot stay and annoy me by his continued presence, nor does he wish it. Death, so-called, it should be remembered, makes no immediate change in the disposition or soul tendency. Hence the undesirable influences and obsessions.

"Your fraternally, J. W. Dennis."

"Buffalo, N. Y.

"Dear Brother:

" You must pardon me for writing you again on the subject of obsession, or low spirit controls. While I was a trustee of the Lily Dale Camp for several years, I sat with a great many spirit-mediums who urged me to so do, and accordingly I have had a chance to see and study more cases of obsession than most people.

"A Mrs. Burdick came once to our house and said she had been in the asylum for the insane for two months, but she declared that she was not in the least insane. I told her she was not insane, and had a sitting with her, and soon discovered that she was troubled by the spirit of her mother, who had become insane in earth-life, over the sorrow caused by her son being imprisoned for wrecking a bank. I had long ago learned that the returning spirits to the earth's atmosphere always manifested in the same way they did when they left, until they had been taught better, and become more self-balanced; so I told the lady to wish—to pray continually that her mother would come to her clothed in her right mind. I also talked to this spirit mother, and told her that she was doing her daughter a positive injury in coming and attempting to demonstrate through her in that excited condition. In less than three months both daughter and mother were well, and have remained so, yet before the mother was taught better she almost continually obsessed her daughter. Obsessions may be of ignorance, mischief or malice.

"A few years ago a lady, who is now speaking before the same society with myself, was sitting with me at my home for development as a medium, and she attained the point where she was controlled by a good spirit who sang through her. One night she was caught, or obsessed by a spirit that threw her into hysterics, and she could hardly keep from screaming aloud all the time. She got cured of the trouble by being controlled by a mesmeric force stronger than the power of the obsessing spirit, yet I believe that she may at any time become obsessed again as all controlled mediums are under certain conditions, open to that danger.

"Martha Pollock, of B——, Ont., was suddenly taken possession of by a devil of a spirit a few years ago, and when she was not in a fight with her people, she would go to bed and lie there, and would not help a particle in work of any kind. She was cured, the spirit being driven away by a Professor Dustin, who was a very powerful mesmerist.

"Grandma Hathaway, up in Dakota, wrote me that she was a medium, and that she had taken Catholic children into her heart and home, and into her bed, and as a result she had been fairly obsessed by Catholic spirits ever since. She could not sleep, but she would not give up the children. She appealed to me for aid in getting rid of the Catholic influence, and so I magnetized paper and sent. This, with my will power and good spirits, did the business, for she wrote me that she could sleep all night without being troubled, and felt well.

"You may know Mrs. Hammett, of Encinitas, Cal., who has been at my house here in Buffalo. She has about twenty demons continually around her, but she declares that she is perfectly free from all spirit influences. (Yes, I knew her well—knew her to be good at begging money for a medium's home—and such a home! Those who went to it soon left.—J. M. P.)

"I. W. W., of Buffalo, a good little woman, went up to Lily Dale Camp as a reporter for the *Buffalo Morning Express,* and became converted to Spiritualism. She joined with others in fighting all kinds of physical phenomena. The consequence was that she became obsessed by a whole host of spirits, that were demonstrating phenomena on the physical plane. She became so violently obsessed that she was sent from Lily Dale in a private conveyance to Buffalo, and put in the asylum in a straight jacket. From a beautiful, intelligent woman, she was transformed into that condition, in which she finally died. She would laugh and grin defiantly at the friends who kindly talked to her. A sad case!

"I know of several old crones seventy and eighty years old that I think must be obsessed by dirty, sensuous, or low spirits, such as hang around cesspools of moral filth. Will I have to meet these lovers of moral carrion in spirit life? I hope not. Give me a sulphur hell in preference, for both sulphur and fire are purifiers.

"I was at Vicksburg camp once, and a prominent healer in our ranks came up to me and said, 'I wish you would go to our tent and treat my wife, she is sick.' I told him that he was a good healer, and should treat his wife himself. The next day he took me into his tent. I sat down with his wife and told her she had a pain in the chest, and was fighting off some spirit control. She said she was, and didn't like to be influenced. I told her to yield and let the spirit come, and she was at once thrown from her chair on to the floor in a strange convulsive condition. It continued for a half an hour. When she became conscious and said she felt better, I did not treat her at all. She told me afterward that she was often obsessed by a son of hers who died at the age of eighteen in convulsions, and that the condition of his health had ruined his mentality, so being attached to, he did not try to leave her. In many cases the spirits have no desire to rise higher, and so stay in the atmosphere of the earth and attach themselves to mortals whenever they can, and in this way partially re-live their earthly lives.

"Fraternally,

"J. W. DENNIS."

"DR. PEEBLES:

"In this material, money-hunting age few take notice of obsessions. They are either denied or not understood by a conservative medical fraternity. It is only those who investigate the laws of life relating to psychology and treat the sick, that can see and be made to understand how very common is obsession both internal and external.

"To a certain extent all diseases originate in the brain, in the mental rather than in any portion of the body. The causes are within, the appearances without.

"There came to me a while ago a Mr. Gould who had been suffering for some ten years from nervousness, partial blindness and rheumatism. Regular physicians could do him no good. He was a medium, conscious of spirit presences. He almost constantly saw faces. Sometimes they took the form of pictures on the wall. He was awakened night after night by peculiar sensations produced by invisible intelligences. They gave him gloomy apprehensions. They haunted him. He became thus influenced, more and more despondent, till he cherished a hatred for all mankind. He would smoke almost incessantly. His disposition was getting soured. He was irascible. Rheumatism partially crippled him for several years, and he was almost blind.

"Such was the condition of Frank I. Gould for many years, a police officer in Chelsea, Mass.,—all caused by external and internal obsession. The case was a very serious one, baffling the medical profession. My spirit physicians in time removed all the external influences, and later the environing internal entities that had become attached to the nerve centers of the body and brain. These forces were dispelled, dispossessed and cast away

by a band of scientific intelligences educated in spirit life for this work. They then placed protecting spirit friends about him. ... The tobacco habit was taken from him, the nervousness subsided, the infesting faces disappeared, and he is now perfectly well, following his employment. To all of this he will gladly testify if so invited. DR. G. LESTER LANE."
Boston, Mass.

CHAPTER XV.

More Letters Relating to Obsessions.

IT IS only justice to say that I have the names and addresses of the letter-writers describing these infernal influences. Some of them occupy prominent and official positions in society. Nearly all of them are spiritists, or inclined toward Spiritualism or Liberalism.

Those obsessed among the ecclesiastical sects are quickly pronounced insane and taken to lunatic asylums.

"DORCHESTER, MASS., Dec. 11, 1899.
"DR. PEEBLES:
"You will remember that some time ago I wrote you about a sick lady friend of mine. It wasn't a month later before she was out of the body. . . And now comes the peculiar part of this case.

"It was Tuesday evening, and we had not yet received the news of my friend's death. I had gone out to spend the evening, and left my oldest son (a boy fifteen years old) at home with a lady that makes her home with us. My youngest son had gone to choir practice before I left. My son had complained of a depressed feeling and a strong desire to cry. He would not cry, but the tears would roll down his cheeks. He said he was not sick, so I went away to visit my friend. After I had gone, my son and the lady I spoke of, were in the room previously occupied by the sick lady who had died. They heard a sound as of a door closing, and my son said, 'I guess that is Frankie (my youngest son).' The lady looked up and said, 'Yes, there he is peeping behind those curtains.' And she got up to catch him, but he was not there. While they were out of the room, the door closed with a bang, and my son opened it and went into the room. Some invisible power quickly seized him, and then came a struggle.

"He was forced from that room, the door banged, closed, through a long entry into the kitchen, and he was thrown to the floor and thrown around so that the lady was freightened and called for help. It took three persons—one a strong man—to hold him. After a while he became quieter. Then Frank came home. After Frank had been in the house a short time, the oldest boy was seized again worse than before. Frank ran for my father, and then came after me. When I reached home, he was in bed, tossing and throwing himself like one in mortal agony. He had to be held, and his face was purple, his eyes starting from his head, and the bed was wet with sweat. He did not know me, and then something like indignation—a mighty power came over me, and I told father to let him go, and I commanded in God's name, that whatever influence it was that held him to go,—*to go*, and not to come back again. My boy in a moment ceased struggling, and looking up, said, 'What is it, mama?' just as if he had been sweetly asleep,— only that he seemed exhausted.

"How can you explain it? Who do you think it was? He has not been troubled or obsessed since. Is he in danger? Do inform me.

"Very truly yours,
"Mrs. L. G. R."

"Central City, S. D., Nov. 13, 1899.

"Doctor:

"I saw your card in the *Better Life* about obsession. Will say that mother, myself and little sister six years old have been troubled for ever a year, and our experiences are something horrible. Briefly, I will state some of them. I have seen many things in the spirit world. I can also hear, and the words are distinct. I could see men and women put all kinds of vile things on us, and the feelings of our bodies at these times were something terrible. The far-distant echoes of words come, and they say, 'I'll make you spoil what you're writing.' They call me horrid names. They made my sister tell horrid fairy tales, and with great difficulty we made her stop, and she would be all in a perspiration and excited over them. When I looked, I could see a clown at the head of her bed, and it followed her for a long time. Many clowns were here some time ago,—seven months, about,— and they threw what seemed to be knives into our bodies, and at each time pain would dart in the place where the knife went. Then two people, a man and a woman, who had been very vicious and had tormented us, professed to be good, and came and pulled the knives out, and put cone-shaped ice into the wounds. Before this same woman burned a branch of what she called the 'tree of death,' and she held this around mama, and her side began to shrivel up, and I rubbed her and we tried to overthrow the influence, which we did, and all was well. After the woman became good, she burned a branch similar to the above which she called the 'tree of life.' She was very bad after all this, and still tormented us, and her constant companion was a big, coarse spirit-man. We sat for communication, and were misled, and we then quit sitting, but the sights have not left me entirely. Spirit people say horrid things and make me afraid. When I sit for psychic development, a voice will say something which makes me tremble, then if I think of mama, I can see a band of Indians, and I then hear many taunting voices speaking to me. It would take many pages to relate what we have seen, suffered and undergone.

"This is a small town, and we have been here two years. From the actions of nearly all the inhabitants, and the crimes committed, one would naturally say, 'This is an obsessed town.' I am hardly permitted by these spirits to write. I was never sick until we came here, and mama was much stronger. My little sister is tired all the time. Can you help us out of these terrible conditions?

"Yours sincerely,
"M. L. S."

"KALAMAZOO, MICH., Dec. 1, 1899.
"DOCTOR PEEBLES:

"I saw your card asking for cases of obsession, and will relate to you the case of a woman in this city. She says in this obsessed state that she is the best medium in the world. She tells the wildest tales. She was in the asylum in this city for about two years. Her health was improved, but she was not changed mentally. I think she gets more stubborn all the time. She tells so much that the spirits tell her, that I have never known her to tell anything that we could rely upon. She sees spirits and gives some tests. She was an unusually bright woman, taught school for seventeen years and was married to a lawyer. He drank, neglected her and two little boys. She left him, and he had her put in the asylum. She is now dependent upon her relatives for support. The lady is my sister, and since leaving her husband she has got the idea that I don't belong to the family—was changed when a babe. When we reason with her, and trying to tell her that it is evil-disposed spirits that tell her these things, she gets very angry.

"Yours respectfully,
" Mrs. P. H. R.

"Baird, Texas, June 9, 1899.
"Doctor:
"Eighteen months ago I tried to write automatically, and after a few sittings I was successful; but it was a very bad spirit who later, for some cause, used my hand. He was a liar and a miserable character. He confessed that he had been the murderer of his life, and that he was sent to me to better him, and for me to do for him some missionary work. As I am a German, he used that language, and recounted to me a great many of his misdeeds.

Not long before these events, I became convinced of the truth of spiritism, but I did not know much of the philosophy, and I candidly believed this spirit, and tried to do something for him, supposing that I could help him. But he became more and more insolent and malicious toward me, so that I could stand it no longer. Then I broke the communications up with him, and told him positively I would have nothing more to do with him.

In revenge, he began to torment me by touching my head day and night, almost constantly, and during the last six months I have suffered intensely from him. I know it is he, but I have never communicated with him since. I am a little better now, but he is always haunting me, and I would be very much obliged to you if you would drive him away. Please give me some advice. You are, so I am informed, one of the best-informed *spiritists,* and there is no doubt that you may know a remedy against this persistent sinister influence. Possibly the cause of all these troubles is my ignorance concerning spiritism. I do not know how to resist him. I pray you give me instruction in this line.

"Yours truly,
"F. W."

"BAIRD, TEXAS, June 27, 1899.

"DOCTOR:

"In reply to your letter, I must say that it would have been much better for me if I had corresponded with you a year ago. A great trouble of our cause is that a great many uneducated and ignorant people are trying to instruct and teach others. They write and talk about things without the least knowledge of hypnotism, psychic law or the matter they are treating.

"When I was first troubled with this controlling spirit, I read that it was our duty to be friendly to every spirit, and teach and help even the worst of them, to receive them with Christain love, etc. As I was very ignorant in regard to Spiritism, and believed that these writers and teachers knew what they were talking about, I accepted their advice. You know the sad result. For six months, now, I haven't let that evil spirit use my hand, and I figuratively knock his head against the rock wall of my house when he troubles me, and I find this treatment eminently successful. I do not speak to him nor notice him. I do not want to revenge myself, but want to drive him away, and I will do it with all my strength and pyschic power. True, he is persistent, but I have a strong will, and he will never be able to break it. His power is continually lessening.

"However, I need help. I am living in a small town of about 1,000 inhabitants. You advise me, besides using my will power, to call a strong band of Indian spirits to help me. I am eagerly willing to do so, but do not know just how to do it. Must I address my wishes to my guardian spirits? I am very well read in the line of philosophy, and am a German writer myself, but do not know much about *Spiritism*. Years ago I was a strong enemy of spiritism, and possibly such treatment was needed to convince me of the truth. Please excuse my poor English.   Truly yours,
"F. W."

CHAPTER XVI.

Obsessions of Methodists and Others.

MONON, IND., Jan. 14, 1900.

"DR. PEEBLES:

"Some time ago I saw your request for experience along the line of obsession, and I wish to give you mine. First, I will relate a case I well knew.

"Many years ago, there was a girl in Watertown, N. Y., named Nancy Hull, who was reputed not of good character, although appearing to be generally. She was taken suddenly sick, and on her dying bed requested the neighbors to come and see her, but there was one proud woman who would not come because she had reason to believe that Nancy had tempted her husband. She called Nancy a vile name, and she passed into the spirit life with deep feelings of hatred and resentment toward this woman; and accordingly she resolved to bring this woman's girls to the same condition that she was reputed to be in on earth. She took her hate with her. She was revengeful. The girls were not led astray, but they were badly obsessed and tormented by this spirit. I knew all the parties concerned, and years later Nancy came to me as a spirit and begged me with tears to obtain their forgiveness.

"In 1887 a lady passed away leaving her husband and four children, the three eldest being girls. Her whole life had been devoted to her husband and family, and in seeking means to keep near them and help them, she found me, and psychically influenced me to go to this town and make their acquaintance. She influenced me so powerfully that my body was at times as much hers almost as my own, and she further influenced me to marry him. I did so, and tried conscientiously to be a good stepmother, but rebellious children prevented a happy home, and I was compelled by force of circumstances to leave. I was not by any means because of this a poor, broken-hearted, sorrowful woman. Then Frances Willard, having entered spirit life, and active as ever to heal the broken-hearted and restore confidence in desolate homes, found me.

"I returned home, and became conscious of spirit presences in the house. One day out in the garden I received this message, 'Nothing will be put upon you but what you can endure, and you will have plenty of help. I wrote many messages to my husband from his first wife, and she urged him to be kind.

"About two years ago, I was powerfully overcome by spirit power, and shook like a leaf in a strong gale. I fell on my knees and prayed for all my relatives, and felt friendly to all, friends and enemies alike. Then this thought rushed into my mind, 'I give you a new name, —"Frances Willard." I felt so spiritual, exalted and loving.

"Some time afterward, Miss Willard sent for the ladies of the W. C. T. U. to come, but the news had gone abroad that I was crazy, and they were afraid. Then the sad thought was 'I come unto my own, and my own received me not.' Unbeknown to me, I had a trial for my sanity, and was asked,—You say that Miss Willard is here?

"I answered, 'Yes. I do.'

"'What does she want? Has she a message?'

"'Yes, it is this,—I want the church to open wide its doors and plant in its vineyard three trees,—Spiritualism, divine healing and the holy purposes of the Women's Christian Temperance Union.'

"On the strength of this spirit message I was reported insane, or obsessed and sentenced to the insane asylum. But before my sentence was executed, my niece from St. Paul came, and persuaded them to allow her to take me to Chicago to a specialist. I went to Chicago and was admitted to the Hahnemann Hospital. I was examined by Dr. Bailey, who reported that I was in sound condition, although somewhat nervous. He also privately told me to go on unto perfection, as these spiritual mainfestations would soon not be sneered at, or be so misunderstood. When I returned home, however, I had the reputation of being insane. I was advised to go to the asylum, and I went. I suffered much humiliation. After three weeks, the superintendent discharged me, with the decision that there was no mental derangement in my case, with the exception of a certain degree of emotional sensitiveness.

"I am regenerated, lifted out of the power of obsessing spirits now, but my environments are not altogether congenial. I am a Methodist and also a Spiritualist. I have reached the end of my stationery, and will complete this letter, and send it with all its imperfections.

"Yours for the truth,

"Mrs. E. H."

"WEST LEBANON, IND., June 27, 1900.
"DOCTOR:
"Since last November I have passed through such a peculiar psychic experience that I scarcely knew what manner of person I was for about two months and a half. Your essay gave me some light on my peculiar condition of mind, and I want to tell you something of my experiences and the cause which led to it.

"I had been a great reader along scientific lines of thought, and a student of the Bible from early childhood. In the past few years my leisure time has been spent with books rather than company, although I have by no means been a recluse. Outside of my home duties, I have done considerable church work, and with this aim in mind, I visited some new comers in our neighborhood, an old gentleman and his wife. The old gentleman was skeptical. He had no faith in the Bible, but believed in the presence of spirits and unseen beings about us. I asked him how he obtained his knowledge, and he explained by showing me a planchette. I put my hand on it with his wife, and it spelled out after a bit, 'Don't want to write. Will write some other time.' It was astonishing to me, and aroused my curiosity.

"I had heard of others writing involuntarily, and so when I came home, I sat with a pencil in hand until it wrote as readily as by my own will. It had an alluring effect upon me. Soon there were seeming contradictions and deceptions. My discernment seemed to be taken away from me. Because of my excitable and nervous condition, I was soon taken away to the insane asylum, pronounced insane. I remained there three months. My stay during the latter part of the time was to prove my sanity to those who had care of me. For the first six weeks, I felt not a care for home, nor daunted in the least because of being there.

"My mind seemed to act rapidly, and I could write a whole book, telling of the things that passed through my mind, the weird, visionary objects presented to my view, and the real observations that came under my notice. My nature was so changed at times that I did not have any ill-feeling toward any one. It seemed that there were two influences working through my mind, so conflicting that at times it was annoying to me. My hand at one time wrote that magnetism built up the mind, and necromancy tore it down, and that I was to show the world what necromancy was doing for it. I cried over this. And although I prayed every day, my prayers were made light of, and I became almost fearful to pray, and then a most beautiful prayer would ring through my head as from another person. The influence at times was terrible. I cannot describe it. I was not myself. I was obsessed. But at last I came out from under that influence, the cause of which I do not fully understand. The Institution did not do it, for I took but few doses of medicine, and did not follow their instructions. But suddenly, this controlling influence left me, and I came to my natural self. What a relief!

"I was not insane, but under some psychic spell. My parents do not allow anything now to come into my hands upon the subject of Spiritism.

"Yours respectfully,
"MARY C."

"DR. PEEBLES:

"A sad case of obsession (called epilepsy by physicians) was treated and cured in four days. DR. A. A. KIMBALL. Here it is in brief:

"During the winter of 1894 there was brought to my office in Northampton, Mass., a young girl by the name of Edith Shepherd, of Florence, Mass., aged nine years. She had developed fine test mediumship at circles which she attended. I was present at one of the circles, and saw clairvoyantly over the head of this girl a very dark evil force, who was seeking to get possession of her. I told her brother that they must be very careful of her, and take particular pains that only good conditions surrounded her.

"In a short time they moved to Leominster, Mass., and the girl began to have what were called epileptic fits. She would fall backward upon the floor, her body perfectly rigid, eyes closed and jaws set. By rubbing her, she would come out of these fits in a short time; but they continued to attack her oftener and with more severity. One day while in a fit of unusual severity, they despaired of bringing her out of it. Suddenly she was controlled by the spirit of a little Indian girl, who said, 'Rub medie quick and hard, and we will try and hold her.' They renewed their efforts, which were crowned with success. The Indian spirit returned, and informed them that there was a band of bad demon spirits who were determined to take the medium's spirit out of her body, and that they were not able to hold their medium longer in those dark conditions, and for them to go back to Florence immediately, if they wished to keep her alive. They came back to Florence, but the 'fits' continued. A lady friend advised the mother to bring the child to me, which she did. While the mother was relating to me the child's condition, she was looking at different articles around the room, when suddenly with a scream she fell backward on the floor. I sprang to her and found her body rigid, jaws tightly set, eyes closed, and on lifting the eyelid, found the eye turned upward, only disclosing a part of the pupil. Upon the face was an expression of the deepest hatred, revenge and maliciousness combined. I raised her in my arms and laid her upon a couch, and sat down by her side placing my right hand on her forehead. Instantly her eyes opened, and with a terrible curse, the spirit (for such it was) demanded me to remove my hand, and followed up this demand with the most bitter curses and maledictions that I ever heard from the lips of a mortal toward the mother for putting her child in my care, and also toward me for magnetically breaking his power over her. Six of these vicious spirits came at this time, to whom I talked and reasoned with, while at the same time my band were throwing upon them a spiritual power to raise them out of the dark conditions they were in to a higher plane of spiritual development. The child was brought to me four days in succession, many spirits of this class being taken from her each day, until this band of evil spirits was entirely broken up. She has had no recurrence of the trouble, and for the last five years has enjoyed excellent health.''

"SALMA, KANS., Dec. 29, 1899.

"DOCTOR:

"I saw your note in the *Temple of Health* asking for accounts of people suffering from obsession. I have an intimate friend who often comes to see me, and we sit alone in a circle. She has very strong psychic powers, and could make a splendid medium, only she is annoyed by a dark, malicious spirit. She sees him clairvoyantly. I really think he would kill her if let alone. My band is powerful enough to keep him away from me, but not

always from her. From what our higher spirit friends tell us, he must be terrible. She does not dare to go under full control. We have reasoned, prayed, coaxed and scolded, but with no success. If you can tell us anything to do, I am sure, we will be thankful. The lady is a bright woman about fifty years old.
"MRS. HANNAH DODDS."

"ARMENIA, SALVADOR, CENTRAL AMERICA,
Oct. 24, 1901.
"DR. PEEBLES.
"SIR: In the *Progressive Thinker*, No. 611, of Aug. 10, I find an article directed to you by Dr. Robert Greer, headed 'Romish spirits,' that led me to imagine that you are about to publish a book on spirit obsession; and as I was most *infernally obsessed* for the space of two and a half years, some fifteen years ago, I have concluded to offer you my experience in the matter, to be used by you as you may see fit.

"I am not really a Spiritualist, and was never present at but two spiritual séances, neither of which appeared to me to be of very much significance, but I have been, as I said before, *terribly obsessed* by two spirits once in human bodies who seemed to me as humanly solid as myself. They measurably ate with me, seemingly slept in the same rooms with me, and traveled with me by rail and steamer over *half the globe*. They produced strange psychic phenomena for my edification; argued and explained to me scientific subjects that I had never studied or even dreamed of, and hounded me with insults and vicious vituperations when I refused to lend my entire attention, sometimes bringing orchestras of men and women with rare stringed instruments, whom, I must say, produced the most delightful, yet weird music it has ever been my pleasure to listen to.

"At first I thought the public was 'daft' for not seeing and hearing what I so dinstinctly saw and heard, but when I began to realize that the public was beginning to imagine me out of my head, *by the advice of my persecutors,* I quit talking about the matter, and so escaped a straight-jacket. That there are both good spirits and wicked demon spirits, I well know.

"I have no doubt but that if you hand this letter to some good psychometrist, he will tell you that I am telling the exact truth, and if you desire me to write out my experience in detail, I will gladly do so, and send it to you *under oath,* as I have always wished to publish it but have refrained through fear of the world's ridicule.

"I am an American born Roman Catholic, and very liberal religiously, and once could write fair English, but have been so long in Spanish America that I have lost the knack of good English, so anything I might write you would probably have to re-write.

"Truly yours,
"Col. P. P. B."

CHAPTER XVII.

Obsessions, Tobacco and Liquor.

"COLON, MICH., June 27, 1899.

"DEAR BROTHER:

"I will try and give you an account of the séances we had with Farmer Riley, that I spoke to you of on the railway train. About four years ago, myself, wife, daughter and a Mr. Cornell drove thirty-six miles to Farmer Riley's home to attend a séance. The séance went well for half an hour, with Riley in the cabinet, when suddenly a slate was handed from the cabinet with something like the following written on it: 'Turn up the curtain, and take the medium out; change the conditions, or we will not have the medium go under control again tonight. JOHN BENTON.

"The slate was handed to Mrs. Riley, who read it, and then requested Mr. Benton to wait a few minutes longer. Soon there came a distinct voice from the cabinet, saying, 'You promised you would not come again tonight, you demon.' Then an apparent scuffle ensued, in which the curtain was terribly agitated, and a man's arm dressed in a black flowing sleeve, similar to that of a Catholic priest was very distinctly seen as it protruded from the cabinet. It looked as though the intruder was getting a pretty severe shaking up,—a thorough thrashing. A moment later something apparently struck the side of the wall of the cabinet, as though one man had thrown another against it in the struggle. Then a slate was handed out with much the same request as before, and with something like, '*that cursed priest is here again tonight.*' Mrs. Riley then threw open the cabinet, and got the medium out. Mr. Riley then requested me to read from the slates, saying, 'I fear it is all up for tonight; that old obsessing priest is determined to spoil the séance if possible.'

"I then said to Mr. Riley, 'Let us change the conditions.'

" 'How can we do it?' he asked.

"I said, 'Let us get Cornell to sing some cheerful songs and play the organ (he is and adept at that), as I think our spirit friends are tired of these old psalm tunes, and I believe it will drive this infesting priest away.' (Tobacco and whisky seem to attract evil spirits. Some priests, as well as some laymen, drink while in their bodies.)

"Mr. Riley thought that would do, and soon he returned to the cabinet. We had to urge Mr. Cornell to sing, as he thought it would disturb the sanctity of the séance. He had scarcely got well to singing before the spirits, several of them, began to walk out of the cabinet. Mr. Eber Pierce's son came out well formed and shook hands with my wife, and firmly clung to her until he was all dematerialized but his hand. We could all distinctly see his hand and wrist when the rest of his body had become invisible. We had a grand time after we got rid of that intruding, obsessing priest. This causes me to wonder if spirits, like mortals, still quarrel and torment each other? Can they molest and break up séances? Can they obsess, infest and injure mortals? Such is my candid belief based upon observation and experiences during the last twenty-five years.

"Very truly yours,
"A. S. Prout."

(Personally knowing this gentleman for thirty years and more, and also knowing Mr. Pierce's son of whom he speaks, I can vouch for the correctness of Mr. Prout's statements, which have been greatly curtailed to save space. A superior clairvoyant attending one of these séances saw dark aural-clad obsessing demons, such as she had often seen in the vicinity of questionable houses, pool-rooms, city dance dens, drinking saloons and gamblers' resorts. These are the hypnotizing, lying, obsessing demons 'reserved unto judgment.' J. M. P.)

"Grand Rapids, Mich., Dec. 10, 1899.
"Doctor:

"Your card incited me to give my experience with evil spirits. When young I got into the habit of drinking. This grew on me until it made a hell on earth for both me and my associates. My wife used to plead with me, and once threatened to leave me. I hated myself for drinking, and made promise after promise to stop, but after abstaining for a week, I would go on another carousal. I could not overcome the desire.

"Attending a Spiritualist camp-meeting, I met a clairvoyant who told me that I was a sensitive, and was influenced by an evil spirit who was gratifying his appetite and base desires through my body. It surprised me. She said that my earnest desire to overcome the habit had also attracted to me good spirits who were trying to rightly influence me. She insisted that I sit for development when I went home, and ask God and the good angels to help me, and the evil ones would necessarily have to leave. I did as she said, and in a short time we got many fine manifestations, and later got well acquainted with the undeveloped earth-bound spirit that influenced me to do evil, and also got acquainted with some of those higher spirits that were trying to help me out of this obsessing influence. It was a hard contest between the good and the evil spirits—a very battle, so to speak. The good would be controlling me and giving excellent manifestations of truth and wisdom, when suddenly I would feel a thrill of other influences low and positive, and the good spirits would be forced away. This evil spirit would sneer at and mock me, and I would plead with him just as I would with a wicked mortal. He said he had got me and would do with me just as he pleased. I kept on, and I finally got rid of him. He said before leaving that as I had made him see things different, he would not bother me any more. That was nearly five years ago, and we have heard from him but once in that time.

"As soon as his influence left me I had no trouble in overcoming that terrible drinking thirst, and it has been nearly five years since I have touched a drop of liquor. I wish that every medium, and every person influenced by spirits from the other world, could see the great harm it does to use tobacco, liquor and be a slave to other filthy habits. These do a great deal toward attracting these undeveloped and evil spirits.

"Very truly yours,
"J. E. WALKER."

(I personally know Mr. Walker. He is now a just, upright and honorable man. The last I saw him a few months since he was on the Spiritualist's rostrum in Battle Creek delivering a most stirring lecture.)

In connection with the above, it is but justice to say to thoughtful Spiritualists and especially to mediumistic sensitives that these letters from the obsessed or the once obsessed appearing in this volume are not only genuine—*genuine* with the writers' signatures attached, yet requesting that only their initials in whole or a part be used. Hundreds of letters written me during the past five years, and perhaps the most interesting of them, if selfishness, occult depravity and psychological sinfulness from the unseen side of conscious life be interesting, I have not published, because a majority of the parties moving in what is termed the "higher circles of social life" utterly refused to have their names, their initials, the village or city where they resided mentioned. Quite a number of these persons wrote me for aid in dispossessing them or some member of their family of an unwanted, uncanny controlling influence. (J. M. P.)

"BENNINGTON, N. H., Nov. 12, 1899.

"DEAR SIR:

"As I have had some experience with undeveloped or evil-disposed spirits, I will briefly state my case. Five years ago this fall I discovered that I was mediumistic, and very rapidly developed into a writing medium, at first automatic, then inspirational, and finally, I became claraudient. Soon, I had unmistakable tests, and knew I was communicating with relatives and very dear friends. Having been a great skeptic all my life, it was so marvelous and astounding that I could not get satisfied, and passed much of my time writing. Ignorantly I opened the door for all grades of spirits to walk in, and being selfish and earthly, they staid, controlling me to the exclusion of all my identified friends.

"Finally, sad as it was, I was obliged to give up all intercourse with spirit-intelligences, and when they found that I would not write for them, they commenced talking, and kept it up tormenting me day and night, for several weeks. The more they found I was annoyed, the more persistent they were, and at last it became unbearable. I had to use all my strength of will to stop it, and I succeeded after a time. They threatened if I would not talk with them, that they would follow me to my death or make me insane. Then I thought it time to see who would conquer. My will was thoroughly aroused. *I would not listen to their talk,* and when sewing or driving, if alone, would repeat hymns and poetry, and when at the table, I was allowed to do all the talking. When retiring at night I would read myself to sleep. They would wake me several times in the night, but I always had a book at hand, and would read myself to sleep again. If I relaxed my vigilance for one instant, they were there ready to commence their everlasting chatter and babble. It was nearly two weeks after I commenced this line of earnest, positive and stringent warfare that I got entirely rid of them. I have not been troubled by the talking since.

"Once or twice a year I try to communicate with spirits by writing, but apparently the same evil influences,—the same demons, always come, and will try to personate some of my friends, but I can readily distinguish the difference. I have about given up all expectations of ever being able to exercise my gift, for these evil-disposed, obsessing spirits will not allow it. I will kindly ask you not to publish my name in this connection, for

I am extremely sensitive about it. I read an article in a Spiritualist paper once, saying 'like attracts like.' This I do not believe. Certainly, it is not true in my case. It is more true that 'fools rush in where angels fear to tread.' I want no more of this obsessing spiritism. Respectfully yours,
"N. H."

"Aurora, Ill., Nov. 7, 1899.
"Dear Sir:
"I am a medium (inspirational) but have had so much trouble in my mediumship that I am doing nothing with it. A constant battle is going on concerning me among the spirits. I have been magnetically held much of the time for two and a half years by a positive spirit who is determined to make me an 'adept.' I knew him when on earth. There is no mistaking the identity. He was a medium, educated, well-enlightened on the subject of Spiritualism, but he wants to dictatorily rule me to the utter exclusion of all other spirits. I knew nothing of his mediumship during his earth life. My acquaintance with him was slight. A spirit Turk also wants to make me an 'Oriental adept.' He has been near me nearly three years, and I have only known recently that these spirits wished to teach me Eastern adeptism, but I absolutely refuse. I have no desire, nor can I entertain the thought of my becoming an adept. My individuality must and will be maintained. The very slight knowledge I have of adeptism is enough. Still the spirit obsessionally holds me. I have used every means in my power to have him leave me, but I am not magnetically strong enough to break his control and drive him away. He has psychic help from another spirit, who also wants to make

me an adept. I have an indomitable will power, but weak magnetism. I am very easily controlled, and to a great degree am at the mercy of these dictatorial positive spirits. I have suffered agonies, sometimes almost worse than death, from two strong spirits rather than give up to their wild, unwise teachings. I think I can safely say no medium has ever made a harder struggle or braver fight for the good of true Spiritualism than myself. But I have about given up the struggle. I have always said if I could not be an honest, truthful medium, I would not be a medium. One of the strong spirits who holds me tells many direct falsehoods. There are three good-principled spirits who endeavor to protect me, and drive the others away, but they are not always magnetically strong enough. There are many good spirit friends who want to aid and be my guides, but are deterred by the two spirits who are determined to master me.

"Two and a half years ago, when my mediumship began, I knew absolutely nothing of the rules of mediumship. I did not even know that evil spirits could communicate. I supposed evil spirits were somewhere kept under restraint. And I did not know there was such a thing as obsession, having never heard the word. I never sat for development, and the phases I have were literally thrust upon me. Intelligent spirits tell me I can develop nearly all phases of mediumship.

"A year ago I could see clairvoyantly, but the two strong spirits—demons, shall I call them—will not allow my spirit friends to show me beautiful visions any more. I see spirit lights, see several forms of life on the spirit plane, but I do not know what they mean. I see small clouds, both light and dark. One of my good spirit friends can rap on the table, touch jars, etc., so that I can distinctly hear. He says he could give me independent voices and independent music, but is not allowed to. I have had many exalting and ennobling communications from my good spirit friends, and if the demon spirits who hold me because they are determined to make an adept of me, would leave me, I could go on with my mediumship and so do great good in the world. I will not allow my individuality to be benumbed or destroyed. I would like to teach and develop mediums, but will never make any attempt under the present unfavorable conditions.

"During the first year and a half of my mediumship, I was held by an undeveloped astral, or earth-bound demon-spirit, but was freed this summer. Never will I consent to be an adept. There is an Indian that stays with me, but can only speak occasionally. He is a noble and beautiful spirit. Loves God and obeys the law, and if he could be permitted to influence me, I could advance and progress, but until that time comes (if ever), I refuse to go on with my mediumship.

"Respectfully,
"Mrs. J. T."

"Toronto, Ont., Nov. 6, 1899.

"Dr. Peebles:
"Referring to your card in the *Better Life,* I will give you a few instances of obsession. I have a sister, a trance medium, not a public medium, in fact, only her most intimate friends have seen her in a trance condition.

"Two winters ago she and I were in a street car when she suddenly jumped up and tried to get off the car without stopping it, but the conductor and myself seized her and held her until the car stopped. All on the car believed her to be intoxicated, but I knew that she was obsessed. As soon as we reached the sidewalk, I pleaded with the spirit to permit her to go home, but all was in vain for a time. At last I got the intoxicated spirit to go home with me. When we got at my home, he said that was the first time he had ever controlled one, or ever been there. I was afraid he would injure or overtax my sister's strength, and I coaxed him, while still controlling, to lie on the bed. All this time my sister was, to all appearances, beastly drunk, using profane and very obscene language to me. Under his control, she behaved, in fact, in a very rude and every way unbecoming manner.

"I was at my wits' end to know how to get rid of him, and sat down by the bed sorrowfully wondering when my sister would again come to herself. I tried all the means I had ever heard of to dispossess him, when about two A. M., I told my husband to grasp one of her hands firmly, and I took the other, making a circle around her. And immediately she was herself again, but oh, so tired, nervous and worn out that we got her into a sleep, that remained until twelve next day, when she awoke, but remembered nothing about it,—so we never told her.

"When in her unconscious trance condition, she personates the dying taking on their conditions. These are sometimes terribly painful to witness. In most cases the spirits taking possession of her are relatives and friends, and they try to do all the good they can. But she has been abused five times by strange, wicked, obsessing demons, one case of which is stated above, all different, however. On account of these obsessing conditions and dangers, she will not allow herself to become further entranced. She resists the approach of every spirit, and

Obsessions, Tobacco and Liquors. 171

so the world has to do without one of the best trance mediums that I ever knew.

"Yours truly,
"IDA E. C."

"VICTORIA, B. C., Oct. 24, 1900.

"DEAR SIR:

"For about seven months I have had and am having a sad and perplexing experience. I sincerely and anxiously hope and trust that you will give the matter your most serious and earnest consideration at your earliest convenience. About one year ago I began to investigate Spiritualism, and became deeply interested in the life its philosophy teaches. I read considerable of its philosophy, but sat only a few times for phenomena.

"In the early part of last May, I received what I believed to be automatic writing, and heard voices from (as I believed) the spirit world. The writing exactly resembled that of my deceased wife, but was, almost without exception, extremely blasphemous and vulgar. At first there seemed many voices around me, quite low, yet distinct, varying in distance from me. These were similar to those of acquaintances (their names being mentioned as if conversing), and the conversations were of the most vulgar nature. Some time later, I became impressed that there was but one voice, and my continuous experience since verifies that impression. I have grown positive of this, and believe it to be one voice. Since I first heard it speak, until today, I have with but few exceptions, listened to nothing but heinous blasphemy and obscenity, copiously mingled with which are continual mental impressions or reflections of a similar character. For some weeks he personated God, and strenuously endeavored to persuade me that my soul was God; that it, or he, had indwelt in man since the atonement, coming down as a soul through a certain race; that I was the last of that race, and was to become God and possess his power on March 1, 1901; and was to reign on earth and in heaven, alternately for one thousand years, and that my deceased wife was to be the queen of the realms and live with me. Later on, he personated both God and Christ by speaking or throwing the voice, as if Christ was in the heavens conversing with my soul, or God within me. And yet, the conversations were mostly scurrilously obscene. He can cause a ringing sensation in my head, which he generally does by repeating the word 'see,' and which exists almost continually. He or it can speak distinctly at pleasure, and intelligently, and of things of which I am not thinking; it can stop speaking at pleasure, but absolutely refuses to do so. Since first hearing the voice (early in May) I have spent the greater part of my time in solitude,—that is, I have conversed very infrequently and but little, have read little or none, and this voice has been and is almost continuously sounding in my head, or apparently near me. He knows every item of my life that I can recollect, and repeatedly refers to them and friends, both by word and mental vision or impression, simply to taunt and annoy me. His conversations generally are most obscene and vulgar, and spoken to tantalize. When reading, he reads with me. When writing, thinking or conversing, he has to a limited extent, the power of confusing me—Can stop reading or speaking when I am reading or writing, if so inclined, but thus far has utterly refused to do so. I seem to be two personalities.

"He has power to terribly influence my temper and passions, and in a manner which I cannot perceive. He has the power to cause me slight griping pains immediately below my waist, which would be preceded by a threat to kill me by gnawing out my vitals. He has power to interfere with my breathing but slightly; also to cause facial impressions, known only to myself. He is an obsessing devil.

"He speaks and sings distinctly. He is intelligent, but wicked. I hear his voice almost continually, but it affects me more at night when I generally reach sleep through fatigue. He also can, and frequently does, cause a spasmodic shiver to pass through my whole system. He tells me he has no knowledge as to how he does these things, yet knows he causes many if not all of them; but he absolutely refuses to desist talking, which I think might remedy the whole trouble. From the first time I heard his voice until today, I have strenuously endeavored to induce him to converse spiritually, and to desist talking, except at times when it would be advantageous to himself and me. But despite all my entreaties, he continues to harass me night and day, and stubbornly refuses to do anything that is reasonable or right. He generally threatens to do the things stated, before doing them.   Yours respectfully,

"C. W. D."

CHAPTER XVIII.

Roman Catholic Obsessions and the False Names of Spirits.

"CHICAGO, ILL., May 25, 1901.
"DEAR SIR AND BROTHER:
"You ask me to state from my extended experience of forty years and more in Spiritualism, something what I know of spirits and spirit-life. In reply will say that I positively know that spirits good and evil do exist, for with clairvoyant eyes I have seen them, and with clairaudient ears I have heard their voices, and spoken with them face to face many, many times.

"Some may ask, 'What do spirits look like?' I answer, just like human beings; some are clothed in different styles of costume, others are nude. Some of the nude are transparent and bright as golden day,—others are opaque and dark as night. From personal appearance, however, you cannot always judge infallibly between good and evil spirits. It is only by their auras and specific acts that you can judge them. Spirits who manifest to you with god intent are good; spirits who manifest with selfish, evil intent are bad.

"Evil spirits will assume wrong names, will falsify and betray. Good spirits never! Pure-minded spirits represent all that is good and true and beautiful, moral and spiritual. The angels of love and light treat humanity always with benevolence, whereas the conduct of evil spirits is always sly, selfish and malevolent. The evil spirits are the very composite of all that is morally bad. They are cruel and remorseless. They will stand at nothing to accomplish their ends, and thieving, lying spirits to accomplish their ends, will hypnotize, suggest, impress, stultify, obsess and otherwise persist in driving us to misfortune. They have done so to me several times. During the past forty years they have been my worst and only real enemies, and often made me think that life was not worth living. Obsession I know to be a fact, and a most sorry one too, to me.

"No later than five years ago they gave me a terrible fall, and threatened beforehand that they were going to do it. This fall did me considerable bodily harm, got me out of business, and laid me up for nearly a year. I have not quite recovered yet. Spirits can make sick, and can heal also. A week afterward, while on my bed in agony, I was visited by three spirit men with clean-shaven faces and in clerical attire. They appeared standing in front of me at the foot of my bed with eyes sternly fixed upon me. They were as real as any mortals I ever saw. The one nearest to my left exclaimed in tones of triumph, 'Ha, ha! We told you we would fix you!'

"'Yes,' I replied, 'but gentlemen, what have I done that you persecute me so? Tell me, and if I can atone for it, I will.'

"Their reply was, 'You are atoning for it now, and you have pretty well atoned for it during the past forty years. When you were young and in your prime, overflowing with the zeal of Protestantism, you antagonized severely the only true church—the old peerless leader of the Christian religion, and the only way to grace and eternal glory. You drew from it many of its adherents, and these drew from it in turn, many more, and many of whom are now here in spirit life—but not of us. They worship at other shrines to the great discomfort of their family ancestors. In spirit life, as in human life, there are many sects and many organizations, but we are of the holy mother church and very jealous of any religious society, or any one that invades our sacred domain, and undermines the faith of our adherents. Our remotest ancestors of the church desire to have with them all their posterity, and all descendants born into the church, and a relentless war is ever waged against all who hinder or oppose the church. Witness our torment in earth life to all those apostate priests and bishops who have seceded from us. To them we are unrelenting and unmerciful. But, you say, as you have often said, that " the mother church is not Christian, but pagan." Perhaps you, although a layman, may think you know more tha nall our holy priesthood since mother church began. They educated us, they think for us, and tell us we are Christians; we believe and are satisfied.

" 'But to the point: For forty years we have been upon your track and hostile to you, and you knew it, but did not fully know why, and yet you covertly attributed to us all your misfortunes. To mar your pleasures, we often made you sick and deprived you of your energy temporarily. Often, too, when you were wrapped in slumber we entered into your dreams, giving you various impressions, how to speculate, but only to despoil you. We made you bankrupt more than once in order to cut off your supplies, and all because we have direct orders from the government of our mother church to so do. Not, however, for the purpose of converting you to our religion, for that would be impossible, now, besides, we would not have you if we could, for with us you would

Roman Catholic Obsessions. 177

ever be a disturbing, heretical element. Our discipline, —our following of you—was to teach you one of life's important lessons, namely, to mind your own business hereafter and let mother church and her communicants alone.

" 'Our treatment of you, we know, has been rather rough, but well meant from our church standpoint. You bore it well, and now our missionary work with you is done. This will be our last exploit against you. We will, therefore, leave you now and haunt you no more forever. What have you to say?'

"I replied, 'Gentlemen, to begin with, I must say that in this terrible fall while descending my own doorsteps, causing me so much pain, I think you played me a vile, scurvy trick. For my sincere and conscientious religious devotion to truth, I think I have paid a severe unjust price, and you call this Christian, do you?

" 'Gentlemen, I do not profess to know it all, but I do know from what I have read of church history that Christ, the founder of Christianity, taught a religion of love, and the church he founded was the church of the golden rule. I know, too, from what I have read, that soon after the first century, because of corruption of the priesthood, the holy spirit, with the heavenly inspiring spirits, withdrew, and the original church in its purity ceased to exist under the name of Christ until about the third century, when a few fanatical priests, with others, banded themselves together and called themselves Christians. They soon began to be wicked and worldly. They built a great priestly heirarchy. They fought and quarreled among themselves about the interpretation of the Master until about 50,000,000 mortals, during those dark ages, were slain, slaughtered and burned alive at the behest, it is said, of the mother church. For sixteen hundred years she has kept up this theological fight and persecution, more or less. Her methods, of course, have changed during these later years of progress, but her malevolent, sectarian spirit toward heretics is just the same, and she would repeat her cruelties today if she dared. For my part, I have no respect for your "mother church." I regard her as a great religious gambling institution, and her church worshipers as dupes and bigots, and of the future beyond the grave her priests know nothing.'

"At this juncture the speaker exclaimed, 'Brothers, let us be going. This man is unredeemable. Let us leave him to be eternally lost, and so bid him adieu.' They seemed as though stunned by this straight-out talk. They vanished to parts from which I hope they may never return.

"DR. ROBERT GREER."

"DANVILLE, N. Y., Nov. 6, 1899.

"DR. PEEBLES:

"Can you relieve me of these obsessing spirits that are destroying my life forces? Five years ago I was called 'a beautiful lady,' loved for my genial womanly disposition. I went to Cassadaga Camp-meeting, and attended a séance. The night after coming home from the séance, I lay in bed nervous, half-conscious and half entranced all night. When I came home, I found myself clairvoyant and clairaudient, and I had a great many remarkable things given me. I was very glad for a time to be mediumistic, and I could tell you a great deal if I could personally talk it to you.

"They say that you can cure obsession. Will you

please cure me of this obsession, and drive these spirits to the hells of their own making? I shall get deranged if I can't stop their hurting me, and thrusting their unseen fangs into my flesh. I suffer the tortures of a burning hell, and I get but two or three hours' sleep out of the night. I am getting so thin that I know they will kill me if I can't get help. You will help me, won't you? I am a maiden lady and live all alone. I can't drive these dirty, infesting spirits away. I try, and they turn upon me, and swear at me, and talk their obscene, filthy talk, and they throw me about physically at times. I have to hear their talking from morning till night, and sometimes nearly all night. O my God, Dr. Peebles, I can't think of a worse hell than I endure, so do drive these devils away from hurting both my body and my soul. It will kill me if I can't get some help. Is not spirit-control a curse? There are two vicious youths, and one low female with them. I don't know if you can see them clairvoyantly. They rush toward me in hideous shapes, and if I drive them away they come right back again. I think they are the demons of the old Bible times. The leader is a witty devilish spirit liking to make fun, and then they will talk so disgustingly filthy, and if I command them to stop, they will swear at me like a vile, dirty tramp in the street. They will mock me, and so hurt me that I will cry out for pain. I am so sick at heart. They have already injured my health. Can you not—*will* you not do something for me?

"Kindly yours,
"Miss Sarah C——."

"NEW YORK, Nov. 6, 1899.
"DR. PEEBLES:
"In my own person I can give you a very extraordinary case of obsession. If you should think of publishing the particulars, please omit all names, as there are those living today who would be socially hurt by making public what I shall now relate as exactly and cursorily as I can.

"It was in October, eight years ago, that I was first made aware of the truth of Spiritualism. Having been raised an Episcopalian, I never heard that there was even such a phenomenon or philosophy as Spiritualism. The fact was made known to me through the mediumship developed in my granddaughter. My daughter living in England wrote me of these wonderful revelations made to her. At this time I was in some doubt as to the truth of the creed—I may say all creeds. I prayed, or rather wished that if a better revelation could be possible, that it might come to me, and it did. It was to me, a present heaven, and I eagerly sought every means of further enlightenment. I sat with a planchette, and after some patience, my hand began to move. After a while, I took a pencil, and found that I could get writing, not automatically, but inspirationally. Then I commenced writing messages from many friends of my youth in the spirit. Still further my mediumship was developed. I heard my friends talking to me. I held delightful conversations with them, and their voices were as distinct as they were in earth-life. I could not see them, but heard them and also their conversation with each other.

"Alas! But a short time did this wonderful happiness endure. I began to hear others, not my friends, talking around me. Later, I heard all sorts of nonsense spoken. I felt crowds around, and in writing messages was interfered with, and conversations were interrupted. One morning, about a month after I had developed this mediumship, as I lay on the sofa in my room (I was boarding at the time), I felt a strange spirit take possession of me. It was a new experience. It was such a sensation, and his voice was clear and distinct to my friends around me, who had been talking to me so tenderly as I rested.

" 'Where is your medium now?' was said in triumph! Then commenced a hell upon earth, with the most cruel tortures. He has held possession, more or less, of my mind from that time to this. I have never been able to get either writing or voice messages without it being changed or added to or destroyed in some way by him. I have been tortured day and night, everywhere, in and out of company. He follows every word I read or write, and is always talking. He is silent for a few seconds, perhaps, at a time, and then talks folly, balderdash, profanity, filth, obscenity, etc. I have spent much with mediums for relief, with no avail. The magnetism from spirit friends was the only thing that helped me to drive him out and let them get near me. I have been driven almost distracted by this obsessing demon. Not a day passes, I may say, without bitter weeping. I have walked the room at night in agony of distress. No words can express what I have suffered. My unmarried daughter who lived with me could not understand me.

"I was advised by my spirit friends to keep it secret, and I did so for two years, but going through a terrible ordeal later, I was obliged to tell what was the cause of my trouble. Of course, it was put down to hallucination.

The world is blind to spirit forces. As I said, my married daughter had developed mediumship in her family, and it was proved to her that it was no hallucination.

"It was little over four years that I had been suffering, when becoming seriously ill, this evil spirit got entire control of me, leading me to act and talk in a very unwise, foolish manner, which my daughter thought was insanity. She sent for several doctors from asylums, who pronounced me insane. They injected a strong dose of morphine under the skin forcibly, as I refused to swallow anything, and in a state of half unconsciousness, I was carried off to the Bloomingdale Asylum. In a few days, getting better of the stomach attack, the psychic control weakened and I became my normal self. I was kept there for three months—a perfectly sane woman! I was never insane, or anything approaching it, nor was there ever in my family a predisposition approaching this malady. Had I been inclined, I might have been driven to it by all I have suffered. My little all was spent in this frightful mistake of my daughter, and so I am left a very poor woman for the rest of my life. I have been to a medium here many times, and her spirit controls have done much for me. Dr. Wise, a spirit control, speaking in the independent voice, informed me that this poor, demented spirit that obsessionally torments me is a Catholic priest, and that he is working out some personal revenge. I never made an enemy in my life, so his revenge is not on me, but on some others whom he can injure through me. There are three demon spirits concerned in this work of holding me and hindering me in my mediumship. Of course, you know that the opposition to all mediums is strong in the Catholic spirit-world. Dr. Wise tells me that (as I have also read) there are dark satellites or zones attached to every planet, and this spirit has been removed to that belonging to earth, but the magnetic tie that he has formed between himself and myself is so strong that his removal does not completely break it. Now he tells me that they are obliged to convey him to another sphere altogether, so as to break this magnetic attraction.

"Last March or April, I was told that it might take some months to become entirely free. However, here I am, still listening at times, to this terrible voice, and not that alone, but realizing the warping of my thoughts, so that my soul is not fully my own. I am enclosed. I am surrounded always with a band of high spirits helping me all in their power. Were it not so, I would indeed, be still in an insane asylum. I sit every evening for influence, and feel at times the near presence of dear ones. All my clairaudient power has been taken away on account of hypnotic interference. I do not go to any more mediums for help, not having the money. My spirit friends help me some with their impressions and magnetic influence, but they have not *all* power. I am certain that there are divisions and moral battles fought in the next stage of existence, as there are in this. I think that the most of those in the lunatic asylums are only obsessed as I was. Doctors do not understand these things, nor did my daughter that put me in the asylum.

"Very truly yours, ——."

"MYRES, FLA., June 5, 1899.

"DEAR SIR:

"Seeing your name in the *Progressive Thinker,* I write to you for help. I am undergoing one of the most terrible ordeals I ever have heard of in my life. For nearly ten months I have been tormented in every conceivable way. Have heard the vilest language, and been accused of almost every possible crime. Things that I have never thought of are thrust into my mind; and my life, and also that of my family, has been threatened. My sight was good at first, and I had to fight hard all night long with a light burning to keep my sight, and they kept telling me they would ruin my life, and so the fight went on. I could hear these demons talk distinctly. They were from the darkest spheres. They almost wholly took away my sight, but still I was able to see flowers and pictures of different kinds, photos single and in large groups. My hearing is good. What I want to know is, what is all this punishment put upon me for? I am unable to work, and I am a poor man, and if they are not taken from me soon we shall suffer from want and hunger.

"I am not a drinking man, and was never addicted to swearing. This mediumship, or whatever it is, was forced upon me. When the fight first began, we held our family prayers and asked help of God in the name of Jesus Christ, and was promised that the evil would be very soon removed if I would keep up my prayers, but instead, the punishment grew severer and more of it, until I could scarcely stand it at all. They kept saying that it was the Lord Jesus Christ putting this on me for my sins. Then I commenced saying my prayers in another way. It was of no use.

"These demons declared that they were my two brothers that went over to spirit life when they were but little children, some forty-four years ago, and that it was because I didn't remember them that I was tormented. They said that it was the Lord Jesus forcing them to do this,—and so it goes on. Every damning thing that can be thought of is put upon me. It would be impossible for me to describe all their horrible talk and vicious threats, and I feel as though I must have relief. If you or any one of your friends on earth or in heaven can send a band of spirits here, they would have to positively force these away before I could know who was talking. I think other spirits have come to my help at times. They sometimes shout to me to come out of doors, they want to tell me what to do. When I go out, there is such a shouting and mingling of contradictory voices; some tell me to do one thing, and others another, until I am tired and wild and mad from listening.

"Now will you, or some of your friends, send a band of good, powerful spirits to take them away?
"Yours,
"J. C. Baker."

The careful perusal of the above letter touched a sympathetic chord in my nature. Seldom a month goes by but that I receive similar ones. Some of them I do not answer. There is a limit to every man's time. And then nearly every person thus afflicted required different advice and different psychic treatment. As Mr. Baker had no objection to my using his name, I here publish the reply that I promptly forwarded him:

"BATTLE CREEK, MICH., June 8, 1899.
"Mr. J. C. Baker,
"Myres, Fla.
"MY DEAR SIR:
"I received your letter several days ago and have given it some considerable thought. Your untoward

psychic experiences are nothing strange to me, because for years I have witnessed and studied the characteristics of these low, obsessing influences, generally caused by demoniac spirits. These are only mortals out of their physical bodies, and I look upon and judge them precisely as I do mortals, by their conduct, teachings and influences.

"These rough, unruly manifestations occur not altogether infrequently in the beginning of mediumship, and especially where persons had previously been connected with some narrow religious sect. These annoying controlling spirits, who have psychically conjoined themselves to you, are what I denominate, restless, ill-disposed, evil spirits. They abide along the border-land of our planet. They have certainly basely abused and maltreated you, and they ought to be ashamed of themselves. If they are not malicious devils, they are ignorant and morally stupid. In either case they are measurably morally responsible.

"Are they not conscious of the fact, that whatsoever they sow, that must they also reap? Have they no conception of pure angel presences above them? Do they not know that there is no possible way of being happy except by being good and doing good to others?

"No! God has not "put this punishment upon you," my brother, as you suggest. God does not send thieves into good men's houses to rob them, but good spirits, good men, and robbers too, are all in the arena of life, moral actors, and the subjects of inflexible law.

"Now listen to my paternal advice. See in the first place that your home and your surroundings are cleanly and inviting, pleasant and harmonious. Cherish perfect faith in God, in the Christ-spirit of love, in the nobility of humanity and in the righteousness of the right.

"Do not give a thought just for the present to Spiritualism, nor to those obsessional controls. Drop them out of your conscious being. You speak of 'going out of doors to hear them.' Do nothing of the kind. Do not hear them. Do not notice them. Treat them with that calm, dignified indifference that you would passing gales of wind. Do not, I pray you, fight them, because fight begets fight. Evidently they are ignorant and almost conscienceless spirits. They probably do these things for fun, or amusement, or perhaps, through downright malice. In either case do not notice them. Avoid all stimulants, liquors, coffee and tea. They are expensive and useless excitants. Be calm, resigned and attend to your daily work as best you can. If you can have some pleasant, genial and spiritually-minded friend in your presence, talk with him. Converse on scientific subjects, on farming, on flowers, on education and the magnificent works of nature; but give no thought or a word of conversation to these spirits. Of course, this low class of spirits will swear and will lie, and there is no way to stop lying spirits coming to us psychically from the enveloping spirit-world, except for us to stop sending, through death, so many liars over there.

"Exercise your own judgment, your own reason, always, in regard to what spirits, good or bad, may say. be yourself; be manly; be positive; be aspirational. Aspiration is prayer. God gave you your reason and judgment to use, and you must use them wisely and firmly. Think good thoughts; read good books. Sing sweet soul-inspiring songs. Make your home a paradise of love.

"I want you to sit one-half hour twice a week, Tuesday and Thursday evenings, about nine o'clock, quiet and passive, and put your left hand upon my signature. Relax and think of the good and the true, the beautiful and the holy. At the same time, or about the same time, I will project through vibrating ether-waves my good thoughts, inspirational prayers and invocations to the angel hosts that do the will of God, for your relief. Have faith in God—faith in the Christ-spirit of love and faith in the regal reign of right; and soon—I cannot tell just how long— you will be conscious of the loosening of the psychological chains that have bound you. You will certainly be relieved of these demoniac influences. God reigns, and the heavens are not only higher than the hells, but they are infinitely more powerful. I have cured hundreds of worse cases than yours in this and in foreign lands. Do not despair.

"Have you any objections to my publishing a portion of your letter, making proper comments upon it? I have so many of this character that it may perhaps benefit others to publish my off-hand reply. If you do not wish to have me use your name, I will not do so.
"Very cordially yours,
"J. M. PEEBLES, M. D.
"*Battle Creek, Mich.*"

Miss Nora Bacheler's Testimony.

This cultured lady, writer and author, of Ashland, Ore., plainly expresses her views and gives some of her experiences as follows:

"I know what it is to do battle with these unseen powers of darkness.

"I know what it is to fight to the utmost limit of endurance for the control of my own organism—my conscious self.

"I know what it is to spend nights of horror and days of unspeakable torment.

"I know what insanity is. I know what evil spirits can do.

"I know what desire impels the suicide, for I have been to the very verge of the precipice; and yet do I renounce mediumship, and the help, the inspiration, the exalted states of mind which it brings? No! I will not throw away a shell which contains a priceless pearl, because a little poisonous viper lies coiled therein. I will dispatch the intruder with all possible speed, and retain the pearl for my everlasting joy and satisfaction.

"This is what every medium must do, throttle the obsessing influences at their first inception, and keep his face ever turned to the pure and beautiful, the exalted influences from the higher realms of spirit life.

"There is a great work which Spiritualism has to do, a work not yet begun, the work of enlightening ignorant humanity upon the subject of unseen and unsuspected spirit influences, and the part they play in human life and human society.

"On this subject of obsession many Spiritualists are as yet woefully ignorant. They seem to me mentally stupid. Those who understand are for the most part afraid to speak. For a theory has been advanced (by those unacquainted with the facts) and has gained much credence, that evil influences will not trouble a person whose motives are pure and noble, and whose character is above reproach; that it is only the evilly disposed, those of impure lives, low motives, vile passions, who bring around them the powers of darkness. 'Like attracts like,' it is said. 'If you are annoyed by depraved and vicious spirits, it is because there is something wrong in your own life, and character. You may be thought a pure and lovely soul by most intimate friends, but in reality, hidden down deep from view, you possess some very wicked traits, or you would never attract such evil influences!'

"What an insult is this! How utterly cruel and heartless to tell a refined, sensitive, tormented and persecuted medium that she has 'attracted' the vile fiends into whose clutches she has had the misfortune, through ignorance, to fall! It is little wonder that dense ignorance and darkness on this subject exist, when such erratic ideas prevail. It is little wonder that mediums whisper their experiences only to one another, and then with the utmost secrecy and many admonitions, fearing lest others may hear and condemn. Away with this opinion. It is utterly false.

"In the last issue of the *Progressive Thinker* there is a statement something like this: An evil spirit cannot endure the psychic atmosphere of a good and pure person; cannot approach or do him harm. Now, this is a bold assumption, a mere theory, without a single fact to support it. I could name, if I chose, no less than nine of my personal acquaintances, as good and pure women as ever walked this green earth, who have been annoyed and tormented by these unseen powers—these fiends.

"The sooner we explode this fallacy the better. It bars the progress of investigation; it keeps the facts from view! it is the cause of withholding knowledge which young and undeveloped mediums imperatively need, for there is danger in mediumship. There is untold and incalculable danger in ignorant mediumship. Innocence and purity are no bar to the approach of fiends incarnate; neither are they a bar to the approach of fiends decarnate. A sensitive instrument can be played upon by an angel or a demon, and until the instrument is sufficiently developed psychically to distinguish between the two, he or she is as liable to fall into the hands of one as the other.

"The world little knows of the wickedness, the depravity, the countless crimes that are directly attributable to the unseen powers of the air. Many a weak-willed, ignorant, unsuspecting mortal is dragged down to infamy and shame because the obsession of psychic powers renders him an easy tool in the hands of vicious and criminal spirits on the other side of the grave."

CHAPTER XIX.

Obsessional History of a Cultured Woman.

"DOCTOR:

"Those who have known me for a quarter of a century will willingly testify to my usual sound health, equilibrium of temperament, general sociability, good character and happy disposition. . . .

"I was a natural investigator. There was no problem that I did not desire to solve. I sought to unriddle the riddles of the universe. I studied the occult. I sought to probe the mysteries of life, pre-existence, reincarnation, and the deep subject of psychic research. All of these and others had charms for me. . . .

"The first symptoms of obsessional influences experienced were seemingly causeless, nervous sensations, weariness, sleeplessness, a feeling of being burdened by some invisible weight; the light duties of life seemed impossible. I was puzzled. These feelings were followed by gloominess, by doubt, and abnormal irritating tendencies, longings for relief, with occasional rays of hopefulness.

"Do not suggest, as one or two physicians did, that I was approaching a peculiar period in a woman's life. I knew better. Woman knows woman best, and especially so if well read in the physiology and histology of herself. The most of physicians are famous for their fallibility.

"In other cases that I have witnessed and studied since my release from the influences of these wandering, unprincipled, earth-hungering, earth-bound spirits, there was an unnatural dissatisfaction with everything and everybody. The atmosphere to them seemed dense, and many objects seemed vibrating about them to no wise end. Discordant thoughts covertly crept into the mind. Magnetic currents seemed to settle on the brain, causing pain and restlessness.

"The activity and decision of the will would seem to weaken, or so vary at times that the best resolutions utterly failed to be realized. Fear and distrust were such growing emotions that a discordant word, a stern look, or harsh sound would cause this half-obsessed person to weep, or to sense smothering sensations of grief, followed by strong resentment and sometimes sneering, caustic epithets.

"All of the preceding symptoms may exist without the least organic disease. Yet physicians looking at the

Obsessional History of a Cultured Woman. 193

outer objective side of things, will in these cases talk of a 'torpid liver,' 'malaria' or 'depleted vitality.' Generally this depletion is in their own non-illuminated brains.

"In the more advanced stages of obsession, the sufferer becomes subject to great dejection of spirits; life seemed a burden, and the imagination stimulated by invisible presences on the low planes of spirit life, run riot. They suspect their friends. They become impatient. Their suspicions dominate their reason. They are obstinate. They turn against their life-long friends, and they are impressed, often forced to say and do things contrary to their own reason in their better, more normal moments. They become irascible in temper, vicious by spells, contemplating suicide.

"These persons are now obsessed. They are slaves. They may hear voices, see strange, weird faces, concoct the wildest schemes, conceive vicious plans, become profane, using the most obscene language, and insist upon thousands of the most abnormal notions.

" Very often these obsessing spirits, pretentious and falsifying, assume to have been on earth great personages. They make wonderful promises. They flatter their poor, hypnotized subjects under the demoniac impressions. They sometimes pretend that God commands them to do certain irrational, abominable and monstrous things, such as to commit murder. Guiteau, the murderer of Garfield, was no doubt obsessed.

"The partially obsessed are often conscious of a conflict between their better, higher natures, and the unseen impressional influences, encouraging and even forcing them to go contrary to the whole calm tenor of their lives. They are tortured with misleading thoughts, with fearful forebodings and temptations to commit previ-

ously undreamed crimes. Oh, how little the majority of mankind knows of the perils that haunt and infest the border-lands of occultism and misapplied spiritism!
"*Chicago, Ill.*   Mrs. H――."

A Personal Obsessional Experience.

This lady further writes:

"For ten years I have been conscious of the presence of spirits. I positively know of spirit existence, and that some unseen intelligences were constantly with me. But my limited knowledge of spiritual laws, and volumes relating to occultism, conveyed to me the only thought that spirits coming from the higher world were true and loving medial powers between heaven and earth. I supposed them all to be good.

"My psychic powers, such as clairvoyance and clairaudience, were gradually developed. I had finally what were denominated several spiritual gifts; but I soon discovered that at times I could not rely upon all that was received. Still, I did not question the spirits. I thought the conditions were not right, or perhaps my thoughts had all unwittingly prevented absolutely correct messages.

"Still developing, I arrived at a point whereby these invisible persons—invisible to those about me—could use my vocal organs for conversing, for reading and for singing. These spirits saw, or seemed to see through my eyes, hear through my ears, and my hands were used automatically for both writing and music.

"My vision at times was very clear, and I was conscious of myriad thoughts vibrating in and through my brain, independent of myself. All that I thought or did became intensified, giving by spells a depressed state of feeling, or a nervousness, uneasiness foreign to my usual better self.

"Different controls affected me differently. Those who had just entered spirit life often transferred to me their idiosyncrasies. Some gave me a choking, smothering sensation. A spirit girl, assuming to be my guardian control, was only using up my vitality for her own selfish purposes, along with others who were injuring me, I will not say whether it was through ignorance or malice.

"Another spirit, seemingly, approaching me on the left side, clearly discerned by my clairvoyant sight, absorbed my vital forces until I felt that entire side weakening. Paralysis seemed imminent. Still another influencing spirit, professing great purity, came to me attired in white, yet drawing some aural force from my spine. The weakness became painful. She threw a magnetic network over and around me almost stupefying, or blotting out my consciousness.

"I had now become enough of a clairvoyant sensitive to measurably see their thought currents, witness their movements, and fathom their purposes. They were shadowy and dark-hued, leaving a dark, filmy trail of substance behind them. It seemed to permeate the walls of my room. They made me feel that I was their servant, that I was enclosed within the walls of their power —a power that I could not fully repel. They projected into my mind vile vagaries and threatenings of insanity. At length, they said positively that they would make me insane.

"Day and night they worked and willed to overcome my will and dethrone my reason. Not being naturally sensuous or immoral, they could not seriously affect my habits or my moral nature. They accompanied me to church, to concerts, to theaters, seemingly relishing the aural magnetisms of others, something as we inhale the fragrance of flowers.

"You have seen the larger boy kick the smaller one, the master beat the servant to make him obedient; so they tormented me, demanding the right to control me physically and psychologically. They affected my eyesight, throwing a mist-like substance about me, which at times would be almost suffocating and blinding.

"Christian Scientists, mental scientists, suggestive practitioners, could be of no benefit to me. Their efforts were failures.

"Antagonizing my tormentors by reasonings, by suggestions, by moral cleanliness, and by making magnetic passes over my head, and changing environments, I kept them in a measure from throwing their hypnotic influence over me; but they went far enough to induce terrible mental sufferings and torturing pains.

"In this sad state of mind I was not entirely alone. With me it was a battle for individuality, for health, and for sanity. To be sure, there were good sympathizing guardian spirits, anxious to assist and protect me; but they had not that insiduous, earthly, hypnotic power that these deceptive, selfish demons had. These, as I proved, had low, sinister motives. Their power was physical and hypnotic. An Irish or an Italian railway laborer has far more physical power over pick and spade than the conductor or division superintendent. Hypnotic power is dangerous unless guided by goodness and wisdom. Here is where these obsessing spirits have a great advantage, and especially so, where we poor mortals have to breathe vice-impregnated air, submit to the filthy, uprising emanations of the streets and the excited outbreathed atmosphere of rushing crowds on public conveyances. . . .

"It may interest thinkers and students of the occult to know how I was relieved and restored to my normal health of body and mind. It was through the instrumentality of Dr. G. S. Lane, Boston. He is an excellent man, encircled by a high and beautiful concourse of spirit intelligences, physicians, surgeons and Oriental healers. Very soon after coming under the influence of his heavenly guides, my condition changed. A heavy atmosphere was lifted from me, my natural strength returned, my power to reason brightened up, my will became re-established and my sight became clear. While Dr. Lane was treating me, I saw clairvoyantly a magnificent Indian spirit standing on his left and an exalted circle of physicians around and above him, removing the dark misty, poisonous atmosphere, that had been environing me—that had been, I might say, projected into the very depths of my brain by these roaming vitality-sapping earth-bound demons.

"Finally, I desire my positive testimony to be stated, and to remain as an abiding witness to the truth of spirit intercourse, spirit influence, spirit control, spirit environment, and also of dark obsessions, external and internal, dangerous and demoralizing, injuring humanity on the earth plane of life. Of course, there is a brighter side to all this, but the facts should all be known. If there is a precipice ahead of the traveler in a strange land, he should be warned of it.

" Spiritualism, pure and proper, is not only a great truth, but a great blessing, when used reverently as a demonstration of a future existence, and as a comforter, bringing beautiful messages of sympathy, tenderness and loving remembrances from our risen relatives and friends.

"If history is to be believed, obsession belonged to all lands and all ages. It occurred in the past. It is rampant in the present; many are obsessed, diseased and do not know the causative agencies. Let not our speakers and writers sheath their swords of truth till the people are better educated upon psychic subjects, and the obsessed released from the thraldom of evil, earth-bound spirits of darkness.

"*Chicago, Ill.* Mrs. H——."

The above somewhat lengthy communication, from a very intelligent lady whom I have had the pleasure of personally knowing, is presented almost verbatim from her manuscript. She is a good writer. Where abbreviated, or the wording modified, the fact, the idea, has been carefully preserved. There are a number of sensitive intermediaries such as Dr. Lane, of Boston, Dr. Kimball, of Maine, Mrs. M. Bergen Brown, of Morgan Hill, Cal., Dr. Yates, of Chicago, and others spiritually gifted with the power of removing these influences, adverse entities of a deceptive, selfish order, and putting these evil-disposed spirits into better conditions for unfoldment.

Absolute and endless evil is out of the question. None, either here or in the after life, are totally depraved; the worst have some shining traits. The image of God is ineffaceable. The divine diamond spark, though dimmed and deep-buried, is glittering within, waiting the quickening fires of inspiration.

Conscious of the Pauline truth that what men sow

Obsessional History of a Cultured Woman. 199

that must they reap, I feel to impress the necessity of a pure, highly-purposed, Christ-like life while in the body. There should be a rich and substantial accumulation of intellectual, moral and spiritual power now. This is imperishable, and from it there is an outflowing, vital, spiritual atmosphere that attracts the good.

It has been one of my great literary endeavors to clearly show that we, the living men of today, are moral actors—are responsible beings and are making and surrounding ourselves with an invisible atmosphere, dark gray, hazy, or golden, or white and glistening as the raiment of angels. Both the visible and the invisible worlds vibrate through this etheric atmosphere. It is an atmosphere which if clear, bright, and positive for the pure, the beautiful and the holy, brings peace and joy and sound judgment and personal power; but on the other hand if it be impure, selfish and clouded, it yields a harvest of unrest, irritability and moral weakness opening the gateway to the obsessing inhabitants of Hades.

It must be considered that all obsessions are not from surrounding unseen intelligences. There is a sort of an ideation obsession caused by an unbalanced, weakened organization. Everything objective and subjective affects these persons. They are like tremulous aspens. They are partly the victims of their own disordered imaginations. They are emotional, suspicious, pessimistic sensationalists, touching the fringe-belt of morbidity, hearing the unheard, and seeing fanciful pictorial presentations, instead of genuine realities. This sort of obsession is remedied by auto-suggestion, will power and hypnotic treatment scientifically administered. The unhealthy or the morally unclean should never presume to hypnotize. It would be very dangerous. The mesmeric treatment in almost all cases is preferable to the hypnotic method. I have used both successfully, and aided by attending heavenly intelligences, constituting a battery of vital force, I have demagnetized the obsessed, freeing them from obsessional thraldom, giving to them their right minds, restoring their health, thus sowing the flower seeds of peace, prosperity and happiness, where thorns had pierced bleeding feet.

CHAPTER XX.

Psychological Crimes Instigated by Vicious Spirits.

THE statement so often repeated that "like attracts like," does not belong to the logician's realm of the universals. It has definite limits. The two positive poles in electricity come under the word "like," and yet they quickly repel. Human beings under all skies are of like origin, like species, and gifted with the innate like—or love of happiness; and yet dislikes, and fierce, brutal wars have occurred, or are occurring in many lands, the strong oppressing the weak, the powerful forcing the feeble against their wills. Might, in the lower spheres, as on earth, makes right. The will is potent. Vice may dominate for a time. Mobs may temporarily govern. The hells are boastful and spiteful. The once crowned heads, the mighty sovereigns, princely social rulers, the potentates of prize rings, continue their proclivities when stripped of their fleshly garments. The law of spiritual gravity brings them into our daily employments and environments. They suggest, they hypnotize, they control, they may and do force sensitives, subversive as it may seem of moral order, to go wrong, doubtless leading them to the commission of criminal acts. Many clear, well-substantiated cases of this kind are on record. Possibly this may be denied. Negations, however, are cheap, and of little consequence. It is affirmations, coupled with demonstrations and experiences that tell —and tell to convince.

The soft palliative sometimes advanced by the psychically uneducated, that an evil-inclined spirit can harm no one unless there is active or latent evil within attracting the evil from without, is not only false and illogical, but absolutely silly. "How can we reason but from what we know?" asked Socrates. The wild savage that with hatchet brains the babe, gives the lie to this theory. Where the highwayman knocks down and robs the kindly bearer of foods and a few coins to a poor widow, is it because of the evil within this benevolent reformer's nature? Perish such presumption! The suggestion is contemptible!

If the afore-named things occur in mortal life, by parity of reasoning and in consonance with law, or through the violation of the higher law, they naturally may occur in spirit life, spirits influencing spirits out of and spirits in fleshly bodies. If spirits can heal, they can make ill. If they can bless, they can curse—they can kill.

Consider the noted case of Alice Hoffman, of New York. She was a bright, happy girl, but refused to marry a young man who desired her hand and heart. At first she encouraged him. Then learning of his vile, licentious habits, she refused to see him. Soon in a drunken fit he fell from the cars and was killed. A few months after this she became nervous, uneasy, melancholy, and at length she declared that she saw this young man's spirit. He haunted her steps till her nerves were wrung to breaking tension. She both saw and heard him speak. He told her of things unknown to herself. He fully demonstrated his identity in many ways. He insisted upon a promise from her to marry him when she came to his spirit plane of life. She refused, and tried to drive him away. A prominent clairvoyant medium saw him about her—saw his close approaches— saw him trying to magnetize her.

The family physcian suggested that this might be "a hallucination." She spurned the idea, declaring that her brain was quite as clear, and mind quite as well balanced as the doctor's or some of her distant friends.

This obsessing spirit failing to control her and extort promises, became angry, talked obscenely, cursed her, threatened her. She was pronounced insane by physicians. Her friends opposed taking her to the asylum, she contending in the meantime that it was Harry's ghost that made her do these things, and who gave her at times "the strength of three men."

In one of her more lucid moments, she said to a sister, "I am going to get well. I am not crazy. I can't help doing these terrible things. I can see all kinds of spirits in the air at times, and there is one great Indian that my angel mother has brought and he gets right in between me and haunting Harry, and he lifts up a great war club. He looks ugly on the outside of his feathery dress, but he is much brighter than this wicked spirit that I knew and at one time thought I loved. I am going to get well. Last night a whole dozen of Indians came with mother

Crimes Instigated by Vicious Spirits.

and wove a kind of a white network all about me. It seems like a white mist. I've felt better ever since,—felt more like myself. And mother said these brighter spirits had taken Harry off with them to their country, and were going to keep him in a school. You see that they don't put me in the insane asylum. I am going to get well, and I am better now. That heavy cloud has all been removed."

This family was unacquainted with Spiritualism. In a few weeks this young lady was nearly well, though a little nervous and very sensitive. Still clairvoyant she sees spirit presences, and has become not only healthy but happy.

I had this much condensed narrative from her sister, several years older and highly respectable, strongly favoring the spiritual philosophy.

Here is an abridged account of the shocking, murderous conduct of Knapp, obsessed by a clique of infernals. This man, a very monster by general consent, confessed to having killed five women. His favorite method of murdering was choking. When arrested, he seemingly relished reciting his crimes.

These were his reported words to a journalist, Hamilton, Ohio, Feb. 28, 1903:

"I always kill from behind," he says from between his teeth. "I get them in front of me. Then I clutch them by the throat, placing my knee on the back, and bend them over. They struggle, but not long. They look into my face, but they find no mercy there.

"I kill them and that is all. How do I know when they are dead? I don't know. When they stop breathing, then I stop choking. I listen to the heart, and if that is done beating, then I am done. None of them ever plead for mercy. They couldn't, and it would have been no use. I couldn't have stopped until they were dead."

"What was your motive in killing them? It could not have been money, as they had none."

"No, I cannot tell any one why I killed them. There was something behind me pushing me on, and I could not resist that feeling. It pushed me on and I killed. Yes, I felt good after it was over. It was quickly done. When the work was done, I felt no regret. I had to do it. I hated womankind. I was forced to kill them. I could not resist the power."

To what extent this wretched man was obsessed, to what extent he was responsible, each must judge for himself. He declared a dozen times and more that he cherished no malice toward those whom he murdered. He killed them, he said, "because he had to," "because some power forced him" to commit the bloody deeds.

"Are these things possible? Is it possible for undeveloped spirits to so obsess, to so incite to crime from their spirit abodes?"

It is certainly possible in this world. There are men among us who enjoy shooting, murdering birds—murdering animals—murdering each other in duels, murdering their fellow-men in war, shooting them down deliberately, stamping on their agonizing bodies and gloating over their dying groans.

History abounds in such instances—numberless instances of maddened savages scalping, torturing, burning their murdered victims. These human monsters die. Are they any better from the dying? Does it make a liar truthful to throw off his overcoat? Does capital punishment make paragons of perfection of those hung or electrocuted? If criminality is possible and certain in this world, why not in the future world? In the realm of the real there is no future world. There is but one world with two—with many aspects. All is one eternal now with God. Transferred to another stage of existence, maintaining their identity, the ill-tempered, passionate, deceptive denizens of the darker spheres would naturally continue their selfish, vicious work in the hereafter, which in time and space is here and now. Diakka-like, they would injure for the fun of injuring. They are simply demons of destruction, afire with envy, passion, deceit and malevolence.

But why do not the good spirits and the angels stop the hypnotic obsessions of these depraved spirits?

A fair question! Why do not senators, congressmen, marshals and policemen, clothed with authority, stop drunkenness, gambling, robbery and murder in this world?

Is it said, "They do what they can?"

That is just the point! Good spirits and the good angels of mercy do what they can. They are not absolutely Almighty. They are not infinite in power. They are limited by law. They minister so far as they can in consonance with their refinement, with moral law, moral duty, and a righteous responsibility.

The lever requires a fulcrum. The would-be-helped should call for helpers. When the prodigal son had satisfied himself that the eating of husks which swine had refused was not the most palatable, health-giving food, he arose, "came to himself," and angel-guided, returned to his father.

The following characteristic account appeared in the *Progressive Thinker,* Chicago: "There are cases where the dispossession of obsessional influences is very difficult. One of these I met in Nebraska. While talking with Chas. Davis, a young man came in and was treated by hypnotization. While the treatment was in process, I clairvoyantly saw a colored person by the young man who I afterward learned was one of those low, unfortunate creatures, nearer a brute than a man, who had been lynched and burned to death in Texas, only a few months previously. The boy was thrown on to the ground apparently with epilepsy, and as the spasm left him, he invariably revealed an inclination to criminality. He seemed full of revenge. This showed the folly of sending that class of creatures to the spirit-world before their lustful natures have been burned out. I have but little hopes that such spirits can be reached by kindness, yet it would be well enough to try it, for if you succeed you may save some other person who may be victimized by him after being expelled from one person. I believe this boy was finally relieved, or taken away from the spirit. I have known several insane people who were merely obsessed, and one of the objects of Spiritualism should be not only the relief of these poor victims, but also the salvation of the obsessing spirits themselves.

These ignorant, hypnotizing operators from the more subjective, unseen side of life often so stultify the memory, so overshadow the individuality, that the personality is temporarily lost. Those thus obsessed wander, they know not where. The function of self-cognition and the attribute of memory are, for the time, completely eclipsed. To wit: Mrs. G. Wallace, a wealthy widow of Wilkesbarre, last November "left some friends on Northampton Street after an afternoon's shopping and started for her home four blocks away. She was well dressed, had $10 in her pocketbook, and seemed to be cheerful and happy.

On her way home a strange influence crept over her. It was so complete that thereafter she had no recollection of what she did. Six nights afterward she was tramping the streets of a strange city, penniless and hungry, not knowing who she was nor why she was there. She knew nothing but that she wanted shelter. She had no recollection of the past, no realization of the present was in her mind. It was like the dead arising into life without memory, like the birth of a full-grown woman into a new world.

Here follows her statement as near as her recollection can cover it:

"I can only account for my strange loss of memory by the fact that for a year or more I had been grieving over the death of my beloved husband. I was greatly worried over the settlement of his estate. I can remember now that I was feeling particularly well and strong when I started out shopping on the afternoon of November 21. There were two railway depots which I had to pass on my way home, and when my memory deserted me, I must have gone into one of these stations and bought and east-bound ticket.

"When the five days' blank was ended, I found myself walking along the streets of a strange city. Since then I have learned that it was Newark. I did not know why I was there. It did not seem strange to me. Neither did I know that I ever had a home. In fact, I did not think to inquire.

"I seemed to have barely enough intelligence to know that I must live, and that in order to live I must work. A drizzling rain was falling and the streets were slushy with melted snow and mud. It seemed perfectly natural that I should be walking about the streets. I did not know an awful gulf lay between me and the past. I did not know the value of names or of circumstances.

"I date the memory of my new life as an unknown from the time I found myself walking along the rainy Newark streets. I became so tired that I could scarcely stand, but nobody seemed to pay any attention to me. In a dim and visionary way it must have come upon me to apply to some person for assistance. I remember applying to a family living near a big church. They were very kind, but when they asked me my name and I could not reply, they sent me away. Even then I did not think it queer that I should be nameless. I must have been something like a child in my mind. It is fortunate, however, that I remembered enough about household work to make it available later on.

"In the evening of that rainy day, Fate led my footsteps into Sumner Street. I was told afterward that it was Thanksgiving eve. I rang the door-bells of two or three houses where food and shelter were refused. The last place I applied to was number 629 Sumner Street, the home of Mr. and Mrs. William Stern. There must have been something in my miserable appearance which excited the pity of Mrs. Stern. At any rate, she invited me in and gave me food and shelter for which I offered to pay with work.

" 'We will talk about that in the morning,' she said.

"On the following day, notwithstanding the fact that I could not remember my name, Mrs. Stern offered to employ me at housework, and I accepted the offer with deep gratitude, as I did not know what else to do. For days and weeks, and it may be months, I worked for Mrs. Stern as a servant. One time, after a long, hard day's work, the strange absence of any memory of my childhood began to dawn upon me. I realized that I had no past. I saw other women with children about me, other women with happy homes, other women with husbands. Where was my childhood, my home, my husband? The thoughts gave me a great feeling of unrest. My life began to look strange and mysterious to me. I began to realize that I could not remember further back than the rainy streets of Newark on that dull November morning.

"Through constant brooding, I grew gradually to realize that I was not a professional servant, that I had lived another life, that I was then somebody else, that children were waiting for me somewhere, and that I had relatives and friends and a home.

"Gradually this feeling grew upon me. It made me so abstracted in my work that Mrs. Stern noticed it and asked me if I were ill. My reviving memory seemed to resemble the shoots of newly-sprouted plants. But they were constantly growing, and each day I felt nearer to the solution of an awful mystery. I believe that the first I really remembered were the scenes of my childhood—the old home, the flowers about the schoolhouse, my school days, and my school friends. But still I could not remember my name.

"As time passed, Mrs. Stern noticed that I was growing more and more preoccupied mentally. I know now that I was mentally traveling over my past life and that eventually I would succeed in tracing my entire history.

"One day while working in the kitchen, it came to me like a flash, the cloud was raised. A voice seemed to say to me, 'You are Mrs. George Wallace, and your home is in Wilkesbarre.'

"My memory seemed to clear as though a dark veil had been drawn aside to let the sunshine enter. I remembered my children and I shrieked with joy. Mrs. Stern came to me.

" 'I know who I am,' I said. 'I live in Wilkesbarre, and I have six children there. I must go to them at once.'

"I was so excited that I could not do my work. Mrs. Stern was very kind to me. I was afraid at first. I did not know what the world would think of me, as I could not tell what I might have done in my peculiar condition. But Mrs. Stern counseled and soothed me, and finally sent word to my sister, Mrs. Kate Crosley, of Sayre, Pa. This was the first step which united me again with my family.

"In a few days there came a ring at the door-bell, and in walked my sister Kate and my oldest daughter Elizabeth. Words cannot describe my feelings. I felt as though I had been snatched from the grave. On the following day we started for my sister's home in Sayre, where I met the rest of my children. I learned then that my home in Wilkesbarre had been rented after weeks of sorrow over my disappearance. My children had been taken to relatives in Sayre, as the belief seemed to be general that I was dead.

"I will remain at Sayre with my children until I am strong and well again. Why the lapse of memory occurred I cannot say. My children believe that sorrow over my husband's death had much to do with it."

The daughter of this wandering mother, Miss Elizabeth Wallace, says in the press:

"Although there was not a clue by which my mother could be traced when she left home five months ago, I never for an instant gave up hope of seeing her again. For many weeks I searched everywhere, and even when the police gave up hope and told me that she was un-

Crimes Instigated by Vicious Spirits. 211

doubtedly dead, I said to them time and again, 'You may think what you like, but mother is not dead. I feel that she is alive and will return to us. I do not know when or how, but I shall not worry.'

"It took five long months to verify my faith, and when the other day I clasped my long-absent mother in my arms, the first words I said were, 'I knew I would find you, mother. I felt all along that you were alive and well.' "

This was a clear case of spirit hypnotism—spirit entrancement, where obsession merged into possession. Often in my hypnotic experiments have I blotted out temporarily my subject's name, which would gradually return unless I positively willed to the contrary. At other times, I have substituted some other name for my hypnotical subject's name, causing very great perplexity and painful annoyance, till I removed the hypnotic spell and restored the right name.

History records many cases somewhat similar to this of Mrs. Wallace—cases of spirit hypnotization, inducing loss of memory, loss of personality, the substitution of another personality, of tri-personalities, and sevenfold personalities, in cases of mediumistic controls and the various grades of entrancement. Hypnotism and trance are twin processes in the psychic sphere of metaphysics.

University psychologists, cognizing these abnormal conditions, are modifying their positions in regard to criminality and insanity. Psychism is becoming more and more of a study with the literati of all lands. The facts that in so many cases called lapsed memory, the parties assuming entirely different names, coupled with strange, distinguishing characteristics and abnormal conduct, induce not only belief, but a fixed conviction that some foreign spirit intelligence has control of body and mind. This conviction is a rational one.

The conscious intelligences may have borrowed these human vehicles, or they may have taken them by force to accomplish some purpose unknown to mortals. The "Watseka wonder" in the Roff family was a case in point—a marked case of possession and the interchange of worlds. These phenomena revive the old apostolic teaching, "try the spirits," for demons may assume angelic names to deceive, gratify and feed the fires of criminality.

CHAPTER XXI.

Obsession and Witchcraft in All Ages.

THE rationalistic Lecky in his history of European morals, expresses the opinion that the doctrine of evil demons, with other Oriental dogmas, was brought into Rome at about the advent of Christ. This is seriously doubted. In fact, Empedocles, Xenocrates, Chrysippus and others disprove Lecky's statement.

Plutarch, who was virtually the founder of the Neo-Platonists, taught that the gods were immortal, free from passion, pure-minded and immune from sin; while the demons were a lower, inferior order of spiritual beings, the subjects of mortal passion. "Mercenary motives" he said "incline them to attach themselves to and to attack human beings."

"Demons," he wrote, "may persuade the gods. They are the impelling forces of wanderings, of banishments, voluntary servitude, rapes and other grave offenses. "Certain tyrannical demons," he further states, "require for their enjoyment some soul still incarnate, being unable to satisfy their passions in any other way, incite to sedition, lust, wars of conquest, and so get what they lust for."

Demetrius, who visited some of the outlying islands of Britain, called them " the islands of the demons," and the demi-gods, the demons tyrannizing and reigning over the people.

There is much in that word tyrannizing. The lower, selfish class of men are naturally tyrants. Like animals, they like to rule the field. There are time-serving tyrants in the next life. This was a peculiar characteristic of the witchcraft periods of history.

Oriental Witchcraft.

Witchcraft was common in Babylonia and Assyria. The readings of recently found tablets in the stone libraries of ancient Babylonia prove this. The Jews took their religious notions largely from Egypt and Babylonia. There are numerous references to witches in the Old Testament. Witchcraft is mentioned four times. It was believed that witches were the instruments through which demons acted.

The word "witchcraft" occurs but once in the New Testament. The Greek word is *pharmakiea,* which means sorcery, and so reads in the revised version. Lord Coke, in the sixth chapter of his Institute, thus defines a witch: "A person which hath conference with the devil, to consult with him to do some act." Arnold pronounced it a "compact between the evil one or his wicked associates." A witch is defined in the Capital Code of Connecticut, A. D., 1642, as "one who hath or consorteth with familiar associates."

The trials for witchcraft during the seventeenth century all implied or were based upon the above theory. Officials presented specific charges against alleged witches for affecting certain deleterious conditions, injuries or torments through the agencies of evil spirits.

There has been a most unreasonable effort in some directions to give the impression that the troubles of those witchcraft times were due to diseased fancies, misdirected imaginations and the "croakings of a few bed-ridden women and silly children." Only those ignorant of psychological influences accept this theory. The facts of the centuries are against it. They were not supernatural; but natural to the psychic plane that produced them.

Evidences of Witchcraft.

There are few more deplorable episodes in American history than those Salem and other witchcraft trials. Scores of cases were formally, legally tried, and after what was considered as good and substantial evidence, the arraigned were summarily condemned to suffer the penalty of death. In these trials, according to Cotton Mather, "to fix the witchcraft on the prisoner at the bar, the first proof used was the testimony of the bewitched (obsessed) themselves." They testified to the facts of their controls. They solemnly declared under oath that they were made to say—made to do these strange things. The Judges seemed to have been men endowed with a profound sense of their responsibility. They may have been prejudiced in their decisions; but they were just men, sincerely desiring to do right. The decisions of the court were sustained by the general sentiment of the people.

Conduct of the Bewitched.

The bewitched—that is, the entranced—would in the presence of their accusers, and also when brought into court to bear testimony, be thrown into "fits," say the old records. They would become insensible and unconscious as do spirit mediums today. They would prophesy. Their faces changed in appearance. All these phenomena were regarded as ample evidence that the accused had mysterious, supernatural power operating upon them. "It cost the court," says a writer of that period, "a wonderful deal of trouble to hear the testimonies of the sufferers, for when they were going to give in their depositions, they would for a long time be taken with fits (entranced) that made them incapable of saying anything." These obsessional entrancements, more common among a certain class of spirit mediums, were then called "fits," "swoons," "hallucinations" and "hysteria." The people were not mistaken in the genuineness of the phenomena, but in the causes of them. They often mistook an Indian spirit for the devil;* and out of this and

---

*"Thou shalt not suffer a witch to live." (Ex. 22:18). This one sentence in the Jewish scriptures, and its interpretation by the bigots of the Middle Ages, brought about a fearful sacrifice of life. Listen to the story briefly told.
  One thousand were burned at Como in one year.
  Eight hundred were burned at Wursburg in one year.
  Five hundred perished at Geneva in three months.
  Eighty were burned in a single village of Savoy.
  Nine women were burned in a single fire at Leith.

similar mistakes came the horrors and fatal wrongs of Gallows Hill.

New England Witchcraft.

Those New England people were religious and heroic. They were conscientious. These witchcraft sights were literally seen. The sounds were heard, and extraordinary works were performed. The age believed in their reality. Denying them was useless. Nineteen persons were executed; and the substantial, sturdy old octogenarian, Giles Cory, was deliberately pressed to death.

These witch works and wonders were quite in consonance with the ancient Delphic oracles, with the demon apparitions and possessions of the medieval ages, with the weird manifestations of the American aborigines, with the fetich, rain-bringing priests of Africa, and with the black magicians of India. Those Hindu wonder-workers practiced and still practice a sort of Oriental witchcraft called black magic. It is given the name black to distinguish it from the gray and the higher white form of occult practices. Black magic is only another phrase for demon obsession. And these low-intentioned, hand-clasping, promiscuous, pitch-dark, midnight séances that show muslin-manufactured spirit faces, suggest the location of

---

Sixty were hanged at Suffolk.
Three thousand were legally executed during one session of Parliament; while thousands more were put to death by mobs.
Remy, a Christian judge, executed eight hundred.
Six hundred were burned by one bishop at Bamburg.
Bognet burned six hundred at St. Cloud.
Thousands were put to death by the Lutherans of Norway and Sweden.
Catholic Spain butchered thousands.
Presbyterians were responsible for the death of four thousand in Scotland.
Seven thousand died at Treves.

The above is quoted from Nation's "Message of Life." We cannot vouch for the exactness of the figures, though they evidently approximate the truth.

buried treasures, or find "social affinities," all belong to the same category. Such spirit séances are the seed-sowing grounds of demonism. Their manifestations are from the hells. They should be shunned as one would shun the dens of slimy adders. They constitute the very essence of witchcraft under a more polished name.

In an interview published in Professor Brittan's *Quarterly Journal,* between Dr. J. F. Gray, of New York, and himself, relative to "Socrates and evil spirits," Professor Brittan, one of the most brillant men that ever graced the ranks of Spiritualism, made the statement that Socrates believed in both good and evil demons, and then established his position by citations from Plato and Xenophon. In his clear-cut classic style, he said, "I use the term 'evil' legitimately, to represent those qualities which tend to injure or to produce mischievous results, whether applied to spirits or mortals. I use it in no absolute sense. I am accustomed to say of some men who disturb the harmony of society by their chaotic passions and selfish, drunken and abandoned lives, that they are evil, as compared with others whose lives approximate the standard of Divine order, and who consequently never interrupt the social harmony.

"Now when I say that Socrates believed in good and evil demons, I would be understood to affirm no more than appears to be virtually conceded in your letter, namely, that some human beings who have departed this life are still disorderly or evil, as compared with those who on earth lived out the conviction that virtue is the only nobility. In other words, those who in this world ' devoted themselves to the animal appetites,' to base theft and crimes, inevitably carry with them the moral consequences of their unbridled lusts. It was this class of demon spirits that influenced and controlled in witchcraft times; and all this is strictly compatible with our ideas of moral law, of the divinity within, and the endless progress of the Spirit.

"Many human spirits are so benighted as to have no conception of the celestial life— are not yet prepared to see clearly and live truly, and the fact appears to warrant the conclusion, that some spirits are now, and will continue to be for a long period, relatively evil."

CHAPTER XXII.

Shall Men Pray for the Dead? Shall We Pray for Demon Spirits?

WORSHIP and prayer are almost universal. They seem to be innate sentiments in the human soul, bubbling up spontaneously as do crystal streams from living fountains.

Wicked, atheistic demons do not pray. They are too self-sufficient. They are boasters. When approaching and controlling sensitives, they generally assume great names. Often they pretend to have been Grecian philosophers, and are afire with the accomplishment of a great mission. Socrates had quite a mediumistic run a few years ago. Great historic names were in the mediumistic air. The Socrates that borrowed money of me through his medium in Troy, N. Y., failed to return it; and when unable to pronounce a Greek word, or tell the

Shall Men Pray for the Dead?

direction of Hymettus (famous for its honey and marble), from ancient Athens, inducing a doubt of his identity, he got angry at me even to profanity. This Socrates could swear in English. Later, he led his medium into the crooked ways of temporal ruin. This man was demon-obsessed. Could he (the demon) be redeemed? Would prayer benefit him? What is true prayer?

It has been said that moles never look up to see the light. This might be expected of burrowing moles; and so swine, feasting upon fallen fruit in autumn time, never look up in thoughtful gratitude to the heavily laden fruit trees from which it fell. Men are more than swine—infinitely more than animals. They, when feasting upon the bounties of the earth, if highly unfolded in the coronal brain region, naturally look up in gratitude to the Divine Presence. Those with depressed, or flattened, top-heads seldom breathe words of prayer or invocation. They are self-sufficient.

While prayer is not a cold repetition of words; while it is not the bending of the knees in fear to some far-off, enthroned monarch; while it is not to change immutable law for selfish ends,—it is aspiration,—I repeat, it is pure and holy aspiration. It is good thoughts spoken or unexpressed. It is the uplifting of the heart's divinest emotions in gratitude to the infinite Oversoul, the absolute One. It is, moreover, concerted thought afire with high and heavenly purpose, reaching through etheric vibrations, to the realms of innumerable spirit intelligences unseen to mortal eyes, and whose mission it is to bless and to help. These angelic intelligences may be called divine helpers. The world's truly great men have been men of faith and men of prayer. Demons of darkness and many mediumistic spiritists influenced by this class of dark, undeveloped spirits, ridicule prayer. They write and speak in the spirit of blasphemy.

Some few years ago the editor of the *Progressive Thinker,* Chicago, called for a spiritistic symposium upon the subject of prayer. The majority of the responses could only be designated as a vicious medley of rubbish. Among those materialistic spiritists denouncing prayer were —— I spare them the mention of their names; but here are some of their sentiments and published statements in the above-named journal: "Prayer is a heathenish practice;" "fear and prayer have done more to damn, demoralize and enslave humanity than all other religious exercises;" "prayer has cursed the human race;" "prayer is a farce, and nothing more;" "prayer is a sop thrown to the crowd;" "prayer is the rankest hypocrisy;" "prayer gratifies vanity;" "prayer is girdled with passion." " It leads to fanaticism;" it is the tiger in the jungle, the coiled serpent ever ready with deadly fangs to strike down the lovers of nature." "Prayer is the dark and damnable shadow on the wall;" "prayer prepares its subjects for hellish deeds;" "prayer robs us of our liberties;" "it is degrading and degrades;" "prayer is cringing, toadying to church superstition;" " prayer either makes a consummate hypocrite of a groveling, yielder-up of manly independence. It destroys our innate sense of right." " It induces a repudiation of personal responsibility, and paves the way to all forms of brutal savagery." But enough! *These,* and more statements of a similar character from materialistic spiritists and the devotees of certain spirit mediums, writing upon prayer with pens dipped in the very gall of demonism exhibit the froth and the foam of the hells. Think of it—ponder it! They carry unconcealed their own comments and moral condemnation.

It is but just to say that Dr. H. V. Sweringen, Luther R. Marsh, E. W. Bond, Geo. W. Kates, E. W. Sprague, Moses Hull, Mrs. Richmond, Dr. George A. Fuller and other eminent Spiritualists took a very different view of the subject. These and other religious Spiritualists are gifted with what phrenologists term "reverence." They are not so demon-influenced as to ridicule prayers, invocations and all soul-felt religious emotions,—emotions which the enlightened world would and do consider sacred.

Shall We Pray for Low, Debased and Wicked Spirits?

St. James, head of the Apostolic College in Jerusalem, gave the command, "Pray for one another," and why not? Why should we not pray the prayers of good will for the living and for the dead? Jesus preached to the "spirits in prison;" doubtless he also prayed for them. And are not Roman Catholics justifiable in praying to saints and angels? If prayers can ascend heavenward, they may also descend hadesward, reaching in tenderest tones down to the Cimmerian spheres of night.

Osiris, when mortal-vestured, frequently prayed to the tutelary gods for aid, and for blessings to rest upon those who had crossed (ferried by Charon) the river Styx. The Cretans prayed Jupiter and other gods to aid the living and the dead. Xenophon testifies that Cyrus prayed for the heroes that had fallen in his battles.

The early church fathers prayed for the "wicked dead"—prayed for the redemption of disorderly demons that troubled the faithful.

St. Hilary, a compeer of Cyril, who wrote about 315

A. D., says: "To those who wish to stand firmly, there is not wanting the custody of the saints nor the blessed guardianship of the angels. . . . There are many spiritual powers that are called angels and the spirits of the just, who preside over churches and persons. They pray for us, and we pray for the dead."

St. Cyprian, who wrote in the year 248 A. D., gave this exhortation: "Let us be merciful of one another in our prayers; with one mind, and one heart in this world and in the next. Let us always pray with mutual charity, relieving our afflictions, and may our prayers for our brethren and sisters, in whatever world, not cease."

Origen, who flourished near the end of the second century, when treating of prayers, guardian spirits and their influence over mortals, wrote: "Who can doubt that our holy fathers aid us by their prayers, and strengthen and excite us by their examples, and the writings they left behind them. The angels of the deliverance and ministering spirits are ever present; come then, thou angel or angels, receive him that is changed from his former error and from the doctrine of demons. . . . I will pray for the dead. I will pray for fallen demons."

St. Chrysostom, called "the golden mouthed," declares that "it is not in vain that oblations and prayers are offered and alms given for the dead. . . Let us not grow weary, then, in affording aid to the dead, by offering prayers for them."

A Great English Spiritualist upon Obsessions.

The distinguished William Howitt, in speaking of obsessions and the infestations of certain mediums in England, says: "With them the approach of spirits is not a visit, nor simply a visitation, but an inroad. They come, the door once open, in crowds, in mobs, in riotous invasions. They run, they leap, they gesticulate, they sing, they whoop, they curse. They are the most merry and the most bitter mockers. Wit looms in their words like flashes of infernal lightning. Pantomine is in their action; laughter in their eyes; and a horror, which no assumption of innocence can veil, is the effluvia of their presence. There is no question with the wretched sufferers of their phantasmagorial assaults, that they are the life and quintessence on hell. Nor is it the mind only of the unfortunate one they haunt; they have a power over his material movements. They move and remove articles; they fling and toss; they hide and steal; they put things where they ought not to be; they take them from whence they constantly should be. Mind, body, soul, memory and imagination—nay, the very heart—are polluted by the ghostly *canaille;* and the sanctuary of life and the dwelling are invaded, disordered, desecrated, and made miserable by them. We have known such sufferers and know them still. They are obsessed by demons, as were many in Christ's time. And yet, they may be redeemed in the future state of existence by discipline, repentance and prayer. Christ's mission extended to both the living and the dead, and the apostle declared that ultimately "every knee shall bow, and every tongue confess that Christ is Lord, to the glory of God the Father."

The celebrated Jung-Stilling furnishes a long list of obsessional cases coming under his immediate inspection. I have seen many sensitives, making no claim to Spiritualism, completely or partly obsessed by dark, undeveloped spirits. Not only have I seen these phenomena in this country, but I saw several well-marked cases in India, and was introduced to one Sivaite priest who devoted every Friday afternoon to the casting out of demons.

A Unitarian Preacher on Obsessions.

The learned and lamented Unitarian preacher, Rev. James Freeman Clarke, wrote: "As regards demoniacal possession, I think that Jesus believed in it, and that he spoke to the evil spirits as though they would hear him. A few years ago I thought that he shared a popular error in this, which our century had outgrown. But within a few years I have been led to believe in the reality of demoniacal possession. I have myself known personally, and also by credible testimony, of at least half-a-dozen instances of persons who seem to have been taken possession of by a low and unclean order of spirits. And the best way of helping them when they were too far gone to help themselves, was to have some other person possessing greater spiritual force, to do what Jesus did, namely, order the spirit to go away. I believe that in certain places and periods, the nervous condition of men is such that the lower order of ghosts may get control of them, and that when Jesus came, it was just such a time and place as this. But Christ's kingdom spans all worlds, and so obsessing demons may be redeemed."

The most fiendish murders ever perpetrated have been by convicts while imprisoned for crime. Only recently in a western penitentiary, one of these fiendish men, nineteen years confined and ever troublesome, stabbed and killed two of his fellow convicts; and while struggling madly to murder the keeper, was shot dead. his last word an oath! Where—what his condition? Is there any reason to expect any immediate moral revolution in such a character? These persons are the demons of this and the demons of the future. Reproof, counsel, punishment in prisons did not save them. Punishment never saves. It startles; it may arrest the wicked in their course for the time being, and it may also lead to serious reflection; but the Christ-power of love, repentance, humility, aspiration, moral effort, wisdom—these are the saving graces!

I have had the demons of the underworld, suffering the bitter, gnawing, galling pains of remorse, come to me, exclaiming, "Help me—pray for me, oh, pray for me! I want the light. I want to see and dwell with those I once knew and loved." The divine spark is never extinct. It is immortal, and capable of being touched by the potent principles of love. God is love.

Possessing the Body of Another.

In "Essays from the Unseen," published by James Burns, London, may be found this remarkable account of a possession, slightly condensed. It is the self-history of a spirit through a very noted medium:

"A person in any world may climb downward as well as upward. It has been urged by men in the flesh, and by advanced spirits too, that the after state of the spirit is a condition of undeviating progress. Now I deny this. I retrograded in my spirit life; on top of many earthly sins, I put a crowning one—I returned to the earth again. I looked backward and inhabited a tenement, and lived in that tenement some four and a half years.

"I stood by the side of the weeping father and mother, over a babe whose spirit was leaving the body. The age or time of its earthly experience was four days; I mean the body had been formed for the reception of a spirit four days. I saw the child's heavenly guide and guardian spirit, and as the spirit of the babe left its house, I saw its guide remove it in his arms, and convey it to spheres in the heavens. I had seen, in my experience on earth, phenomena more wonderful to my philosophic mind than any during my existence out of the body, therefore the wondrous fact to me was a mere fact of conscious individuality out of the body, which led me no nearer to the conception of a Supreme ruling Mind than did the stars which in earth-life I had seen and noticed, and whose motions had been one of my favorite studies —whose immense distances I, with others had calculated. To sum up, I felt that the fact of the mighty moving masses of matter whirling in space was an infinite, onward, and ever-present fact to me on earth, besides which the mere fact that I was in spirit-life faded into insignificance. The one had led me no nearer to God than had the other. I was not religious when inhabiting my earthly body; and I cared little for companionship, when entering the spirit world. I longed for earth's experiences again.

"Unaided by prayer or petition to God, I determined to choose for myself a tabernacle which I could again inhabit and again venture upon earth's scenes, feeling again the passions which had faded but were still held. I determined to find a habitation for my spirit in the body of this new-born babe. In its transition I took advantage of that state in which the spirit of the child was leaving the body, before the mechanism of the physical organization had ceased to act. I succeeded, and in this fragile habitation I, a spirit of a previous sixty-seven years of earth's experiences, took up my abode. My active, restless spirit was perfectly imprisoned in this body. It was ten months ere I could manifest the power of speech through it. I was afraid of crushing the tender fibers of the brain by using them too roughly. At ten months I was able to talk fluently. At two years I could argue with doctors of divinity from the proofs afforded by the Hebrew writings of the prophecies respecting the coming of the Mesiah. At four years I was able to talk fluently English through this body, and some four thousand Latin words. At that age I entered into studies with the greatest anatomists living. I was then enabled to meet in argument the most noted divines, ignoring the authenticity of Bible records. I was too anxious to bring my talent forward in its habitation: my architectural studies, my mathematical exercises, performed at the age of four years and four months, were the wonder of all the leading minds. Fluently I could answer all questions in history. Passionately fond of mathematical studies until the brain formation collapsed—broke—understand me perfectly, because I am incapable of conveying my ideas to the outside world, as through this glass (taking a tumbler off the table) would be incapable of holding water were I to control the arm holding it and dash it on the floor. The envelope was no longer fit to contain the spirit; I abandoned it, having had for four years and nine months a second earth-life. . . .

"Occupying this self-chosen habitation but four years and nine months with immense difficulty and through incompetency, when, for the first time, dawned the fact—there must be a God."

Whether the autobiography of this spirit is to be considered authoritative or not, I express no opinion. It certainly belongs to the realm of the possible, and has many clear, satisfactory corroborations.

This spirit refused to give his name before taking possession of this infantile body; but said he belonged to a prominent European family. It will be noted that this spirit admitted that he retrograded in returning back into a fleshly body. It was not reincarnation, but the re-possession of a human body for a season.

Rancy Vennum and Mary Roff.

Similar to the foregoing was that remarkable case of the Roff family, known as the "Watseka wonder." Of this case of possession, referred to by Professor James, of Harvard, and Dr. Hodgson, I can speak knowingly, positively, for Mr. Asa B. Roff, only recently deceased, was one of my patients several years ago. I knew him not only intimately, but knew his cultured daughter, Minerva Alter, sister of Mary Roff that possessed the body of Mary Lurancy Vennum. It was my further privilege to know other members of this excellent Roff family, and some of the Watseka citizens who were witnesses of this singular psychic,—not of a "double consciousness," but of an actual re-possession again by a spirit of a human body.

The history very briefly told, is this: Miss Vennum when about fourteen, had a series of attacks called hysteria. She was so annoyed by spells of hearing her name called out of the silence by night that her mother frequently slept with her.

Not feeling well on the eleventh day of July, she fell to the floor, apparently dead. She thus lay five hours. When falling at other times, she declared that she saw spirits, describing and identifying them. In these further trances she saw angels and beautiful spirit scenery. Physicians, the Rev. Mr. Baker, and others pronounced her insane, and proposed putting her into a lunatic asylum.

At the crisis, Mr. Roff and Dr. Stevens, of Janesville, called, finding her sitting by the stove, hands upon her knees, eyes staring wildly, thoroughly obsessed. Dr. Stevens, by magnetic treatment and a strong will, dispossessed the evil influences; and then Miss Vennum said, "I see many good, bright spirits here, and among them one Mary Roff," whereupon Mr. Roff remarked promptly, "That's my daughter Mary. She has been in heaven these twelve years."

Counseling with the spirits, it was here arranged that Mary Roff take the place of the former wild demon influences. Miss Roff had many strange experiences before she passed to the spirit-world. On Feb. 1, 1878, she took complete control of Lurancy's body, and dressed to go home to Mr. Roff's residence.

From this time "Rancy" Vennum did not know her parents, and took no interest in family affairs. In fact, it was not her, but Mary Roff dwelling in her body, and she hourly pleaded to go home.

Mrs. Roff and her daughter, Mrs. Alter, hearing of these strange things, called to Mr. Vennum's, when Mary Roff, in Lurancy's body, rushed to meet them. She threw her arms around their necks, and wept for joy. On Feb. 11, 1878, the Vennums sent their daughter (her body possessed by Mary Roff) to Mr. Roff's residence, where she was perfectly happy. She knew where everything was about the house, and talked of hundreds of things that happened when she was a girl in her own body. She said the angels told her that she was to stay with them till some time in May, "a happy, contented daughter, and a loving sister in a borrowed body."

While in Mr. Roff's house, she did not know the Vennums, nor would she recognize them. She declared that she frequently saw spirits,—frequently went to heaven, naming those whom she there met. Some of her tests were remarkable.

On May 7, she told Mrs. Roff that Lurancy Vennum was coming back into her body again. It was a sad and tearful hour. Mary, after saying good-by sat down, was entranced, and Lurancy had control of her own body. She looked anxiously, wildly around, and asked, "Where am I? I was never here before."

Mr. Roff replied, "You are at Mr. Roff's, brought here by Mary to cure your body."

Lurancy wept and said, "I want to go home."

In about five minutes the change came again, and Mary was once more in Lurancy's body. She was overjoyed, asking them to sing her girlhood song, "We Are Coming, Sister Mary." Her conversation at this time, though joyous, was exceedingly serious. She informed them that the good angels told her she could not remain long, as her work was about done; but she assured them that she should often return to them as a loving spirit, and expressed the fear that they would not be able to recognize her. She had been the instrument under angel guidance of seeing Lurancy's health restored, of giving almost unbounded joy to her parents and relations, and of adding tangible proofs of the future, immortal existence.

Mary Reynolds' Possession.

Among other well-authenticated accounts much like those previously narrated, is that of Mary Reynolds, as referred to or described by Rev. W. S. Plummer, Professor Upham, Major Ellicot, professor of mathematics in the United States Military Academy at West Point, and others.

When about eighteen years of age, this Miss Reynolds was attacked by what were denominated "fits." Physicians not being able to distinguish between "fits" and trances, she was treated medically. Passing into one of these trances, or a profound sleep, it was found impossible to waken her; but after some hours she awoke herself, but she had lost all consciousness of her former self. She knew neither her parents nor the relatives of the family. She was ignorant of the details of daily life; but acquired knowledge with the rapidity of mature womanhood. In every respect she was another person. Her states of consciousness were changes at times every few months, and always taking place when going into a trance-sleep. These were called her first and second states—each a distinct personality—an obsession.

This was not a "double consciousness," as certain pseudo-scientists have stated, but two single consciousnesses, manifest as two distinct individualities, alternately dwelling in one body. Dr. Plummer in summing this case up, says:

"The phenomena presented were as if her body was the house of two souls, not occupied by both at the same time, but alternately, first by one then by the other, until at last the usurper gained and held possession, after a struggle of fifteen years. For not only did she seem to have two memories, each in its turn active, and then dormant; but the whole structure of her mind and consciousness, and their mode of operating seemed dissimilar, according to her states. Her sympathies, her method of reasoning, her tastes, her friendships, and the reasons which led to their formation, were in one state wholly unlike what they were in the other. She had different objects of desire, took different views of life, looked at things through different mediums, according to her state."

The foregoing interesting instances, psychological and occult, with others of a similar nature that might be named, present overwhelming evidences to my mind, that they were possessions pure and simple. These are not miracles, but in consonance with the reign of spiritual law.

Obsessions frequently merge into complete possessions, and their characteristics for good or ill depend largely upon the earthly environments and the dominance of the controlling intelligences. "By their fruits shall ye know them."

This chapter cannot better be closed than by using the tender, hopeful words of the good Quaker poet, Whittier:

"In the economy of God, no effort, however small, put forth for the right cause, fails of its effect. No voice, however feeble, lifted up for Truth, ever dies amidst the confused noises of Time. Through discords of sin and sorrow, pain and wrong, it rises, a deathless melody, whose notes of wailing are hereafter to be changed to those of triumph, as they blend with the Great Harmony of a reconciled universe!"

CHAPTER XXIII.

Do Demon Spirits First Hypnotize, Then Obsess and Possess Subjects?

MAN is a trinity in unity, constituted of a physical body, an etheric soul-body, and pure, essential spirit. The spirit is the enthroned king. It is a potentialized portion of God; it is immortal. It is beginningless and endless. The body is its outward vehicle, as matter in its varied grades of refinement is the garment of God.

Matter being passive, inert, is used by the conscious spirit to build up and manipulate the atoms, ions and ether substances for the purpose of external, bodily manifestations. It is grand to think, to feel, to consciously realize that one's self is a Spirit—a spiritual entity—a thinking, reasoning son of God, gifted with the possibilities of upreaching ideals and mighty powers of unfoldment, ever pointing toward the goal of a glad perfection. And yet, man acts, functions on the finite plane of existence; he cannot control the lightnings that flash, the thunders that roll, the volcanoes that burst in madness, the floods that immerse cities, nor the clutching cyclonic maelstroms of the ocean. He is the subject of law, of magnetic currents, countless psychic influences, and multitudinous mental concentrations everflowing from social surroundings and invisible sources. This leads directly to hypnotism, and to the hypnotic or psychic influences of demoniac spirits.

What Is Hypnotism?

No thorough student ever uses hypnotism and mesmerism interchangeably. They are not synoyms. Having practiced one or the other of them for years, and withal, being connected officially with the Psycho-Therapeutic Society of London, lecturing occasionally for the same, I speak by the book, and define hypnotism thus: *A temporary sleep of various degrees; a mental condition exerted upon a sensitive subject by a conscious operator, influencing or controlling the voluntary powers.*

Professor Quackenbos, of Columbia University, defines it in a similar manner near the beginning of his volume entitled, "Mental and Moral Culture." His different treatments of the subject, however, are a little confused, if not contradictory. But near the last of the book he gathers up the threads of his argument and says in language unmistakable, that, "Will-power has nothing to do with hypnotic suggestion; neither the will-power of the operator nor that of the subject. Above all, he (the party influenced) is in no degree subject to another will" (page 268). This is a strained statement. True, the positive operator does not absolutely annihilate—does not perfectly paralyze the negative subject's will; but overshadowing, *does* influence it.

Here again I must stoutly affirm that hypnotism, animal magnetism and mesmerism, though similar, are all unlike in origin, force and influence. In practicing the last two, there is the impartation of the vitalizing, odylic fluid from the mesmerist. Hypnotism—suggestive hypnotism—is purely mental. It has its limitations. It may be used wisely or wickedly. It necessarily carries with it a strong tendency or moral coloring of the operator, whether in the world visible or invisible.

Can Spirits Hypnotize? Can They Mesmerize?

Emphatically, they can. The vast majority of them are neither gods nor angels, but men and women, such as walk the streets today, buying and selling, speculating and theorizing, preaching in pulpits, and punching balls in smoke-pickeled pool-rooms,—these men and women, stripped of their fleshly bodies, people the immediate, over-arching, spirit-world, retaining their identities, their memories, their leaidng life-purposes; hence, they as naturally as necessarily cast backward glances—naturally influence, hypnotize and exert their will-power upon those to whom they are attracted. Here comes in the hypnotic law of mediumship and the danger of demon influences.

What Is the Will?

While man is a self-conscious intelligence, will is an essential and prominent feature of his personality. Will, or power of self-determination, is essential to a moral being. Will is a directing energy from within. Will is the guidance of our own conscious activities. Any premeditated act of the will is an expression of the inner, diviner man.

Now the question arises, can hypnotic influence, dangerous as it is,—can low spirit influences while leading astray, completely paralyze or annihilate the human will? Assuredly not! The will, allied to consciousness, moral conscience, essential spirit and God himself, cannot be destroyed, cannot be annihilated. It may be shadowed, eclipsed, influenced, controlled temporarily, but cannot be utterly and perpetually paralyzed—annihilated. To this end the authoritative Mansel says in his metaphysics, "The will is only one necessary element of the whole personality, and it is never wholly obliterated, nor is it capable of being annihilated by effort of thought or any variance from ordinary law."

The annihilation of the human will by mortal or immortal, is unthinkable. It may be, as aforesaid, weakened, it may be perverted, but never completely paralyzed by man or spirit beyond restoration. A thousand abuses do not nullify one divine principle—one right use for holy aims. Angel ministries, sweet spirit-influences in the line of divine order, stimulate and quicken the will to holier and more heavenly work; while demon influences cloy, deflect, degrade, delude and bewilder, leading to perversion, error, vice and most painful obsessions.

Can the Hypnotized Be Made to Commit Crimes?

Such is not my personal experience with subjects. But my experience is not that of others. Before exercising my psychic powers, I universally tell my subjects that my motives are good, that my aims are moral and conscientious—that if they have pains, I will remove them, and that I will impress them with a healthy, cheerful, happy, uplifting influence. This I do, and this I have conscientiously ever done.

And here I wish to introduce the testimony of one of the most powerful hypnotists, that I ever met—one who for thirty years has been a demonstrator in practical hypnotism and psychology, both in private and public. I refer to that author and hypnotic practitioner, of Boston, Mass., Prof. A. E. Carpenter. He says without the least mental reservation, that "it was thought at first that a person hypnotized could be made to commit a sin of any kind, and that a woman's honor was at the mercy of the hypnotist. In fact, it was thought that once a person had entered the hypnotic state anything might be done with him or her. Criminals could be made to confess, and important secrets wrenched from the subject's under-consciousness without reserve. This is largely a mistake, as the early operators is mesmerism learned long ago in this country.

"This may be laid down as a rule in regard to the limits of hypnotic suggestion. No fixed moral conviction can be overcome, nor will any vital secret be revealed by the subject in any stage of hypnosis. There is always a reserve of latent will that is called into action in extremity, an existing auto-suggesting of conscience that cannot be completely broken down. All stories that you have ever read or heard contrary to this general proposition you may safely count as the product of some person's imagination. This is the way it should be.

It would be a fearful misfortune if we were so constituted as to be likely to enter a mental state in which we should become absolutely subject to another's wicked will. While there is scarcely any limit to the power of suggestion along the lines of benefit to the subject, there is always this reserved moral conviction, backed by the instinct of self-preservation and innate justice that acts as an auto-suggestion, constituting a safeguard to the subject from injury to himself or others through him in this higher hypnosis."

It is quite needless to say that De Puysegur, Broussay, Colonel de Rochas, Prof. Alexander Wilder and other distinguished hypnotists, psychologists and metaphysicians sustain in a degree the views of Professor Carpenter,

This well-known mental scientist and author, Professor Wilder, thus writes, "The hypnotized person, whose individuality is rendered temporarily dormant, becomes more exquisitely sensitive to the aura and influence of those whose influence is concentrated upon him. And so also, we often operate on one another by our presence, and by the concentration of our attention through the silent energy of our will. The individual will of the hypnotized, or one in the mesmeric trance, is dormant, but the real inner self is as much awake as ever, and the subject cannot be induced under an impulse to commit a malicious crime. The conscience, the authoritative 'ought' within, forbids it. Temptation to do a deed, is not a commission of that deed. Induced tendency is not an accomplished reality." Professor Wilder further assures us that "influence is reciprocal, and as a spirit may obsess a human being or an intermediary, it is reasonable to presume that a human being may obsess a spirit in turn."

That hypnotism is shamefully abused admits of no denial. The potent will-power of a selfish, wicked man is extremely dangerous. He throws out that venom force which may imprison. African voudous are hypnotists. Hypnotism has often been efficacious in breaking up families. And notwithstanding the testimony of Professor Carpenter,I believe from the consensus of testimonies of those high in authority,—adepts in psychic studies and experiments, that hypnotists acting persistently on low moral planes may induce—*may lead to the commission of blackest crimes.* This with me is a mature conviction.

Do Demon Spirits First Hypnotize? 239

These traveling hypnotists that infest city and country in winter time, hypnotizing the unwary in public halls for amusement, or money-getting, are to be shunned as one would shun a raging fire, or a rushing oncoming flood of water. They are mountebanks and tramping vampires. They open the way, if their lives are depraved, for obsessing demons. Their suggestions and their ways lead to death.

Tri-personalities and Spirit Controls.

Much ado of a mystical character has been made by psychic research societies about dual and triune personalities. The words used, often polysyllabic, have mystified rather than elucidated, occurring phenomena. Much of this mystification has resulted from not properly drawing a distinction between personality and individuality. They are not synonyms.

Personality (*persona,* Latin) is constituted of consciousness, quality, imparted attributes and other characteristics inherited, acquired or transferred. A spirit-entranced person is seemingly and visibly, another personality, but not another individuality.

Every student of rational Spiritualism knows that a spirit-entranced person, and especially if unconsciously entranced, may be another personality, a dual personality, a tri-personality or a sevenfold personality, temporarily by turns, providing seven different spirit intelligences occupying different planes of spirit existence, control the mentality. But said person is never a dual or triune individuality. And why?—Because the individuality is the original *I AM* of the man. Lexicographically defined, it is an entity, being, oneness, distinct existence. It is, therefore, the equivalent of the *divine ego*, the uncompounded, invisible, indissoluble spirit center of life—God incarnate. This, though non-manifest in natural or hypnotic sleep, is nevertheless, the central conscious force—the essential power—the king immortal upon his throne! Individuality is the essential man. Personality relates more to his mental garments, and manifold environments. These may be changed by suggestion, by hypnotism and by the will-power in entrancements, exhibiting varied personalities. The much-talked-of "subconscious" is a myth.

The diamond, however deeply buried, however encumbered with rubbish, is a diamond still. And so the individuality, the conscious spirit, is spirit still, and as such it is absolutely indestructible.

Obsession, in an important sense of the word, may begin with conception. A certain spirit desiring to accomplish some purpose, may in the very hour of conception, so infuse psychic forces, qualities and pre-mental impressions into the germinal life—may so suggestively affect the mother as to incite, impart the life-tendency of the child. This, rather than Hindu reincarnation, accounts for unlikeness in children—explains idiosyncrasies, and offers the key that unlocking, tells the why and the how of the born genius.

There is an impelling personality behind the genius or the moral monster. And so obsessions pertain to personalities rather than individualities. Having sown the suggestive seed, they may, if so disposed, hypnotically affect, twist, disfigure and mold the person's life-plans and conduct, be it that of the heavenly, or of the lower, baser type—demoniac in fact. Relating to these untoward influences, Miss S. C. Clark, Lynn, Mass., in her

Do Demon Spirits First Hypnotize? 241

very interesting volume entitled, "Pilate's Query," writes:

"We are immersed in a seething sea of spirit-life, in spheres of conscious spirit-existence. Multitudes of souls pass from earthly embodiment every hour. Most of these remain in the borderland of mundane existence; their attractions are all here; they are unable to get away. Floating through our atmosphere, these wandering entities chance to meet or are attracted by a certain personality. They become entangled, as it were, in the aura surrounding that person; sometimes they cannot get away; often they cling desperately, as you know, from the desire to have a body to use. The ability to free such a one is an imperative need in the healer's work of today. Until he thus casts out unclean spirits, he is not doing the perfect work of Christ. 'He cast out the spirits with his word, and healed all that were sick.' A clear distinction is made between these separate needs. The disciples likewise were commanded to heal the sick, cleanse the lepers, and cast out unclean spirits."

Miss Considino, of Chicago, assured her friends that while feeling in the best of health, a feeling gradually seized her, and she lurched forward unconscious. "I had had similar spells (trances) before," she remarked. She was a psychic sensitive. After twenty-eight hours she found herself in a hospital. The attending physicians pronounced it a "strange case of coma." Ignorant as physicians generally are of psychoses, trances and the obsessing influences about us, what else could they pronounce it?

The following were marked cases of obsession, if not posession:

"Dr. William Clifford McDonald left the Harvard

Club in this city (New York), in April, 1901, and has not been seen since.

Arthur David Hammond disappeared from the Park Row Building in December, 1902. He was a sensitive.

"Rev. William H. Dexter, principal of the Normal Academy, Nyack, disappeared from the Fifth Avenue Hotel in Nevember, 1899.

"Rev. A. Waldo, of the University Settlement, was found in February, 1902, after an absence of six years. He was doubtless hypnotized or spirit obsessed."

Here is an obsession case high in authority. When Queen Dowager, Maria Christina, mother of King Alfonso of Spain, left recently for Vienna, the English and Continental journals contained the following:

"Up to the time of his ascension, Alfonso was a devoted and dutiful son, and the fondest of relations existed between him and his mother, who was regent during his minority. His conduct has been toward her of late, so disrespectful, not to say brutal, that it has given rise to stories of mental aberration as the only explanation. For years she had cared for him, watched over and guarded him, and brought him through a childhood of feebleness and illness to finally take his place on the Spanish throne of his fathers, and now, when he has an opportunity to pay, at least in part, for her loving care over him, he has turned against her, even going so far as to threaten to have his guards turn her out of the palace.

"His behavior to this mother has not been the only sign of eccentricity, to put it mildly, that the king has shown. He has manifested an utter disregard of all precedents, especially military, and turned out the troops at the barracks for an impromptu review at daylight, and has quarreled with his ministers, opposing them on many propositions and refusing to sign papers which they have presented him.

"One of his latests freaks was to come down from his apartments stark naked, declaring that clothing was superfluous, and parade the palace for half the day in that naked condition, defying any one to touch his sacred person."

There could scarcely be a clearer case of obsession bordering on insanity. As previously expressed in this volume, a large majority of the insane in lunatic asylums are obsessed by ignorant or selfish, malicious entities that people the enzoning borderland spheres about us. Can these terrible conditions be obviated? Can obsessed prisoners be freed? Can these spirits themselves be freed from self-imprisonment and be redeemed? These questions are answered in the succeeding chapters.

CHAPTER XXIV.

Can the Obsessed Be Relieved, and Low, Obsessing Spirits Be Saved?

HERBERT SPENCER'S test of reality is persistency. This test is just as applicable to the appearance of apparitions, ghosts, spirits, demons and angels as is the universal belief among all tribes and nations of the immortality of the soul.

Only the uneducated, or doggedly wilful, deny in the

present cycle of time, the existence of entities, of various moral grades of invisible presences in our midst. Who are these unseen attendants—what their purpose, and to what extent do they affect us? These questions will not down.

Dr. Lyman Abbott wrote in the *Outlook*: "For reasons stated in my 'Life of Christ,' I believe not only that there really was, but that there really are now such phenomena as demon possessions."

Prof. William James, of Harvard University, writing on the mediumistic trance in relation to the "Psychical Research Society," says, "We believe in all sorts of laws of nature which we cannot ourselves understand, merely because men whom we admire and trust vouch for them. If Messrs. Helmholtz, Huxley, Pasteur and Edison were simultaneously to announce themselves as converts to clairvoyance, thought transferrence and ghosts, who can doubt that there would be a popular stampede in that direction? We should have as great a slush of 'telepathy' in the scientific press as we now have of 'suggestion' in the medical press. In society we should eagerly let it be known that we had always thought there was a basis of truth in haunted houses, and had as far back as we could remember, had faith in demoniacal possessions."

The above is a fair statement of the average American cowardice. What will the people say? is the common remark. The majority sneeze when a few, of the reputed great, take snuff. "Have any of the rulers of the Pharisees believed on him?" was the inquiry in apostolic times. There are spiritists today, many of them, who know of the fact—the terribly distressing fact that thousands nowadays are obsessed by selfish, evil-

Can the Obsessed Be Relieved? 245

disposed spirits, as there were in the time of Anaxagoras, Socrates and Virgil's Cumean Sibyl. But they deny these facts, which are as stubborn as painful. Their stock words are, "It will hurt Spiritualism." The honest, conscientious response is, " If the facts—if plainly stated truths—will hurt Spiritualism, then, be it hurt." The ship is all the better after the removal of the barnacles. No truth can perish. The building stands after the scaffoldings have fallen.

These obsessional cases are frequently brought to the attention of the public. The following is a narration by Dr. G. L. Lane, Boston, of a case coming under his treatment.

"A few years ago there came to me the wreck of what was once a beautiful lady of middle age. Her sister took her to me, she said, as a last resort. She was a pitiful object. She had not known peace or a good night's sleep for years. Degenerated, fiendish spirits talked to her, and threw upon her vision ugly and obscene pictures, turned her against her husband and children. Her husband was and is postmaster of a large city near Boston. She contracted heavy debts in his name, would jump out of the window at night and walk to relatives miles away, and finally had to be strapped to her bed. Her husband had fully decided to place her in an insane asylum. She thus tells her own story of her trouble and restoration:

" 'I was an invalid for fifteen years, suffering with more or less severe pains in my head during the time. I could not see my friends or family for weeks consecutively, and was under the care of trained nurses. I was then treated by a New York specialist for over a year. In trying different treatments I experienced partial relief for a time, then relapsing into my former condition. I resorted to mental and Christian Science, and was treated by a dozen or more at different times, experiencing some little relief temporarily, then dropping back again into my old state of despair. Sleep was almost unknown to me for weeks at a time, and at last my case was pronounced hopeless.

" 'The nerve fluids of my body seemed almost exhausted; the suffering of my brain was terrible, and my room, in my more quiet moments, was filled with strange faces and forms. I could hear voices incessantly addressing me, filling me with terror and despair, until my only thought was to end my life. No one need tell me that these faces and these voices were hallucinations. I know better. I was clairvoyant. I saw, I heard, I knew, and I still know the condition and its causes. It was obsession. In this critical state I was relieved by Dr. G. L. Lane, of Boston, and I am now a well and happy woman.

" 'Mrs. ——.' "

What the Most Efficacious Means of Dispossessing the Obsessed?

When spending a few months in Madras, Bangalore, and other cities in Southern India, making occasional pilgrimages with parties out upon the hills and afar off by old temples, once sacred places, now in partial ruin, I there witnessed very characteristic obsessional scenes. The psychically influenced native would be called among English-speaking people, a medium, or an intermediary sensitive. I witnessed also corresponding phenomena among the howling dervishes when filling my U. S. Consular office in Asiatic Turkey. Also in company with

Can the Obsessed Be Relieved? 247

Mrs. Higgins and others, of the Museum School for Buddhist girls (out at the Cinnamon Gardens in Colombo, Ceylon), I attended and witnessed a demon dancing scene, and later north of Kandy, Ceylon, in the forest by an old Buddhist rock temple, I saw these obsessed natives go through with the strangest, wildest contortions as a prelude to the phenomena that brought prophecies and vulgar poems from the demon gods. They were simply exhibitions of unique obsessions, not altogether unlike the disorderly dark circles of spiritists, where fortunes are told, and hypnotic schemes are concocted to secure some credulous miser's hidden treasures. This spiritism, as afore stated, is a sort of modernized Babylonian necromancy. Its devotees, hypnotized by disembodied denizens of Hades, divine for money. It is promiscuous spirit commerce with a high tariff. It is from beneath and naturally gravitates toward the dark and the darker regions of the invisibles.

When in Canton, China, the guest of Dr. Kerr, physician and missionary, we chanced to speak of the spirit manifestations in America, when he coolly exclaimed: "Why, sir, these manifestations are very old in this country. China is an empire of spiritists." And to prove it he took me out to temples, shrines and booths where I witnessed spirit-writing and other forms of mediumistic phenomena. It is no doubt the consensus of opinion throughout the enlightened world today that these psychic phenomena are largely the works of invisible spirit intelligences, very similar to the demon infestations that characterized the Jewish people of Christ's time.

These weird obsessions belong to all countries, to all periods, and to all conditions of life, from the lowest to the highest. Each nationality, each city has its peculiar aural sphere. The sphere, the aural emanations of New York are very unlike those of Philadelphia, and those of Philadelphia are decidedly unlike those of London. Sensitives at once cognize these diverse conditions. And so each individual has his own environing sphere. Swedenborg remarks that " these spheres flow from the thoughts of every one. Those that go forth from the angels are so full of love and wisdom that they affect the inmost life of all with whom they are present. I have sometimes perceived them and have been happily affected myself." *

Selfish, hypnotizing spirits often push their way into these individual spheres, and so dominate the personality, first obsessing, then possibly possessing the person to the very verge of ruin.

It is naturally asked here, where are your exorcists? Who is empowered to cast out, force away and better the condition of these poor earth-bound spirits?

Listen to the message of old: "And when he had called to him his twelve disciples, he gave them power against unclean spirits, to cast them out, and to heal all manner of sickness and all manner of diseases." Mark 10:1.

"And when the even was come, they brought unto him many that were possessed with demons, and he cast out the spirits with his word, and healed all that were sick." Matt. 13:10.

Note the phrase, "his word," and back of that voiced word was the *"I will, be thou clean,"* and back of this were the glorified spirits of Moses and Elias,—

---

*Quoted from James Barton Stewart, *alias*, a very intelligent lady of Chicago, cured of obsession.

and back of these, that legion of angels, and back of these that Christ-heaven "cloud of witnesses," and back and above these Almighty God, the Central Consciousness, the life, power, love and wisdom of the universe.

That dark demoniac spirits have the power, either through ignorance or selfishness, to disturb or absorb the vitality, to cause nervous irritability, to partially paralyze, to infuse poisonous auras into the emanating spheres of those they desire to injure or make ill for some purpose best known to their infernal selves, admits of no doubt to those versed in psychoses and the variant branches of occult study.

In the passages above quoted it will be observed that these spirits are spoken of as "unclean spirits," and the casting of them out is connected with "all manner of sickness."

In the early days of Christianity, when it was spiritual rather than sacerdotal, and when love to God and man was the only test of discipleship, evil-influencing spirits were magnetically disengaged, or cast out by the disciples and by the many truly inspired believers. Hence the passages: "And the seventy returned again with joy, saying, Lord, even the demons are subject unto us through thy name. . . . Rejoice not that the spirits are subject unto you, but rather rejoice because your names are written in heaven." Luke 10: 17, 20.

Saying nothing more of the evangelists, it is said (Acts 19) that "special miracles (spiritual manifestations) were wrought by the hands of Paul; so that from his body were brought unto the sick, handkerchiefs or aprons, and the diseases departed from them, and the evil spirits went out of them."

Why Is Obsession Allowed?

It may be asked, why do not good, pure-minded, exalted spirits interpose and prevent obsessions? Just as wisely ask why good, honest officials on earth do not prevent all vice and wrong-doing. Spirits and angels are not endowed with infinite power. They do what they reasonably can. The attitude, the will largely governs there as here. A selfish, positive spirit, with base motives and a potent will, may obsess where a sensitive, refined, negative mother is spirit life might fail to counteract the obsessing influence. A clique of Cork Irishmen with picks and spades might not only do more work on a railroad than the same number of artists or Yale professors, but they could doubtless conquer them for a time in any material combat. There is natural law in the spirit world; but law is not always adequate in any world, short of the angelic, to prevent all selfish wrong-doing. God governs by universal, not special, laws.

I anticipate your inquiry, "How may I know whether I am influenced, controlled by a good or a bad spirit?"

By your sensitized perceptions, your intuition, your reason, and your highest judgment; otherwise expressed, if a spirit's approach and influence causes nervous irritability, permanent exhaustion of vitality, and sad gloomy forebodings; or if it induces envy, jealousy, and ill-feelings, assuming some great name, consider it a parasite, a hungry cormorant, a cimmerian demon, and say, promptly, positively, *"Get thee behind me, Satan!"*

Is There Evil Anywhere on Earth?

It is sorrowfully admitted that there are public teachers who teach that there is no evil in this or the future life,—all is right—"all is good," say they. What is termed evil is only "undeveloped good," which logic continued compels us to say that a purposed lie is undeveloped truth, and rape undeveloped virtue. These doctrines are the dogmas of darkest demons.

This is a world of comparisons. There are valleys and marshes where slimy serpents crawl, and towering sun-kissed mountains where the air is ever pure and bracing. Contrast exist all about us. They are real. Furious madness is just as positive an emotion as is calm, collected sympathy. Those who cannot feel, who do not know, who cannot cognize the difference between heat and cold are physically paralyzed, and those who do not cognize the difference between good and evil are already smitten with a most deplorable moral paralysis. Their spiritual natures are benumbed. It was the inspired Isaiah who said, "Woe unto them who call evil good, and good evil, and that put light for darkness, and darkness for light." These doctrines are the doctrines of conscienceless demons.

What Steps Are to Be Taken in Obsession?

Those believing themselves troubled, obsessed by these spirits of moral darkness, should rectify their daily habits in regard to hygiene, associations and trains of thought. They should retire to some pleasant apartment, and having shut to the door, converse with them kindly, candidly, just as though they were clothed in their fleshly garments. Tell them they are not wanted. Plead with them to withdraw and look to the higher intelligences for instruction. Impress upon their minds that they are immortal, and that there is an eternity of progress, beauty and glory open before them. Tell them that gratification will sink rather than help them to rise to heavenly heights.

If this method does not suffice, be more positive, commanding them in the name of all that is high, holy and divine to depart. There was a period of several years in my long-life experience that I was afflicted and annoyed by these smooth-tongued, yet scheming, lying demons. As Paul fought with beasts at Ephesus, so I fought these wandering ghosts with thoughts, prayers, and a mighty, positive will power. I commanded and demanded that they depart, calling in the meantime upon the angels of God, angels of the living Christ, to gaze upon them, and aid in removing them—removing them, to be taken to disciplinary spheres for mental and spiritual treatment.

The work of redemption is not confined to any one sphere of being, Jesus preached to spirits in prison. And there is "joy in heaven when one sinner repents,"—when one demon turns to God for light.

If one fails to release himself from these hypnotic controls of demons, what then? Call upon an exorcist —one empowered to demagnetize, and remove the hypnotic cause. Egypt, Greece and Rome, in their palmiest days, had their official exorcists. About the middle of the third century, Cornelius of Rome had fifty exorcists, readers, operators and door-keepers. Exorcists were much lauded in the Hellenistic period.

Plutarch relates that the Magi advised the demonized to read and repeat the "Ephesian Letters" when alone and quiet (Sympos. vii: 5). It is said that Crœsus uttered them on the funeral pyre. Hesychius and Clement, of Alexandria, referred to these letters and also to the fact of music being used as an aid in cases of exorcism.

Can the Obsessed Be Relieved? 253

Justin Martyr says to Trypho: "Though you Jews exorcise any demon in the name of those who were among you, either kings or righteous men or prophets or patriarchs, it will not be subject to you. But if any of you exorcise it in the name of the God of Abraham, and the God of Isaac, it will perhaps be subject to you " (Dialogue, e. 85). Though there was evidently much superstition and many quaint notions mingled with the exorcists' methods all along the days of antiquity, still the fact, the underlying fact of demonism and exorcism, remains like immovable rocks. It may be truthfully said that in the Roman period of the Antonines, especially that of Marcus Aurelius Antoninus and in the times also of the early Christian Fathers, exorcists were among the cultured and influential classes. Some of them were supposed to have supernatural power. Whatever their powers might have been, they were natural to the spiritual plane of existence.

If a person is conscious of troublesome, obsessional influences, if invisible familiars haunt, converse with them. Tell them frankly they are injuring you. Then change your environments. Seek some mountainous district, where the air is pure; avoid all promiscuous spirit circles; keep the thoughts upon things moral and spiritual, observe all hygienic habits, and pray for divine help. Having done all these things in the Christ-spirit of love and truth and failed of relief, then call upon some healing exorcist, commissioned by a convoy of angels to cast out demons and restore the sick.

When in India the second time, I spent much of my time for months in "casting out devils," that is, in demagnetizing the victim, and removing the obsessing demons. My success was almost marvelous to myself. I was conscious of but one failure. I have also removed hundreds afflicted, tormented by the demons of the tartarean spheres. I command—I speak the "word" in the name of the Christ.

Sickness may be caused by transmitted tendencies, climatic conditions, ignorance and violation of natural laws; hence, is not always caused as certain extremists have taught, by thought—by thought transferrence, hypnotic forces and obsessional influences. There are cyclonic storms, zymotic diseases that have no more to do with hypnotism than they have with Calvinism, or Unitarianism, while hysteria, misanthrope, supersensitiveness, one form of epilepsy, stupid mutterings in insomnia, wild imaginations, nervous convulsions, loss of nerve vitality, somnambulism and several phases of insanity belong largely to the category of obsessions and possessions.

The exorcist—the man that treats obsessions—should be exemplary in conduct, clean in habits, religiously aspirational and spiritually minded. He should also be firm and positive in his convictions, aided by a legion of angels—angels that delight to do the will of God.

CHAPTER XXV.

Kindly Probations and Dire Obsessions.

"AND Saviour shall come up on Mt. Zion," exclaimed the inspired prophet Obadiah. Saviours are soul rescuers. They are altruistic workers and helpers.

"Thou shalt call his name Jesus," said the message-bearing angel, "for he shall save his people from their sins;" not from the just and adequate punishment, as cause and effect, due their sins, but he shall save them from sin, or from sinning, by teaching them to keep and obey the moral law. "Being reconciled," said the apostle Paul, "we are saved by his life." It is character, it is life, the purity and holiness of life that saves in all worlds visible and invisible.

The event called death is but the hyphen that connects the two aspects of one world; it is the severing of the co-partnership existing between the earthly and the more refined, etheric spiritual body. It in no wise changes the characteristics or natural tendencies of the person. The ignorant do not die into wisdom, nor the barbarian into the blissful angel. Identity is as abiding as the stars. And God bears the same loving relation to souls discarnate that he does to souls incarnate, the divine voice being, "Obey,—live and enjoy, or sin and suffer," the suffering being disciplinary rather than retaliatory.

Mortals at death enter the underworld or the upper-worlds with as absolutely substantial bodies as they now have, yet more ethereal. The stars differ in brilliancy. The auras of spirits differ in the future world. Some shine with transcendent brightness, others are as dark as the shadows of Erebus. There are intense sufferings in those Gadarene spheres. Memory is the undying worm. God builds no hells, burns no man's fingers here, curses no souls there. Effects follow conduct and habits as dust the wheels of the carriage.

Men are the architects of their own hells and heavens; they reap what they sow. They are moral beings, having the power of choice. The door of mercy is never closed. God's tender mercies endure forever. He is unchangeable. The angels call, and souls are constantly coming up, some slowly, yet surely, through tribulations deep. The Christ of Galilee is still toiling through million agencies to redeem undeveloped, obsessing spirits. Many hearing, quickly, gladly, partially awake to the light, and repentantly pray for more light. I have had spirits come to me through intermediaries, suffering the bitter, biting, burning agonies of remorse, and pleadingly say, "Pray for me, oh, help me! I pray you show me the light!"

To such I always speak firmly, yet in the tenderest tones of sympathy and kindness, assuring them that we are brothers all; that the wisest make mistakes, that the worst have their better moments and their good thoughts, demonstrate that the divine principle is never utterly obliterated; that there is still hope; that the Christ of the ages is still saying, "Come unto me all ye that labor and are heavy laden, and I will give you rest," that angel mothers in heaven still love, and that pure, unselfish love in all worlds is undying, immortal.

With these sympathetic words I extend the hand of fraternal friendship, and further say, Come up higher, brother, where the sun of wisdom ever shines, where the flowers of affection ever bloom, and where every motion is melody and music itself.

The gospel of true Spiritualism, the synonym of pure Christianity, ever speaks the commanding word, "Despise none, despair of none; aid the prodigal on the way to his father's house." The heart, in all worlds, softens at the echoing sounds of angel footsteps, softens as they tell that spirit life is real life, an active life, a social life, a retributive life, a constructive life, an ideal life, a progressive life, and that in the better land of immortality there are evergreen groves, meandering streams, deep mossy banks, musical birds, stars of diamond beauty, golden skies darkened by no clouds; there are also fields, fountains, gardens, schools, lyceums, massive libraries, universities of wisdom, hierarchies of the gods—everything to delight, to educate, and unfold the soul—these, all "these shall be thine," was an ancient spirit's promise to me in tones that thrilled my being's depths, "when thou art worthy, when thou art worthy."

The lamented and very learned F. W .H. Myres wrote in that great work of his near the close of his life these impressive words:

"Pondering deeply, I see ground to believe that the state of souls after death is one of endless evolution in wisdom and in love. Their loves of earth persist; and most of all those highest loves which seek their outlet in adoration and work. . . . Yet from their step of vantage ground in the universe, at least, they see that it is good. I do not mean that they know either of an end or of an explanation of evil. Yet evil to them seems less terrible than a slavish thing. It is embodied in no mighty potentate; rather it forms an isolating madness from which higher spirits strive to free the distorted soul. There needs no chastisement of fire; self-knowledge is man's punishment and his reward; self-knowledge and the nearness or the aloofness of companion souls. For in that world love is actually self-preservation; the Communion of Saints not only adorns, but constitutes the life everlasting. Nay, from the law of sympathetic telepathy it follows that that communion is valid for us here and now. Even now the love of souls departed makes answer to our invocations; even now our loving memory—love is itself a prayer—supports and strengthens those delivered spirits upon their upward way. No wonder, since we are to them but as fellow-travelers shrouded in a mist; "Neither death nor life, nor height nor depth, nor any other creature can bar us from the hearth-fire of the universe, or hide for more than a moment the inconceivable oneness of souls."

Faith Merging into Knowledge.

The illustrious Henry Ward Beecher, when referring to the great English reformer, Robert Owen, to Prof. Robert Hare, of the Pennsylvania University, and other atheistic materialists brought to believe in God and immortality through spirit converse, said that "Spiritualism strengthens faith." It does this and more; it gives the candid, conscientious investigator knowledge of a future existence. It had not only given me this knowledge, but it has strengthened my trust in God and my faith in Christ and in the redemptive power of true heaven-illumined Christianity. "By this," said Jesus, "shall all men know that ye are my disciples, if ye have love one for another." In this Christian discipleship I glory.

There must be a marked distinction made between Christianity and churchianity. The one is from above, the other from beneath. The one teaches the doctrines of Christ, the other the commandments of men formulated into creeds—creeds that cramp and bind the conscience. Jesus did not form nor authorize the formation of any new sect. He gave the "new commandment, that ye love one another," saying "feed my sheep;" then adding, "other sheep I have which are not of this fold; them I must bring also, and there shall be one fold and one shepherd."

Churchianity, crimsoned with the blood of slain millions for opinion's sake, formulates creeds, builds up walls of partition, condemns heretics, hoards up ill-gotten millions, constructs gaudy cathedrals, pampers and bows to the tyrant fashion, caters to policy, engages in wars of conquest, encourages Sunday-school cadets and boys' brigades. In brief, while making measurably clean the outside of the cup, churchianity is steeped in the worldliness of the world, and sad to say, the clergy with few exceptions, aid and abet this popular war-encouraging churchianity, thus crucifying afresh the Christ of the ages.

It is the potent Christianity of the living Christ that civilizes, that casts out demons, and still sings the angel song—"peace on earth, good will to men."

Considered with reference to religious cycles and Messiahs, Jesus stood upon the pinnacle of Hebrew Spiritualism, the great Judean physician of souls. As God is Spirit—that is, the Infinite Spirit—presence acting by the law of mediation, the Apostle, with a singular clearness of perception, pronounced the Nazarene "the Mediator"—that is, an intermediary between God and man.

The persecuted and martyred intermediaries of one age become gods in succeeding ages.

But if Jesus were only divine man, "elder brother," wherein, then, you will perhaps inquire, consisted His moral superiority over others. If I rightly understand His essential and peculiar characteristics, His pre-eminent greatness consisted in His more spiritual conceptions, in His fine well-balanced organization, in His Christ baptism, in a constant overshadowing of angelic influences; in the depth of His moral aspirations; in the warmth of His sympathies; in His deep schooling into the spiritual gifts of Essenian circles; in His soul-pervading spirit of obedience to the mandates of right, in His unwearied, self-forgetting, self-sacrificing devotion to the welfare of universal humanity, and His love for and perfect trust in God.

The leading thoughts ever burning in His being for acceptance and actualization were the divine Fatherhood of God, the universal brotherhood of man, the perpetual ministry of angels and spirits, disciplinary retribution for all wrong-doing, and the absolute necessity of toleration, charity, repentance, forgiveness, love—in brief, good works. And these, crystallizing into action as a mighty reform-force for human education and redemption, I denominate the *positive religion,* and consider it perfectly synonymous with Spiritualism—Spiritualism as a definition and practical power in its best and highest estate.

This pure religion and undefiled, established in men's hearts and lives, and not on "sacred" parchments, alone, would soon be felt in states and kingdoms, promoting peace, justice and charity, rendering legal enactments wise and humanitarian, and causing the sweet waters of concord and good will to flow over all the earth for the spiritual healing and moral uplifting of the nations. This is Christianity—this is Spiritualism, the religion of the soul, the inborn religion of all rational men. Only the few hear its voice. It was so in olden times when there "came a voice from heaven," and the people standing by and hearing, said, "it thundered;" others said, "an angel spake." Spiritism with its rude, noisy phenomena and obsessions, hears the thunder only, Spiritualism, the " still, small voice" of the angel, pleads lovingly, saying "come up higher." Its witnesses have been the luminous suns and stars along the ages. When Whittier the Quaker poet, accompanied by an English philanthropist, visited that eminent Unitarian, the Rev. Dr. Channing, for the last time in Rhode Island, their themes of conversation were anti-slavery reform, progress, peace, toleration and human sympathy. Mr. Whittier, referring to it afterward, wrote these tender lines:

"No bars of sect or clime were felt,—
  The Babel strife of tongues had ceased,
And at one common altar knelt
  The Quaker and the priest."

Thus may, thus do the hearts of the good and erudite ever blend in unison. Such fellowship constitutes heaven on earth. If you cannot walk peaceably, religiously and fraternally with others, go your way, brother, kindly leaving the road behind you for others. Heaven, as London, may be reached from different directions.

A Prominent Writer.

In *Medium and Daybreak,* London, March 11, 1894, I find the following from Hudson Tuttle under the heading "Obsession—Uncontrollable Desire to Kill."

"I was sitting," says Hudson Tuttle, "with a circle of friends around a large walnut dining-table, which was moving in response to questions. The intelligence claimed to be an Indian, and to the request said he would sketch his own portrait, by my hand. I held a piece of chalk, the size of a small marble, and automatically my hand drew a grotesque portrait. We all laughed, and my father, who had quitted the table, and seated himself on the opposite side of the room, said: 'It looks like Satan.'

"Instantly my mind, from light and pleasant thoughts, was changed to fierce and *unutterable hatred.* Anger turned the light to bloody redness, and to kill was an uncontrollable desire, under which I threw the chalk, with the precision of a bullet, hitting the offender in the center of the forehead, with a force which shivered the chalk in pieces. Had it been larger, serious consequences would certainly have resulted. Of course, the séance was at an end, but I could not escape that terrible influence for the evening.

"The study of this séance, showed me the danger which menaced the sensitive, and gave the key to a *class of crimes* which hitherto had remained inexplicable.

"We often hear of those who have been trusted for years, and models of honesty and fidelity, and moral uprightness, without warning, committing some heinous crime against property or person. They usually say they were seized by a sudden and uncontrollable impulse, and regretted their acts as soon as accomplished."

Spiritualism Not Mere Spiritism.

As Christianity must be differentiated from creed-enforcing churchianity, so Spiritualism must be differentiated from spiritism. The words are unlike. They should never be used interchangeably. *Al,* an Arabic particle, is a prefix to many words, and is the equivalent to a definiteness of mental and moral qualities. It has still more potency when a suffix. No classic writer confounds office and official, idea and ideal,—intellect and intellectual, then why spirit and spiritual, or spiritism and Spiritualism? A murderer is a spirit clothed in a fleshly body, but he is neither a spiritual nor a spiritually-minded mortal.

China today is a nation of phenomenalists, and obsessions are common in every city. Crossing the Atlantic a few years ago, the Korean minister to Washington, D. C., was my cabin-mate as afore referred to; and he related to me by the hour the wonderful spirit manifestations of his country, and the accompanying depressing, and the prevailing soul-tormenting obsessions. The Maoris of New Zealand are spiritists, holding converse with their dead in caves dimly lighted by kauri-gum knots. Mormons as often said and never denied, are spiritists, boasting of their gift of tongues and other spirit gifts.

Are these Oriental races and polygamy-practicing sectarists Spiritualists? Furthest from it possible! Believing in spirits and spirit phenomena no more makes a true Spiritualist than believing in the laws of mechanics makes a skilful engineer.

Hypnotism, often the attendant of anti-theistic spiritism, unwisely selfishly used, is extremely dangerous. It weakens the personal will, and often proves the promoter of dire mental diseases,—such as hysteria, neurasthenia, obsession and possession.

In Spirit Life "94,000,000 Years."

A man, sunken-eyed, spare in body and hollow-cheeked, recently came to me from southern Michigan, where twenty years previously he had been hypnotized in a public hall, becoming soon after a medium, speaking much of the time in an unknown tongue. It was to me gutteral gibberish. I inquired his name. It was unpronounceable. I asked him how long he had been in the spirit world. His prompt reply was 94,000,000 years.

"What has been your employment all these aeons of time?"

"Visiting the stars and planets, grasping all their laws," was the pompuous answer.

At this point I stepped to my library and bringing out a Crookes' radiometer, set it in the sunshine. The within machinery began to spin rapidly. "What causes the rapidity of that motion?" I asked.

"It is the force of my will-power. I am willing it to move."

"Are you?" I said, pushing the radiometer into the shadow, dark and sunless. The motion of the wings stopped. "See," I said, "the force is gone."

Coolly he remarked, "Yes—I've taken my will-power off."

This bare-faced falsity arousing my positive within, I stated in solid English, "You are a pretender, a deceiver, a base falsifier. Your will has nothing to do with this radiometer. You've sapped this man's vitality, you've made him a physcial wreck, you've fooled him

Kindly Probations and Dire Obsessions. 265

and shamefully lied to me. Now, sir, do you leave. In the name of truth and the living Christ I demand and command you to leave, and with these stirring words, I stepped to the medium, clapping my right hand upon his forehead, the left upon the back of his neck, and slowly moving it downward resting a moment over the solar plexus, then passing it still downward and outward. I stood by this obsessed subject probably five minutes, breathing a magnetic breath occasionally upon his head and exerting a strong exorcising will-power.

"What are your sensations,—how do you feel?" I inquired of this man.

"Can't hardly tell. I feel strangely and yet strong. It seems to me, doctor, that you weigh a ton. You are awfully powerful."

It is not I alone, was my reply. There is a messenger band—a sphere of conscious power behind and above me. It is potent, penetrating and uplifting. These immortal intelligences thrill and fill my being's depths with a spiritual force that at times is absolutely overmastering. Did not Jesus say, "Thinkest thou that I cannot pray to my Father and he shall presently give me more than twelve legions of angels?" Prayer lifts the soul into vibratory unison with angels and hierarchies of arch-angels who ever delight to do the will of God.

CHAPTER XXVI.

Swedenborg and Obsessing Evil Spirits

OFTEN has the statement been made, especially upon the continent of Europe, that Emanuel Swedenborg, oldest son of Jesper Swedenborg, born in Stockholm on the twenty-ninth of January, 1688, and educated at Upsala, was the greatest philosopher and Spiritualist since John's time of Patmos record. Though founder of what is denominated the "New Church," and a man of great erudition for that period, he was infested at times with evil spirits. This fact is based both upon the testimony of himself and his friends.

In the two large volumes of Swedenborg's life by William White, a cultured English author and bookreviewer whom I had the honor of personally knowing, lucid accounts are given of this Swedish seer's personal habits, associations and psychic experiences during his twenty-seven years' converse with angels, spirits and demons.

At one time, Swedenborg, upon reliable authority, pronounced himself "the Messiah." And Mr. Wesley inserted in his Armenian magazine for January, 1781, strange accounts of Swedenborg while lodging in Mr. Brockmer's house. He seems to have been entranced, or controlled, by demons, for he "foamed at the mouth, and made otherwise a frightful appearance."

Coming into the house at another time, he pulled off

his clothes, rushed out and rolled in the mud in the gutter. Mr. Brockmer took him to a lodging and put him under the treatment of Dr. Smith, Mr. Sheer-Smith, also, with whom Swedenborg staid for a time, was "affrighted with him by reason of his talking in the night. Sometimes he would stand in the doorstead of his room as if holding conversation with some unseen person, and divers other strange things accorded to the insane." The Rev. Mr. Beorgman, minister of the German Church, Savoy, London, Mr. Mathseus, Mr. Hindmarsh, and others are mentioned in testimony of these idiosyncrasies, all of which go to prove that he was the subject at times of demon infestations.

When in London, Swedenborg commenced a Spiritual Diary, which he kept up for seventeen years. Dr. Tafel printed these diary manuscripts in twelve volumes. These we quote from run from 1747 to 1749, continuously. Treating of evil spirits he wrote:

"I can attest that they are so dreadful and horrible as to be indescribable. The Devil's most deceitful machinations are unutterable, yea, inconceivable; for there is nothing bad in man which he does not stir up to mischief. . . . These direful attempts of evil spirits, which I have often experienced, are rather to be consigned to oblivion than published. By them I have learned that unless the Lord had been essentially present, I could not have held out a single moment, but must have inevitably gone to perdition. . . .

"Sept., 1747.—From experience I have learned that evil spirits cannot desist from tormenting. By their presence they have inflicted pains upon different parts of my body; upon my feet, so that I could scarcely walk; upon the dorsal nerves so that I could scarcely stand;

and upon parts of my head with such pertinacity, that the pains lasted for some hours. . . .

"Jan. 8, 1748.— It was stated when I was going to sleep, that certain spirits were conspiring to kill me; fearing nothing, I fell asleep. About the middle of the night I awoke, and felt that I did not breathe from myself, but, as I believed, from heaven. It was then plainly told me that whole hosts of spirits had conspired for my suffocation, but as soon as they made the attempt, a heavenly respiration was opened in me and they were defeated. . . .

"Jan. 11, 1748.—Spirits often wish me to steal things of small values, such as are exposed in shops; so strong is their desire that they actually move my hand. . . .

"Jan. 30, 1748.—Coming home today, I was sad. My melancholy was induced by a troubled spirit who told me he had reckoned himself among the most famous of men. He had devoted himself to metaphysics, and now discovering what worthless phantasies they were, and how they had hidden the divine truth from his eyes, he called them filth, and was full of sorrow. . . .

"Feb., 1748.—It has sometimes, yea, rather often happened, that pleasant flavors have been changed in my mouth to nasty. Twice, if I mistake not, sugar has tasted like salt. . . . These changes are induced by spirits. . . .

"March 14, 1748.— There are among spirits many who love white vestments, and indeed so passionately, that they incited me during several weeks to buy such vestments. . . .

"March 20, 1748.—When spirits begin to speak with man, care should be taken not to believe them, for almost everything they say is made up by them, and they lie. If it were permitted them to relate what heaven is, and how things are in heaven, they would tell so many falsehoods, and with such strong assertion, that man would be astonished. Wherefore, I was not allowed, when such spirits were speaking, to believe anything they said. They love to feign. Whatever may be the topic discussed, they think they know all about it; they form different opinions concerning it, and conduct themselves altogether as if they were perfectly well informed; and if a man listens and believes, they insist, and in various ways deceive and seduce him. . . .

"Oct. 20, 1748.— Seeing some boys fighting, I felt a very high degree of delight flowing in from certain spirits; whence it is plain how much they love enmities. I discern the character of spirits at once by the feelings they insinuate. I do not, as people generally do, credit myself with whatever enters my mind. . . .

"Nov. 2, 1748.—Evil spirits wished to cast me under the wheels of carriages in the street. Today I noticed particularly their constant endeavor to do so; and was enabled to perceive that such mischief is their passion. . . .

"There are sirens who wish above all things to be incarnate. When I eat, they wish to eat. I have been infested with them for several days. They strive to appropriate the almond cakes, pears and pigeons on which I feed, and to possess my body. . . .

"Nov. 27, 1748.—I had a feeling of shaking hands, that not I, but some one else grasped the hand. A spirit said he took the hand. Hence it seems a spirit had possession of my hand with its sense of touch. . . .

"Some time before the faculty of conversing with spirits was opened in me, I was impelled to commit suicide with a knife. The impulse grew so strong that I was forced to hide the knife out of sight in my desk.

"I have now discovered that Sara Hesselia was the spirit who excited the suicidal impulse as often as I saw the knife. From this it may appear that men may be unconsciously infested with spirits who hated them during their life on earth."

Again I must refer to A. J. Davis, the seer. In his "Diakka," he informs us unreservedly that there are spirits morally deficient, and " effectionally unclean,"—that their chief business in continuing about this world is "jugglery, trickery and witticisms, victimizing others, . . . secretly tormenting mediums, causing them to exaggerate in speech and falsify by acts; unlocking and unbolting the street doors of your bosom and memory, pointing your feet into wrong paths, and far more."

That eminent scientist and author, Prof. William Denton, wisely wrote, "The miser returning, curses the fatal appetite which binds him in the metallic chain forged by his own avarice; the sensualist lives here again by attachment, lives in the agonizing retrospect of lost delights for which the nature of spiritual existence furnishes no satisfaction."

The distinguished Judge Edmonds, of New York, was gifted with what is often termed "open vision." Some of the more remarkable of his visions he recorded. Here is one:

"Quietly sitting in my room, earthly walls and all material things fading away, I saw in the far distance a country peopled by great numbers. The country was diversified, some portions being darker than others, devoid of forests and flowers. There was a great variety in the shade of the atmosphere, from a light gray to a nearly black. From above sunbeams seemed to flash in at times, exciting a momentary wonder among these people.

"Coming nearer to my vision, they seemed busy. Some were conversing and gesturing; some were angrily discussing; some seemed to be accusing others and fighting; some seemed to approach fleshly human beings, clinging to and living in their odylic envelopes, exciting in, or transferring to them their own thoughts. . . .

"I approached one of these dark places, and there saw a miserable human being. He was ghastly, thin, haggard. He knew no means of escape from that dark habitation, where he was all alone. The most violent of human passions were raging in him. He was walking back and forth like a caged animal.

"There was a little light in this place, but it was an awful one. It was a lurid, flame-like light. His eyes were open and staring like burning coals, straining to see something. The darkness was horrible to him. He had no companion but his own hatred and the memory of his evil past. I saw him while walking lift his clenched hands and curse his Maker. He cursed also the false teachers who had pretended to tell him the consequences of a life of sin, yet knew so little of them. They had told him of a hell of fire and brimstone only, and he believed there was none. . . . If you could have seen the agony that was printed on his face, the despair and hatred that spoke in every lineament, the desperate passion that swelled his very being in defiance of God and man, you would have shuddered and recoiled from the sight; and what aggravated all this suffering was his ignorance that there was any redemption for him. . . .

"Working himself into a passion, he cried, 'Oh, for

annihilation!' He howled at times like a furious maniac. The worms of memory—memories of selfishness, dishonesty, crime, murder—were gnawing on his being's center. . . .

"I saw others wandering in a grayish light; these I was told were those who had died in drunken fits, or had come to these abodes in some vehicle of vice or crime. Their eyes were staring, their hair straggling, their frame half covered in scarlet brown or muddy-tinged garments. These were often engaged in accusing others. Sometimes their monotony was varied by reaching the spheres of mortals in lascivious houses, gamblers' dens of hilarity and drunkenness. Here they sought to relieve their earthly lives of lust and carnal delights. In a measure they seemed to succeed through some law of attraction. And yet the success was momentary. They quarreled among themselves, while seeking out mortals to further gratify their propensities,—gratify them by entering their aural surroundings and inciting them to commit deeds of darkness, either through ignorance or hate of God, spirits and men,—poor, unhappy, horror-stricken souls!" This was obsession.

In another vision of scenes in the lower under-world of spirit life, he saw spirits whose "exteriors and environments were coarse and painful to behold, and their interiors were largely in correspondence. The murky air was full of jarring discords, and the denizens were of a fighting, wrangling nature. Inquiring, I was directed to two women in a quarrel over their jealous social relations, and murdering each other, the one dying immediately, the other living a few days to rave in accusations of anger. The man causing the jealousy had committed suicide. And, like Judas, they had all gravitated to their own places. . . . Angels descending to these abodes dazzled the denizens with their brightness. They considered their appearances illusions, and continued their orgies." These poor, unbalanced souls "had made these hells for themselves. Their pains were retributive and disciplinary. I was shown some who through contrition and repentance, were on the way to better conditions. Angels and good spirits are untiring in their ministries, and God's 'mercy endureth forever.' Blessed are those who descend to teach—who lovingly preach to and become instruments in the redemption of demons. These in the grand consummation shall see the travail of their souls, and be crowned as saviours."*

Tallmadge and a Catholic Obsession.

Among the able and substantial men of the West in the line of spiritual science is the Hon. J. R. Tallmadge (relative of Ex-senator N. P. Tallmadge, and once governor of Wisconsin), who recently wrote thus of obsession:

"In what has been called an opening cycle, which was especially noted by the appearance of Jesus, there seemed to have been the influx of a great spiritual wave, and psychic control became common; with it many obsessions rendering one of the especial features of the commission delivered to the apostles, the 'casting out of devils.' . . .

"My introduction to Spiritualism some fifty years ago was in a merry mood, suggesting that 'we sit around the table and see what there is in this spirit business we have heard about.' Within five minutes after

---
*See "Immortality: Our Homes and Employments Hereafter" (300 pages), Banner of Light Pub. Co., Boston.

being seated, a lady of the family was entranced, and like the twinkling of an eye, our merry-making was turned into deep astonishment, awe and profound interest; thus having in our own family one of the best psychics I have known.

"Some six years later she and husband settled on a farm bordering a settlement of German Catholics, a few miles from the large St. Cloud monastery. A family of that faith had occupied the house. On the occasion of a call at their home I found that we had what I little understood at that time, an obsession on our hands—a Catholic priest the obsessing intruder. She was removed to my home, never returning to the house, soon going into an involuntary fast lasting twenty-five days, taking no nourishment except a bit of bread and butter and a half teacup of coffee each morning.

"I could exorcise the intruding priest, but he would return when I was absent. 'These go not out except by fasting and prayer.' At the end of the fast she was entirely released from the hypnotic power of this Roman Catholic priest. The most of the insane are the subjects of obsessions. These obsessing, earth-attracted spirits frequent the lake steamers, the lowest quarters of our cities, second-class hotels, gambling saloons and brothels, exciting crime and subsisting largely upon the emanations in restaurants and kitchens, abstracting the vitalizing elements from the foods, thus psychically starving their victims.

"Nearly all at least of the fraudulent mediums," continues Mr. Tallmadge, "were psychics; thrown out into promiscuous surroundings and a thought-atmosphere of fraud, without the requisite protection through which they could hold possession of their own sphere and guardian influences. Without understanding the new realm of forces opened through psychic development, we left a narrowly opened door unguarded, and whatever the predominating influences below, such was the quality above; like opening the street door of our dwellings with entire freedom for any to enter and avail themselves of a privilege or an abuse of it. Of course a dominating development of moral purpose is a strong protection; although the lady referred to possessed a most lovely, unselfish nature, with admirable poise of character, it was not sufficient with the surroundings to ward off the obsession. This abuse, lacking wisdom and understanding, has been a prominent cause of the unpopularity of Spiritualism."

Correctly speaking, Spiritualism is not "unpopular." It is the antithesis of materialism. It means immortality. All Christians rising reverently above sect, bow religiously at the shrine of Spiritualism, the foundation principle of which is God. Said Jesus, "Spirit is God," and Proclus of the Neo-Platonian period, breathed about the same thought when uplifting his eyes to the blue heavens, he reverently exclaimed, "God is Causation!"

A Professor's Obsession.

The following is a remarkable case of obsession in high life. I wish I were permitted to give the name and residence of the professor. It would carry weight.

This gentleman was noted for his good, common sense, scholarly attainments and a liberality tending toward materialism. Here is his abbridged account:

"Commencing on a Fourth of July, and continuing for two or three years, singular incidents occurred in my life—strange thoughts now and then flashed into my mind, jealousies bordering on malice would affect me. I would feel profane." He was strongly affected at one time to go into liquor-saloons. He had, withal, become nervous, and his health was gradually failing. He had become a puzzle to himself.

Sitting one evening in his study reading, his hand was forcibly seized, became spasmodic, and he felt impelled to write. Reluctantly, he complied, and after a few circular scrawls, calming down to legible words, he automatically wrote this: "I have you—have you in part now. I have tried for years to control you. I have much to say. You disliked me. You opposed my policy and kept me out of office. At heart you were my enemy. You shall pay for it. I have the advantage now. Revenge is only justice. I have followed you."

"What is your name?"

"No matter. You know me, or will."

"No, I do not recognize you. You seem excited, restless. Are you happy?"

He wrote, "Far from it. . . . Wait a moment. I am losing my power. Your will opposes me. You are afraid."

A few weeks later, "Your will keeps me away. There's an old man here. I think he was a Quaker. He says he is your father. He opposes me, yet looks kindly at me. I am losing my power. Pray for me, a poor wretched man bereft of my body and friends."

"With pleasure I will pray for you, and pray to good spirits to help you."

"Months passed and I again felt his presence strongly. I yielded."

"Well, here I am again. I have but little power. Your will is against me. I see the folly of revenge. You do well to keep me away from you. . . . Pray for me. A light—a strange light covers me. I shall now leave you forever."

From this time on the gentleman began to regain his health, his equanimity of temper and his natural spirit of cheerfulness. Since this obsessional episode he has refused—willed against any psychic controls, but is conscious of and susceptible to spiritual impressions. He is an earnest and efficient toiler in the line of educational employment.

Hold this thought in mind, O seekers after truth! O sensitives! whenever an invisible intelligence affects your health injuriously, makes flaming prophecies, assumes a great name, shows nervous irritability, hatred, or a gleam of sensual vulgarity, quit your occult sittings at once—quit and seek better, higher environments. Read books rich in science and elevated moral thoughts; search for associates of refinement, culture and religious aspirations. "Keep thou a clean heart," said the old prophet.

CHAPTER XXVII.

Written Correspondence with Demons.

They Speak for Themselves.

RECORDS of spirit writings may be found in the ancient Hebrew Scriptures and in Grecian and Roman literature.

The ten commandments were written "upon tablets of stones." David gave to Solomon the pattern of the porch and the houses, and the pattern of all that he had by the spirit. "All this," said David, "the Lord (a spirit) made me understand in writing by his hand upon me."

"There came forth the fingers of a man's hand, and the king saw the part of the hand that wrote." (Dan. 5:5.)

Writing mediumship, conscious or automatic, has been a frequent phenomenon among spiritists for half a century. With some sensitives the hand alone is used; others employ the planchette, or ouija board.

Mr. Joseph Hartman, a writer for the press, an author, a new churchman of the most liberal stamp, residing formerly in Philadelphia and later in East Pittsburg, Pa., became interested in Spiritualism through newspaper reports, and resolved to investigate it. Accordingly, sitting at a table with his children, it moved, answering questions. A planchette being used afterward, his son Lou developed writing mediumship, and later his daughter Kate began to automatically write, draw flowers and rural scenes. In 1880 a very intellectual daughter of his, Dolly, died at eighteen. Her communications from the spirit side at first were delightful, and seemingly perfectly truthful. Soon Mr. Hartman detected falsehood. Intensifying the searchlight, he proved it. The discovery quite stunned him. But these cunning demon intelligences tiding the matter over, the investigations were continued and different séances visited. At length, Mr. Hartman himself became a writing, clairvoyant, clairaudient and trance medium, with other hypnotic phases. Some of his performances under these invisible controls are almost indescribable. He was pronounced by some insane. He was not insane, but obsessed.

These demons, professing at times to be his friends, deceived him, made him ill, choked him, nearly starved him, pretended to be the Lord, almost forced him to commit suicide, made him dance, kneel down and pray and deny the truth of spiritism in a railway station. They actually tortured him, and then again they would write very intellectually through his hand. On a brief visit to him and his family, I witnessed his writing. It was rapid and with some very clever passages. But putting my hand over and above his, not touching it, their writing immediately ceased. Inquiring why, they said there was a white mist all around me and a bright aura from my hand that interfered with and destroyed their power.

The following communications speak for themselves. I believe in justice, in equality, and in hearing what treacherous, deceiving demons have to say in their own behalf.

"March, 1883.—I had held no intercourse with my spirit 'band' for six months, having become disgusted with them. But a short time prior to this date I opened correspondence with Dr. J. M. Peebles, author, lecturer, physician, etc., residing in Hammonton, N. J., with the purpose of showing him that spirits communicating with us are certainly not our friends, but as far as I could judge from experience and investigation, they were base pretenders, artful liars, and degraded devils. It was thus the following correspondence originated:

" 'The spirits with me address you the following:

HARTMAN.

" 'PITTSBURG, March 17, 1883.
" 'Dr. Peebles,

" 'DEAR SIR: At Mr. Hartman's request we address you a few lines. We are not in agreement with him as he says. We are anti-Christ, with all that is involved in that term. We are in continual combat with Mr. Hartman. We find that we can do but little to move him from the fixed position he has taken. He understands us too well, and knows the use we sustain relating to his life. . . . It is our special business to tempt and try him in every possible way, and lead him into what is evil and false; and we have been doing so for years, but not consciously to him until more than a year ago, when we commenced controlling him, so that we found him to be a very excellent writing medium. Then we began a series of plans and plots to mislead him through his affections for and confidence in his spirit daughter, Miss Dolly. We succeeded in making him believe he was in communication with her, and at such times he and we were very good friends; but we were deceiving him then in a terrible manner; but it is our business to do that.

Written Correspondence with Demons. 281

" 'This delightful state to him lasted until we attempted too much in her name, and tried to fool him by saying that his daughter Mary vas very ill, and that he should go home at once. Next morning, for the sake of correcting that blunder, we made another more fatal than the first, for we now said that Dolly had not been there on the previous evening, and that he must have been a false spirit, as he had discovered; and now Dolly was present to expose the deception, vindicate herself and claim confidence. . . .

" 'He was a monopolist in the message business, and we had our fun and delight for several weeks in fooling him; answering for any name he desired to hold intercourse with. But he often suspected and detected us in lying; but we could always blame it on some other fellows, and promised to keep them off next time. That is our great advantage over mortals, and most people will accept our explanation; but he was always doubting our identity. . . .

" 'Thus by degrees he discovered our true character, which we had to confess, and arrived at a better understanding with him. We then commenced tormenting him like hell; and having his open ear through which we had been speaking to him, we now bent all our force on that organ, and constantly talked to him night and day, never letting him sleep a moment. Then we persuaded him that he must live abstemiously on account of his health, and we directed him in eating and almost starved him.

" 'Thus we weakened him and brought him under control, and made him do whatever we commanded, until we made him act like crazy. We were mad as hell at him for resisting us; and now that we had him in our power, we did put him through the roughest, funniest, crookedest, most infernal experience he ever had. At last, to cap the climax, we assumed to be God, and in his name commanded him; and he obeyed, contrary to his judgment and inclinations; and thus we treated him for three weeks, in which time he did not sleep a wink. Then by degrees he rallied under some force superior to ours, which he called the Lord, who in fact we supposed it was, or we should have taken him out of the body. In fact, however, we cannot do that; but in our zeal we thought we could and he thought we would; for he supposed that we were Deity operating in him; and in this condition we held him bound so that he could not move in the least without our permission, until he could endure the torture no longer. Then he would break away from us; and the first time he did so, we were enraged to such a degree that we who had been personating God, now in our hot anger swore at him in the name of God in such a dreadful way that he at once discovered our true nature, and rejoiced to get out of our hands.

" 'But we could not release him, and still talked to him, trying to soothe him; and by degrees, by our arts, we again got him into his former state, under control, and again tortured him for hours; when he broke again, and thus alternately many times until he recovered, and we lost his open ear and the use of his hand both. Then only by influx or dictation could we reach him, and that power by degrees partially wore away, but through which we have some hold on him yet.

" 'We used to operate on him so as to shake his hand after he had recovered; but he was afraid to write until we persuaded him good spirits would now come to him. Then he timidly tried us once more, and to his disgust we turned up again declaring our hostility and determination to lead him to hell. But we cannot scare him, and he is not afraid of us "devils," as he calls us, and which in fact we are; but we do not like the name, and out of respect for our preferences he calls us Jones, Brown or Smith, providing we behave decently and use no bad language.

" 'At last we know each other pretty well. He knows our purpose and fights us with Scripture and new-church arguments, and we fight with materialism, naturalism and Ingersollism. We are damned spirits. . . .

" 'All this "message" business is fabricated by associated evil spirits who read the minds of a "circle," as you would read a book, and then pretend to be their friends. We warn you against the sentiments of Mr. Hartman's first letter. He is all wrong as you see. We know all about it, if we are evil spirits; and we have no fear of God or anything else, and hate the name of Jesus. God is not anything—all moonshine. Mr. Hartman has limited us to this sheet; but he never before has allowed us to write as we do to you; but today he has granted us a privilege, which is now ended.

" ' Yours respectfully,
" 'JAMES MONROE,
and several other American citizens, all in hell for having lived wicked lives while on earth.'

"To our letter sent with the above, Dr. Peebles replied under date of March 17. We insert only the last paragraph of his letter.

" 'I think quite seriously of answering, or replying to this "band" of spirits that have written to me through your hand. What do you think of it? Most truly thine.
" ' J. M. PEEBLES.'

"Having perused the letter, my 'Twelve' expressed a wish to address another letter to him, which I granted, and is given as follows:

"'PITTSBURG, March 31, 1883.

"'DEAR BROTHER PEEBLES: We are delighted with another opportunity offered by Mr. H. to briefly address you again. We see he has some reserve in his mind in respect to publishing our message. He wants no publicity in these matters. He is at present very reserved. Formerly while he thought it was all right and emanated from good spirits or friends, he was very bold and outspoken about it; but our severe treatment of him has made him averse to any notoriety.

"'We have revealed to him our true nature as he has stated it, namely, that we are his evil-attending spirits, and it is our office by appointment by some overruling power, to tempt, try and torment him, and finally bring him into our society if we can do it. He recognizes our office and the use it is in regenerating man, by compelling him to resist our machinations as sins or evils of life and falsities of faith. We own that this is our delight; but it does not seem to be his way of thinking, and we have debated the case with him time and time again, trying to persuade him to accept our views, and deny Jesus, Christ, God and everything belonging to such preposterous belief. But he is exceedingly stubborn in his way of thinking, and resists us steadily. . . .

"'He is almost invulnerable to our influences, and is so sensitive to our impresisons that he at once recognizes our work, and attributes it to us directly, and does not impute it to himself, as if it were his own thoughts, but charges them to us, and we have to confess, for he has thoroughly found us out, and cannot be imposed on to any great extent.

"'We thank you for your expression of pleasure or interest in our letter. We hope you and Mr. H. may find new pleasure in future acquaintance, personal or by writing.

"'He gives us only this sheet, so you see he is our master now; but when he crosses into our territory, we shall see if we cannot turn the tables on him. Now he smiles very serenely at that, and we wonder at his indifference to our threats. We try all sorts of ways to scare him, and he only laughs at us, and then we get mad.

"' Ever your friends,
"'ONLY ALICE.'

"Dr. Peebles' Letter to These Profane Evil Spirits.

"'To the Spirit Band influencing Mr. Hartman.
"' HAMMONTON, N. J., April 7, 1883.

"'BROTHERS: Through the kindness of Mr. Hartman, whom I have never had the pleasure of meeting, I am in receipt of two letters from you, written from the spirit side of life through his hand.

"'You perceive that I commence by calling you brothers; for however, we may differ in our theories, or whatever our moral conditions, we are the offspring of God, and therefore brothers. Aratus, the Greek poet, Cleanthus, the stoic philosopher, as well as Paul, the Christian Apostle, taught, "We are the offspring of God," the infinite consciousness and life of the universe, and being the offspring of God, being his children, being one great brotherhood, whether in the mortal or immortal sphere of existence, does it not seem reasonable that we should love and thank God,—help and do good to one another so far as we reasonably can?

" 'And yet you admit in your first letter that you began a "series of plans and plots" too "fool" Mr. Hartman. You further confess that it is your "special business to try, tempt and lead him into what is false."

" 'After he detected you in personating others, convicted you of falsehood, and, resisting your influences, refused to be controlled by you, you admit that you were his "bitter enemies;" and, to further use your own language, "commenced tormenting him like hell."

" 'While disliking to have Mr. Hartman call you "devils," you call yourselves "damned spirits," and say you are in hell for "having lived wicked lives on earth." So far all is clear, for your admissions and your conduct are in perfect accord. You have no secrets.

" 'And now permit me to kindly ask, if you propose to always remain in "hell"—Hades—that lower stratum of spirit existence, to which Jesus descended when he went and "preached to spirits in prison?" True, you may have your "fun" at times, just as poor drunken sots in our world have their seasons of frolic and fun, in dirty, smoky, filthy, lager beer saloons. But to me their fun is nonsense, and their saloon resorts earthly hells. All men at times must have aspirations for something better, higher, and more heavenly. And this no doubt is in a measure your experience. I mean to say that you have seasons of reflection, of meditation, and of aspiration for the good, the true, and the beautiful. You must have them, for you are made—evolved if that be preferable —in the image of God.

"'And here I have forgot that you say "there is no God, it's all moonshine and we hate the name of Jesus."

Your declaration that there is no God is a wild assertion and nothing more. Better and almost infinitely wiser personages than you, seers, sages, philosophers, angels, —affirm that there is a God, both personal and impersonal, and referring to consciousness, intuition, revelation and purpose in nature, they demonstrate it. Philosophers base the personality of God, not upon shape, avoirdupois or locality, but upon intelligence, will, and purpose. And then why should you "hate Jesus?" Did he ever injure you? I confess you astonish me! What would you think if I should tell you that I hated the rose that yielded me its fragrance, that I hated the sun that caused the flowers to bloom, and the fields to wave with their golden harvest? And yet Christ is the spiritual sun, "The Way, the Truth, the Life," and a Saviour!

" 'Poor, frail human beings need a Saviour. A man or a spirit might just as well attempt to lift himself up by his own ears, as to expect to save —perfect—himself. We all need helps, and helpers are saviours. It is only through divine help, divine love and grace from the invisible, with effort on our part, that we conquer.

" 'And right here let me impress upon your minds that having survived the death of your bodies, you can have but little doubt of immortality, but little doubt that you will exist through eternity—a never-ending eternity! And where, and with whom do you propose to so exist? In the brawling hells with plotting, selfish demons, or in the higher heavens with seers and sages, saints and martyrs, prophets and apostles, and glorified hosts of angels, the leader of which may be denominated, "The Lord of Glory."

" 'Oh! I beg of you as the children of a loving Father in heaven, I beg of you as brothers of a common human ity—as conscious, thinking, influencing spirits, to look upward prayerfully, to look to seers and sages, to Confucius, Plato, Gautama Buddha, and the Christ who said "Come unto Me," look up to the compassionate Jesus Christ who loves you, as he loved and tenderly prayed upon the cross for those who hated, mocked and murdered him. And further, I beg of you in the name of our fraternal brotherhood,—our visible and invisible humanity, to no longer deceive, falsify and tempt others to do wrong, but strive to do right, cherishing no hate, concocting no scheming, selfish plans, and speaking no untruths. What you sow, that sooner or later you must reap, this is justice. Labor then and struggle to reach your highest ideal of perfection. Personally I know by checkered earthly experiences of over eighty years that only in being right and doing right—being good and doing good, for the love of good, can I be happy."

" 'Permit me to ask, Do you love flowers and music? Do you love your kind, tender and self-sacrificing mothers, who so lovingly carried you in your earthly infancy upon their maternal bosoms? You certainly have not forgotten them. Do you see them in your present condition, and do you now enjoy their society? Do you love little children, so sweet and innocent, and do you have their society in your present sphere of existence? If not, why not? Just think it over seriously, and answer for yourselves.

" 'I write, or reply to you in the kindest spirit, for I feel kindly toward all moral intelligences, whether in this or in the spirit world; for the most perverse and wicked have some good emotions, and the wisest and best are not absolutely perfect.

" 'Before closing, I will further say that *I* most sincerely believe in God, in disciplinary punishment for sin, in the necessity of repentance, the beauty of faith, and in salvation through Christ (the Christ-spirit of purity, love and truth) and the efficacy of prayer. And before shutting my eyes in sleep tonight I shall pray for you, aspiration is prayer, good thoughts are prayers. Spirits in Hades—the lower spirit ones—have frequently come to me through intermediaries and pleaded of me, imperfect as I am, to pray for them.

" 'And now, good-night, and may God the loving Father of us all and His holy angels enlighten and bless you. Truly thine,

" 'J. M. PEEBLES.

" 'P. S. By Mr. Hartman's permission I should be glad to have you reply to this, and I give you the privilege of asking me such questions as you feel inclined.

" 'J. M. P.'

" 'PITTSBURG, April 8, 1883.

" 'DEAR DR. PEEBLES: You are a very kind-hearted gentleman to take the trouble to write us so kind and instructive a letter. We are under many obligations to Mr. Hartman for permitting us to write through him, and now we find a friend in you who sympathizes with us on account of our lost condition. We accept your kind attentions with many thanks; while our true nature is such, that if you were within our sphere or influence we would do you all the injury in our power.

" 'We have no respect for your authorities whom you quote "that we are all the offspring of God." No, sir! We are not offspring of God. We deny God, as we said before. We are not one brotherhood, for we are of different natures, from different parents, and occupy different spheres here, as men do different planets. Who made all the spheres and different men? Nature. Who ever saw God? No, sir, we are not sons of God. Where is perdition? Who made perdition? Who made Judas? And why did Jesus call him the son of perdition, although he was one of his chosen disciples? Jesus recognized two states, two classes of men and spirits, demons and angels. Who made the two classes, God, man or the devil? It is not important that you answer that query, but please recognize the fact as preached by Jesus, the very name of whom we hate. Why?—Because his followers are a set of fools and idiots, worshiping him as if he could save them. Save them from what—from whom? Why, bless your soul, doctor, we are saved just as much as we desire to be saved.

" 'You suggest "reform," "cease from tormenting." Why, that is our delight, and we should "die" if we had no delight; if there were nobody to torment. What would you be if you attempted to change your hereditary and acquired nature? Can you do it? We are what we are, and we can be no different, nor can anybody else. It is our genius to be just as we are. How can we be different when we have no inclination to be anything else?

" 'Our delight is to fool and tempt and try all who are under our influence. If you do not know that spirits are constantly with you, doing the same thing, then you have lived long to little purpose. If you suppose that you are not tempted and fooled every day of your life, then your wisdom is that of a jackass. Why, damn your conceited —— Do you know anything of this life at all?

" 'Thank you. We are satisfied with our condition; we do as we damn please, and are under no obligation to

God or any other man. We are our own masters, not slaves to superstition, creeds or theology. No! no! none of that, doctor. Plotting and planning to fool, and deceive, and mislead, is our business. We enjoy it. Mr. Hartman has asked us, "Who made it our business, who appointed us to such unholy work?" We are self-appointed, self-directed, and we reap the delights of our work by seeing our victims suffer torments and torture, as we did when we had Mr. Hartman under full control, and in a state of despondency and desperation, so that he expected to land in hell. This we persuaded him to believe, because he believed in God, angels and other such nonsense. He was our subject and slave. We commanded and he obeyed. Then we were in *our delights*. His torments were the best fun we ever had.

" 'But we are now under his control in a measure. At least he does not obey us, and we do in part obey him, and we cannot help it, when he commands. He understands our relations, and has partly stated them in the letter written Saturday night (the author's letter written to the Doctor).

" 'We are his bitter enemies, and we cannot help it. We want him to come and live with us, but he says he hopes he may never find the way to our sphere. You see, he despises us. He calls us "devils," "dogs" and "dirty beasts," because he thinks our lives are such. Nor do we deny it. Our lives are just of that sort. It is true he pities and commiserates our state, but it does no good. He, nor you, nor any mortal, nor immortal, can change our depraved disposition. We elected ourselves to this life when in the world, and when we came here, we simply came into the enjoyment of our interior wishes and hopes. Nor would we change if we could. Besides, we have been adjudged by our own desires, inclinations and determinations.

" ' "Do we always expect," you ask, "to live in hell?" Why not? How are we to get away from what we have loved all our life? Hell is our delight, and the more we can bring here, the more we are delighted; for then we enslave some of our fellows, and can raise mobs, create uproars, and put down those who rule over us, and punish them for having treated us with severity for disobedience. We are always having fights, mobs, uproars and insurrections among us, and this is our delight. Have you ever seen hell on earth? Do you not see that some men delight in such things? Those are the "boys" who naturally come here without much coaxing.

" 'As to remorse, regrets and aspirations for higher things, they are all "bosh" on this side. We only regret that we cannot do more mischief, fool more people and torture them as we did Mr. H. As to heaven, that is rather far off. Where? What ? We see in Mr. H.'s mind many things of imagination respecting heaven. Those are the things we try to destroy and falsify. But they are impregnable. He is the biggest fool we ever had under our jurisdiction. We have suggested worldly pleasures to him, but he gets awfully provoked, and threatens to deprive us of this pleasure of writing, and using his senses to perceive things in this world, as we see through his eyes, and now see each word as it is written. So you see when we are not in rapport with him, we cannot see anything in the material world, and it hurts us if he shuts his eyes, and does not permit us to see.

" 'You think we may have a love for "the beautiful and true?" For beautiful women we have a most ardent love; but it is entirely animal; on earth we sought to seduce and in truth, we now strive to pervert, whenever we can; and that is partly our office with Mr. Hartman, and the result is, he fortifies himself with more truths, and beats us every time. The upshot is, that we are helping him in our perverted way to strengthen himself in his truths, and now he has no fears of us. And that unexpected result arises from our mistakes.

"'Our declaration that there is no God is worth just as much as yours, and a thousand others that there is. Are we not over here where you think God is? Yet we have never seen Him, though we talk about God just as people on earth do; and if you believe He is personal, where is He? Who is He? You say He is the Spiritual Sun of this world—the great *positive mind*. Who told you that? Some spirit who was reading your mind, and making you believe he was an angel. Be careful that you be not fooled by the "good spirits" who come to you pretending to be angels. Mr. H. knows how that is himself.

"'"Jesus never hurts us," you say. We do not know. But why should men make fools of themselves worshiping Him who was a man? Mr. H. says He is the *Divine-Human Man*. But we do not agree on that point.

"'If you love roses, flowers, children and other objects which contribute to your pleasure, we can only answer that we are perversions and hate all those things, even children, and there are none with us. They are somewhere else. Mr. H.'s thoughts are much like your words, and we have many times discussed these subjects, until he has about given us over to our perverted lusts and hatreds.

"'We suppose we had mothers on earth, but we do

not remember them. We have none here. Our society is composed of similarities, and we have our delights entirely different from what you think. Excrementitious substances are more delightful to us than all your roses, flowers and perfumes. It is true when in rapport with those whose interior senses are open, and we can come into their natural senses and the things in their natural memory, we can in some small degree enter into the same pleasures or delights that our mediums do. But we are more at home in our own spheres of delight, and you would be astonished to know in what our delights consist. We are adulterers, fornicators and all that sort. We still have our wives; we are all free-lovers, and roam where we please, and suffer for it sometimes, too. But we cannot help it. Mr. H. abominates us for our evil lives, and would send us into our darkened caves if he could do it. But he thinks there is a supreme Power on this side who partly governs us and regulates our relations with men on earth. So that he submits like a little gentleman, and discusses matters in a rational, philosophical manner. His book of experiences partly prepared, as he has informed, you, will show that we are not so wretched and miserable after all, and that we have planned and perpetrated many jokes, generally at his expense.

" 'You speak of man and spirits needing a Saviour, and Jesus Christ you consider as "a Saviour of mankind." Yet He did not save Judas; He did not save innumerable hosts of damned spirits. There is a great deal of theology on that subject—creeds—and so forth. Surely we are not saved from our life of lusts and love of torturing and tormenting others. Spiritists have much to say relating to "undeveloped," "degraded" spirits, as those who come in a fooling, deceiving way. We tell you all spirits are not of equal powers. Some have more magical ability than others, and are more artful in their methods than we are, and can perform more tricks; and thus the world is led blindfolded into the pit.

" 'That is our business, however; and we are getting a strong hold on the mercenary multitudes, and that encourages us. Very few combat us as Mr. H. does. Spiritists are generally easily persuaded by whatever is said from this side, little dreaming of our real character. But it is our business to fool them and tell them interesting things, especially respecting affinities, generative intercourse, whenever we can get a "circle" that will stand it. But Mr. H. will have none of that. He stops us whenever we approach certain genital topics, while on others, rational, intellectual, theological or moral, he gives us a broad field and wide range. He is peculiarly sensitive on some subjects.

" 'You spoke of "eternity" as if we might have any fears of that. Our time is present. The past is not counted. We have no future. It is all now. And time present is when we act and live. When in rapport with Mr. H., we can see something terrible in his mind relating to eternity. But in our own conditions, separate and apart from his atmosphere and thoughts, there is absolutely nothing thought of it.

" 'Your appeal to us to cease our course on this side is worth just as much as if you would appeal to a river to change its course, and run back to its head-waters. Our course is fixed, and certain and unchangeable. There is no deviation of purpose or delights. Suppose all evil spirits were changed by omnipotence into angels, how could man be regenerated without some opposite force of evil? You must get more into the interiors of man and creation before you can comprehend the use of contending and opposing forces. While we see your blindness and kindness, we can only thank you for your tender love for us; but it is contrary to our nature to hope or pray for your or our own happiness, as there is no Being to whom we could look to answer our supplications. We do not pray. We have no worship. We are naturalists, or materialists, of the Ingersoll type of men. He is doing good work for our cause. He will be a "boss" devil among us when he comes over. We will give him a grand ovation when he reaches our side of the river and show him beauties that he never dreamed of; and we will laugh together at the mistakes of Moses, and at his own much worse than those of Moses. Bully Bob!

" You and Mr. H. are both big fools for denying yourselves such pleasures as your natural inclinations might dictate. We would persuade all men to do so. There are some very virtuous (?) spirits nowadays, that pretend to be angels of light, whatever that may signify in Mr. H.'s mind. (You see we construct our writing from words in his memory.)

" ' "Do we love music?" At home, in perdition, we have none. We are not affected by music only when with our medium. A few evenings ago he gave us some enjoyment at a concert of stringed instruments and metallic horns, when we had a pleasant discussion respecting the correspondence of the different instruments.

" 'We hate children, except females well grown up, and we love them from lust. Why cannot you understand the states of the damned? We are only lusts personified. We enjoy them.

" 'If you suppose we ever "have some good emotions," and if you mean by that what we see in the medium's mind, and which we have often seen manifested in him, we have only to say that he is a soft, chicken-hearted old fool, whenever he gives up to any such nonsense. We don't like baby feelings. We like hard, harsh, heroic pluck and not tom-foolery in a man. Our women, however, have emotions like vixens, and fight like she-devils that they are.

"'This, good friend, is all darned nonsense. You see, we are just fooling Mr. H. and you. Do you suppose that we are going to tell you any of our secrets and mysteries? Now, Mr. H. smiles, he knows us so well; and he may add a P. S. probably, saying it is all true. But we will save him the trouble, and admit that our statements are as near correct as we can make them through a medium that we hate, and who only permits us to write this letter for your accommodation. We offended him last night, and he cut us off instantly, and we did not know if he would ever let us write again; but the receipt of your letter today changed his mind.

"'When you say spirits have asked you to pray for them, you ought to know that they were appealing to your pious belief and practice, and were thus striving to win your favor. If you could just then have seen their faces, you would have seen some good acting. Why, we told Mr. H. how to pray to the Lord, and soon after swore at him as only angered devils can swear, and that revealed to him our true natures.

"'We thank you a hundred times for your good wishes, but they do us no good. We will ask only one question. When you die, where do you expect to land? If you come to our city, you might find business in your profession as a lecturer, teaching us how to get out of hell. Very truly yours, ignoramus.'

"The above was forwarded by next mail. And the next séance I had, I said I thought they should apologize to the kind gentleman on account of their unbecoming language. They replied that they were only waiting for an opportunity to do so, and hoped I would permit them when 'we' got home. The following, therefore, automatically through my hand is the 'amende honorabale.'—HARTMAN.

"The Apology.

"'PITTSBURG, April 15, 1883.

"'DEAR BROTHER PEEBLES: Several days ago we asked Mr. Hartman to give us a chance to apologize to you for our ungentlemanly and un-Christian language, used in our answer to your very kind letter. We have asked him what we ought to say. He replied, "that we should say nothing but what is true and sincere." At first we thought we could not say anything, as we are such liars and perversions of all that is good, true and sincere. . . .

"'He wished us to let you know our true character without reserve. So we did; but we now see that we did great violence to your good intentions, and now we sincerely repent that offense, and earnestly pray you to forgive our malicious words. Nay, more, we will ask you to continue praying for us; for since we know that you and Mr. H. pray for us, we begin to hope that some good may come to us yet; for although we are very bad, we know that our presence with him is doing us some good, for he generally speaks kindly to us, although we treat him in a very wicked way; and we often learn from him things which we never knew, even matters relating to our own world, in which he is deeply interested, and

Written Correspondence with Demons. 299

of which he has made a patient study in the writings of Swedenborg and other seers; and as we are always present with him, we also read through his eyes, as we cannot through any other man's eyes. So we travel with him and see the objects in the world, cities, country, mountains, streams and all the beautiful objects, animate and inanimate, and still our perverse natures lead us to torment, tempt, and curse him in a very capricious manner; and yet he endures it, forgives us, and prays that God in his mercy may lessen our burdens and torments, so far as it is possible with divine order.

"'This hurts us, and arouses our worst states. But there are hours when it does us vast good, and we lament our hard lot, especially when we see his aspirations to reach heaven and angelic society; for all this we clearly see and try to prevent by all our arts, for we want his company in our society. But he repudiates our ways, inclinations, and purposes, and prays God to deliver him from our influences, if in accordance with his mercy and order. . . .

"'If these higher intelligences pass through such states or ordeals of purification, then we may. It now seems to us, that we may hope for some better conditions later. But in fact we have despaired of ever reaching any much better state, unless the Lord gives us a new will and some better understanding, or love of what is good and true.

"'Now, Doctor, in the name of God, continue supplicating the throne of the Most High in our behalf. We are very wicked; this we frankly confess. Our delights have been to do evil; and being associated with Mr. H., as evil spirits are to some extent with all men, we could do no otherwise than our evil propensities inclined us;

hence we deceived, fooled, lied, persuaded in the name of God, but now we are not happy; and he seems to be measurably beyond our influence, and we are somewhat under his, for good we may now hope.

" 'Forgive us for wishing you harm. We did not relish at that time your lecture or appeal to us. We were provoked and wrote from our worst states. We have some better moods, as Mr. H. knows, for we often spend pleasant hours in conversation; though he generally gets disgusted with our frivolous, trifling, fooling, childish or devilish ways. May God bless you for your good wishes; may you continue your good work in propagating the gospel of truth and righteousness, and at last receive the just reward of those who serve God, which we did not in a right way when on earth. Good-by. We will sign no name, as we have none. All names are false, signed this way.' "

These demon entities wrote after their apology some bitter things, closing with these words, "We are irretrievably lost and damned."

The general drift of the foregoing letters affords a clear presentation of the mischief, the diabolical motives characterizing souls temporarily lost in the dark regions of moral obliquity. And further, they most effectually overthrow the much-lauded writings of some spiritists who say that "knowledge is the world's saviour." Knowledge does not save these obsessing spirits. They were far from being ignorant. From their perverse plane they reasoned well. They were not cowards. They were decidedly intelligent. While morally low and cunning, they were intellectually brilliant, close-observing, and knowing. "Knowledge," then, is not "the world's saviour."

Intellectual men and spirits are the most dangerous unless that intellect, that knowledge, is governed by a high moral purpose and guided by wisdom. Unprincipled forgers are good penmen; bank-embezzlers are expert accountants; train-robbers are skilful mechanics; that learned scientist and linguist, Roloff, murdered his wife and child, and sank them in Cayuga Lake, near Ithaca, N. Y. Dr. Webster, professor of chemistry and the sciences in Harvard University, owing Dr. Parkman a debt which he could not liquidate, murdered him and employed his chemical knowledge in disintegrating and destroying the body with destructive acids, to conceal his guilt. Did knowledge of books or science and warfare save British and Boers from recently crimsoning with blood a hundred battlefields? The greater the intellectual knowledge, the deeper the plot may be, the blacker the crime. Hartman's obsessing spirits were intelligent and wicked, relishing and rollicking in their wickedness. And yet, their apology to me shows that they were not beyond what Tennyson terms the "larger hope."

These demon entities, haunting, obsessing Hartman, and writing themselves as "irretrievably lost and damned," were neither. They were not totally depraved. Down deep under inherited débris and encroaching environments there glittered a spark of the divine,—the inbreathed incarnation of God, the divine impress,—that uplift of Divinity. God's love is eternal. These poor, earth-chained spirits, pronouncing themselves in their despair, "devils," are our brothers,—and sons of God, falling where we stumbled. They must—they will be rescued. The promise was that the Christ should see of the "travail of his soul"—the Christ that preached to the spirits in prison,—"and be satisfied."

CHAPTER XXVIII.

Internal Obsessions as Explained by a Discarnate Spirit — Further Experiences.

DOES not water pervade the sponge, and the finer physical substances permeate the coarser? Do not insects wriggle and work their way into and under the bark of proudest oaks and elms? Do not worms pierce, reach into and feed upon the pulp of pear and plum? Is not the air we breathe filled with invisible ions, atoms, and molecular forms and various germs?

Reasoning from the physical and visible, to the unseen and impalpable, and pondering upon obsessions in their various forms, external, internal and infernal, I wrote to Dr. G. Lester Lane's circle of controlling intelligences asking them to inform me what they meant by their repeated phrase, "internal obsessions?"

Here follows their answer, omitting only what they said complimentary of myself and work for human enlightenment:

"We now proceed to reply to your inquiry from a truth-center on our plane of existence. You say in your letter to us, 'When a spirit clothed in its soul-body enters (if it does) into a living, fleshly human body, it compels that spirit-entity to vacate it for the time being. This is called obsession, but is it not rather straight-out possession?'

"Certainly, it is, my brother. Obsessions and possessions, you will remember, are very unlike. The one generally exists without the other. You will also consider that we see forms that you cannot see—that what you call solids are not solids to us. They are at most but mist-shadows, and we are continually seeing what you denominate matter passing into matter, as the hand into the glove, and matter passing through matter, as light through panes of glass. We dwell in another, in a higher and more ethereal state of existence than you, and can descend to you under proper conditions, but you cannot ascend to us in your physical vestures.

"And as you see millions upon millions of sands, leaves of grass, and leaves on forest trees, so we see what you cannot see; we see unnumbered—absolutely unnumbered quintillions of the most delicate substances, refined ethers, atoms, atomic entities, and atomic forms, afire with life, and many of them are vibrant with conscious life,—vibrant with the forces and principles of life. And these, more or less of these, some of which have lived in human forms, enter into human organisms. This we call internal obsession. Some of these undeveloped entities enter through ignorance, others as animated, floating atoms, and others as etheric personalities clinging in thought to their former earthly environments. An atomic entity, or a spirit once dwelling in a human body as man, undeveloped, depraved and in no wise spiritualized, and attracted to magnetic, unguarded persons, fastens to and seeks solace in the aural atmosphere, in the company, or in the brain, and there remains unless those on the higher planes of life should insist that it rise to a higher, superior state of life, and not crave and selfishly cling vampire-like to the form of a human being.

"Psychically clinging to an individual for a time, this spirit, either ignorant or malicious, becomes magnetically and sympathetically so much a part of his or her obsessed life that whatever the person does or thinks, this spirit entity enters still further into relationship with the party, so that ere long it finds itself almost a real part and factor of the person's life, with many associations to stimulate it to continue in mortal flesh. Later this familiar or obsessing spirit finds itself in touch with the nerve centers of the brain, still retaining its personality to a certain extent, and when augmented by other entities, they gradually come into full power, swaying the person's mind till it becomes a center for their work, and sometimes for demoniac work and for insanity. At this stage individuality is impinged upon, if not invalidated, and subjected to a condition so dark that outside guardian influences fail to release the conscious imprisoned spirit. This depends upon the will—the stubborn wills of the obsessing demons. Angels even, are not infinite in power. The most exalted spirits and circles of spirits are neither omniscient nor almighty in power. Jesus, the Christ, could "do no mighty works" on certain occasions. The time had not come.

"If these atomic entities, or rather, if these positive, undeveloped human spirits known as mortals, were evil-inclined, if they were gross and selfish, and immoral in their earth-life, they naturally if not necessarily produce a radical change in a person's disposition and tendencies, inducing and tempting them to drink to gratify their lowest passions and most vicious propensities. If personalized and materialized, they produce criminal acts. Neither policemen nor legislatures of earth life have but the faintest conception of the causes of the majority of the terrible crimes that blacken your world of flesh.

"Some of these atomic forms—forms known by dif-

Further Experiences. 305

ferent names in different spheres—that we see and sense, clothed from within and enlivened by the divine spark of life, are entities and real verities, which, if they were ever temporarily vestured with either a physical or a spiritual body, have deteriorated or retrograded externally back to atoms of life,—to mere, floating, restless entities. Spirit life and spirit forms are graded something as is matter and material forms in your darker world of the sense perceptions.

"It is a part of our work in this higher life to remove these entities from those infested by them. These entities coming in contact with certain elements, chemicals and low spiritual environments, manipulate, take in, and impact enough of ethereal substances to make themselves seen by clairvoyant visionists. Our mediumistic instrument, and his marital companion often see these haunting, obsessing personalities as in mortal life, thereby convincing those gifted with clairvoyant sight of the character of these internal spirit entities that we are dealing with and removing.

"When we have removed these offending spirits, we see that they are removed to spirit hospitals, or reformatories, and placed in the hands of experienced physicians and care-taking nurses for spiritual development. These, when rescued, educated and redeemed, often return to assist in the deliverance and moral uplifting of other unfortunates. Often when these become fitted they are placed as protecting guardians about sensitives.

"Owing to the fact that our medial instrument is at the present time (owing to nervo-exhaustion), out of the closest touch with us, we are quite unable to do full justice to our thoughts and their proper expressions, hence we ask for due consideration and charity."

Personal Experiences in the East—Guardian Spirits.

During one of my journeys in Oriental lands, I stopped at Madura to visit a Parsee physician with whom I had long corresponded. And while conversing upon the bubonic plague, Hindu characteristics and occultism, he incidentally mentioned mesmerism and pitri-obsessions. This opened the way for a free discussion of the subject, and resulted in a somewhat prolonged stay to engage in "casting out demons." The news of my psychic powers spread from Brahmins down through other castes to the Pariahs.*

My first subject was a Brahmin woman, married, but living in the parental home. The father, a wealthy Brahmin, came for me in his carriage. Comfortably seated in a queer-shaped seat on the second floor of this quaintly constructed building, and indulging in some conversation through my interpreter. I called for the woman "vexed with an evil spirit" to be brought into the room. At first she seemed stupid, stolid, and absolutely indifferent. Speaking to her, she made no reply; but soon showed an uneasy feeling. A few minutes later she became quite spasmodic, the eyes wildly gazing about the room.

At this crisis, conscious of a down-pouring of invisible forces, I called for a dish of pure water. When brought, I dipped my hands into it several times, and then began sprinkling the floor, while marching around her, audibly repeating the words, "*All power is from God—all power is from God, through Christ, through angels and ministering spirits.*" Then stepping back several feet in front of her, I said in a commanding tone, "*Look at me!*"

---
*See "Three Journeys Around the World: Life and Magic in India," (470 pages, illustrated), Banner of Light Pub. Co., Boston.

Further Experiences. 307

Refraining for a few moments, the father said, "Obey the Doctor. Look at him."

She now looked at me with a sort of a cold, sardonic stare. Personally, in the meantime, I felt as though I weighed a ton. The spirit was upon me. My eyes determinedly, incisively fixed upon her, I stepped to her quickly, placing one hand upon her forehead, and clapping the other upon the back of her neck, I breathed upon her top brain. In a moment or so she began to tremble, then to shake spasmodically, violently then uttering a dolorous groan, she fell upon the floor. The father, frightened, lifted her partly up.

I continued to keep my left hand upon her head, while the right hand was extended backward and the palm upward. Soon her nervous spasms ceased, and opening her eyes, she sprang into her father's arms. It was a joyful hand and heart clasping. The daughter was herself again.

Invoking my invisible helpers to throw a protecting power about her, and to remove the obsessing, intruding spirit to some imprisoning reformatory to be touched by the purifying saving fires of the higher life, I prayed that he might be instructed, enlightened and saved, to become in turn a helper to those similarly afflicted. Often the reformed inebriate makes the most successful temperance advocate, of which John B. Gough was a striking example.

Many were brought to me during the coming weeks to be demagnetized, dispossessed and relieved. Whether in far-away India or in this country, I seldom fail of removing the intruding demon spirit. In fact, I may say never, if I can have the proper conditions and social environments. Nearly every one that I have dispossessed and cured, desire their names to be kept from the public. This is right.

No two cases, owing to organization and temperament, can be treated exactly alike. In certain cases I prelude the deliverance by magnetized remedies. The physical system requires cleansing and invigorating. It is recorded that in New Testament times "some went out only by fasting and prayer."

Symptoms of Obsessing Influences.

*"Usually the first symptoms of obsession are weariness, physical and mental nervousness, sleeplessness, a feeling of being burdened by some invisible weight, making the light duties of life seem impossible. All of life's prospects begin to look more and more gloomy. There is an impelling haste in what the nervous sufferer says, —and a marked sensitiveness, ultimating in great irritability.

"Often the atmosphere appears dark and dense, rendering it oppressive to breathe. Common objects sometimes appear to vibrate, causing discordant thoughts. The activity of the will, memory, reason and purpose perceptibly commence to fail in the ratio that this foreign external influence gains ascendency.

"There exists a state of fear, distress, jealousy, suspicion, wherewith the least discordant word or stern look will cause weeping, or resentment and anger. Connected with this, there is a weakening of the vitality, and fre-

---

*These symptoms and experiences are from the notes of a most estimable and intelligent lady graduate, Chicago, Mrs. H——, the husband of whom is a prominent business man in the city, and a member of the Board of Trade.

quently an abnormal strengthening of the passional nature.

"All the preceding symptoms may exist independent of any organic or functional disease. The most expert, old-school physician can detect no bodily disease, and their most robust treatment is absolutely useless.

"In the more advanced stages, those obsessed sufferers are subject to impressions to do things contrary to their reason, strange temptations, threatening voices, disturbing touches and burning desires to do the most extravagant things, using profane and obscene words. Not infrequently these obsessing entities induce physical diseases, these being caused by mental, chemical and vital inharmonies."

CHAPTER XXIX.

An Obsessing Spirit Forced Away from His Victim.

AGNES PERRY furnishes a thrilling account of the forcing away of an attaching demon, in the *Light of Truth*, of March 28, 1904. Here follows the abbreviated account:

"This estimable, yet obsessed, woman residing in Chicago was rather advanced in years, refined, of more than ordinary intelligence, rather negative in temperament and deeply interested in reading along lines of advanced thought. She was clairvoyant and clairaudient to a considerable degree. Her mediumistic unfoldment came in her own house, and her gifts were exercised only in private, and her magnetic influencing band was not strong enough to ward off these persistent, intrusive and demon designing spirits.

"When bathing or dressing in her apartments they would approach and laugh in a jeering obnoxious way, suggesting vile offensive thoughts. Sometimes they would control her vocal organs, voicing rude, vulgar and coarse expressions, until her life became almost unbearable. She begged, pleaded and commanded them to leave her, but they only laughed mockingly and continued their torments.

"She learned satisfactorily that the leader, the 'chief instigator' of the licentiousness, was one who on earth had been a physician, practicing for the money there was in it. He was of the kind who could easily torture a fellow being to see what effect a certain drastic drug or treatment would have on the human organism. He was atheistic with no belief in a future life. Both his morality and his spirituality were seemingly wholly undeveloped.

"He died—and astonished to find that he still lived —lived; yet finding no directing Divinity, he began roaming about with no purpose. Finding that he no longer needed to work to exist, he came in touch with this sensitive, he hypnotically attached himself to her, beginning to show his malicious power by making her unhappy. She had met him but once in earth-life. It was now a clear case of vicious obsession.

"She called upon Dr. W. Yates, of Chicago, telling her sad story, when almost instantly the doctor influenced by a powerful band of spirits, began talking to this obsessing spirit and reasoning with him.

An Obsessing Spirit Forced Away.

"The lady, being clairvoyant, could see them all quite plainly and repeated the conversation as she heard it. Red-feather, an Indian guide, talked with him, trying to persuade him to give up his evil ways. The spirit seemed to be thinking of what was said to him and at last said reluctantly that he might go, but if he did, he would send some one in his place. The lady said to the spirit, "If I can do anything to help you, or teach you better things, I am willing to do so, but I will not have spirits with evil thoughts and purposes about me, nor will I submit to the control of every roving spirit that may be pleased to use me. If I cannot have good spirits, I will have none of you."

"She could hear his answer quite plainly, 'I will come to you when I please and as often as I please, and you can't help yourself.'

"The doctor warned him to be very careful or he would surely be punished for his wickedness, at which the spirit became still more abusive in his language.

"Finding persuasion was of no avail, Dr. Yates called on a tried and true friend in spirit-world, laid the case before him and asked for help. It was promised and given.

"This good spirit, with the assistance of some powerful Indians from the band, took the obstinate spirit in charge, forced him to leave the lady's atmosphere, bound him with what seemed to the clairvoyant's vision, to be heavy magnetic chains, and took him to an isolated place in the realm of spirit which they said resembled 'Devil's Island,' where poor Dreyfus was incarcerated. There they told him, he must stay till he overcame his wicked thoughts and was ready to progress into the light.

"When the other influences who had associated with

him in his nefarious work saw what was done to their leader, they scampered away in fear.

"The lady is conscious of perfect relief from the tormentor and gratefully acknowledges her indebtedness to Dr. Yates and his kind spirit friends.

"A Chicago physician who knew this man well in earth-life said, when he heard this statement of facts, 'It is very like him. He was a good doctor, but of his morals the less said, the better.' "

It is quite time that spiritualists arousing themselves from their slumbers relating to these unreliable, diverse and demon influences, should study psychosis and the interrelational laws connecting the visible with the invisible. And further they should consider that undeveloped obsessing spirits, behind the screen, are often the inducing causes of the frauds laid at the doors of our sensitives. The frauds and deceivers of earth do not become paragons of perfection by the removal of their fleshly garments.

A Psychological Crime—An Obsessed Boy of Fifteen Shoots and Kills His Mother as Commanded by Spirits.

The *Chicago Tribune* of May 29, 1904, contains the horrifying account of a lad only fifteen years of age impelled by voices—repeated spirit voices—coolly shot down his mother. Briefly stated the facts were these.

The lad was a favorite of his mother. A very strong attachment existed between them. This was so marked that in the family he was known as "Mother's boy." Only three weeks before he killed her, at the imminent risk of his own life he saved her from being run over by an express train, no ill feeling, no quarrel, no outburst of passion preceded the fatal deed.

An Obsessing Spirit Forced Away.

The family was English, the father a lawyer. The boy stated deliberately that he shot her because he "heard a voice commanding him to so do" and he had no recollection of firing the deadly pistol. The boy's name was Frank Rodgers, and both his father and uncle are solicitors as they are termed in English courts.

After shooting his mother whom he tenderly loved, he took his little sister to the nearest hotel, requesting the landlady to "care for her as things had been upset at home."

The Impelling Voice.

The most remarkable evidence adduced in court was that of Dr. Octavius Ennion, the family physician, who was summoned to the house immediately after Mrs. Rodgers had been shot. To him the boy volunteered the statement that he heard voices urging him to murder his mother.

"On the night I shot my mother," Frank told him, "I went home and had supper. Afterward I went upstairs and got the revolver and went down to the breakfast room. I felt an almost irresistible impulse to shoot mother. I refrained, however, and went out. The impulse came again and I went back into the house.

"A voice distinctly told me to do it. It said, 'Do it and do it quickly.' I do not remember firing or pointing the pistol, but I remember hearing a muffled report, and then I stumbled against the door. That is all I know about it."

He also told the doctor that for two or three months he had been constantly haunted by the feeling that his mother was close behind him and that when he turned his head he saw an apparition of her, which slowly vanished.

This painful case occurring at Mildreth, Cambridgeshire with no objective adequate cause for the murdering of a mother with such accompanying words and phrases as "a voice," "the voices," "strongly influenced," "an irresistible impulse," "an apparition" which slowly "faded," etc., are all the words of spiritism, with its oft-attending obsessions.

Still, Ever-Recurring Questions.

Are there fallen angels? Are there evil spirits? Is there really any evil in the world?

To state without equivocation, as do a few sophistical idealists, that "all is mind," "all is good," that "everything is right," and that there is no evil in this competitive, warring world, is equivalent to saying that right and wrong do not exist in contrast, side by side, something as do flowering vines and poisoning ivies. The existence of contrasts is axiomatic. Denial of such facts constitutes not only a terrific stretch of common sense, but a direct denigration of observation and all intelligent experiences. The contemplation of such moral obliquity is painful.

Think of it! "All is mind," "all is good," "all is right!" And here comes in the stereotyped and oft-repeated phrase, in justification "all is right in the Absolute." This may, indeed, be true! But, how do you know? How did you get into the counsels of the Almighty to warrant such an assertion? By what process of ratiocination did you discover the secrets of the Absolute? Is not this pretension a species of internal, egotistic obsession? What can be more puerile? Be sure evil as an all-conquering entity, objective and permanent does not exist. Such evil, useless and endless, could not possibly enter into and eternally reign in a universe of Unity, of Divine Order, of Infinite Goodness, and of an omniscient, immutable *One*, energizing and encircling all things.

How Can Fact and Philosophy Be Reconciled?

Reason, exercise the highest judgment upon this and all subjects. It is true that abuse, that misrule, misplacements, and purposed crimes black as night, abound more or less in all communities. Denial of this is self-stultification. But these misplacements are incidents natural to imperfect mortality. They are the stony steps, voluntarily taken in the pathway of evolution. They are self-imposed crosses to be overcome. The right warped and twisted out of proper fitness, becomes the wrong. A man may be as emotionally and positively mad as he may be glad, and either madness or merciless malice eclipses the spirit in temporary darkness. And yet, above the clouds the sun shines.

Progress, not completion, is the proof of the divine love of the changeless Reality. Evil, not an end in the divine economy, is its own disciplinary punishment. Misfortune later on may become a fortune. It is unwise, therefore, to burden the air with pessimistic laments.

Many of the most painful phases of life lead along over rocky highways to the richest spiritual unfoldings. The corn dies in underground darkness before it sprouts and springs up into the summer sunshine, laden later with an hundredfold harvest.

Evil spirits may be, are being reached, redeemed and reconciled to the divine order.

The Auras of Spiritual Bodies.

It has become a scientifically established fact, recently admitted as such, that each individual is encircled in a shadowy aural atmosphere. Clairvoyants have been affirming this for a full half century. It rested upon the testimony of their personal clear-seeing. Spirits often describe these enzoning spheres. And now it has been discovered, by the aid of this new-found metal, radium, a metal as yet very difficult to obtain, and one whose heat, light and wonderful activity loses nothing from constant contact with air, water or any form of matter—that this odylic aura is really a revelator of moral attainment.

By the aid of this radium light, this aural atmosphere may be seen enveloping the human form, differing qualitatively and quantitatively in dulness and brightness according to the mental development and moral status of the individual.

This luminous, enveloping emanation, outflowing from, and connected with both the physical and the soul-body, is magnetic or electric, attractive or repulsive, according to the personality. Invisible to most eyes and complex, it extends off from different personalities from one to three and thirty fet, and further in some marked individuals. From this extension of this od-force aura arose the saying, "He is gifted with great personal magnetism."

This emanating aura is the lever, the psychic soil that low, attaching spirits largely employ to implant the psychic seeds of obsessional inharmony, diseases and destruction. To the independent clairvoyant this aura appears like a cloudy, vaporous substance, ranging in color from dark and repulsive, to gray, to leaden, to light, to azure, and to a dazzling golden. It is a revelation of the real character.

This surrounding atmosphere is pleasant, health-giving and morally inspiring when emanating from the truly good and the spiritually minded, whether mortal or immortal. Some persons carry health, peace, sunshine and happiness in their presence. Their touch is a baptism of soul-felt joy; their smile a blessing, and their warm hand-clasp a benediction of purity and sweetness. The psychometrist depends largely upon this encircling atmosphere to read character.

Often am I asked to give my estimate of the planchette. This little instrument under several names, and harmless in itself, is to be shunned unless in the hands of conscientious investigators. Mirthfully used for curiosity or fortune-telling ,it opens the gateway for obsession, and invites, as do large promiscuous séances in ill-aired, dirt-decorated rooms, the demon denizens that people the underworld of moral darkness. Angels incarnate or discarnate, admire cleanly bodies and pure minds.

CHAPTER XXX.

Spiritism and Demonism Versus Spiritualism and Angel Ministries

RUDE, fun-provoking spiritism with its varied paraphernalia, its selfish seekings and dark séance accoutrements, is virtually the synonym of Babylonian necromancy. Appearing among the Jews, it was as wise in the lawgiver Moses, to condemn its "peepings and mutterings," as it is for high-toned Spiritualists and religionists to expose the frauds that masquerade under the name of Spiritualism.

This present-day, promiscuous, helter-skelter spiritism exhibited in theaters, ill-ventilated and cobweb decorated halls, is the racially modified demonism of Jewish and apostolic times. It is similar to the black magic of India, of which Mme. Blavatsky, with her marvelous physical phenomena and accompanying frauds, was, as the Brahmins of Madras informed me, a practical and a practicing exemplification.

This lucrative-loving spiritism is largely the witchcraft, qualified and revised, of the seventeenth century in England and European countries, and later in Cotton Mather's time in New England. It is diakkaism, *plus* fraudulent tricks and obsessions all about us. These diakka (demon-spirits previously referred to, see "Diakka and Their Earthly Victims," by A. J. Davis, pages 13-15) "amuse themselves with jugglery" and circus witticisms, "invariably victimizing others; secretly tormenting mediums, causing them to exaggerate in speech, and to falsify by acts, unlocking and unbolting the street doors of your bosom, pointing your feet to wrong paths, and far more." What a telling phrase,— "far more!" That is, far more than exaggeration, falsehood and jugglery. Dr. A. J. Davis further says of this diakka demonism under the name of "crude spiritism," that "there is no kind of alleged obsession, no species of assumed witchcraft, no phase of religious insanity where such psychology is not possible," x x "These spirits are continually victimizing sensitive persons, delighting in psychologizing and dispossessing them of the use of their will."

Spiritism is no more a moral truth than is telegraphy; nor is it a congeries of divine truths, for many of its received communications, frequently in direct opposition, are often later proved to be falsehoods. This is not denied. And further, spiritism is not a philosophy; neither is it religion, but a psychological fact as prominent among Chinese, Hindus, Koreans and the red Indians of the Rocky Mountains, as among the camp-meeting spiritists, with their test-hunting, wonder-seeking crowds. I repeat, it is a fact—just one fact among the millions that cluster about and figure in this great world's stirring, whirling activities.

The Open Door to Obsessions.

It has been vehemently said by materialistic-inclined spiritists, "We've no use for any God;" "Jesus Christ was a Gnostic myth," or a "priestly make-up," a "Jewish beggar and tramp," "stealing the colt upon which he rode into Jerusalem," and "religion is an old troglodyte superstition." Vulgar statements of this character, as unhistoric as uncultured, injected into certain spiritistic books and journals and profusely advertised, constitute that stimulating compost of the demonism which later flows out as the sickening vomit of the hells. The authors of such irrational teachings aspire before and after death to be leaders. Boasting, strutting, they would sooner reign in Plutos underworld than serve in heaven. They have never dreamed of such graces as modesty and humility. They mistake ambition for aspiration, and policy for principle. When influencing or obsessing sensitive intermediaries, they often assume great historic names to the better compass their ignoble ends.

This American side-show spiritism is not new. It is as old as hoariest antiquity. It stands for converse with the denizens of the lower spirit world. It is simply newly-veneered necromancy. It is one phase of magic. It is, as conducted, the open door to inroads from the diakka regions of darkness. The great body of Chinese are spiritists. The Koreans are spiritists. The African voudous are spiritists. The Mormons—as a thousand times declared—are spiritists, and the late Congressional Smoot trial was proof emphasized and reclinched. But, are polygamy-practicing Mormons really Spiritualists; are their elders allowed to appear as exponents upon our platforms, and in our Spiritualistic temples?

Considering its accompanying selfish schemings, its advertised fortune-tellings, its coal-field searching and social-affinity hunting, spiritism is the broad, open gateway to obsession, and is dangerous just so far as it is lawlessly promiscuous and unprincipled. It was this covert undertone demonism that produced the Woodhull free-love movement. It is the central combative force today of that coarse atheistic irreligion, which often climbing up onto rostrums and camp-meeting platforms, induces confusion and disorganization, repulsing the candid, serious-minded investigator.

Nevertheless, spirit phenomena, ever varying under diverse environments, require the closest, calmest study. Whatever the phases, to whatever height they may ascend, or depths descend, they are so inextricably interwoven into the web of human life and the destiny of men that they cannot be ignored by those who consider them unnecessary or unwise. Abuse must ever be distinguished from right use. Spiritism is on the earth to stay. It aids in exterminating materialism by provoking thought and research into those finer forces that tend upward, and take hold of immortality itself.

Forget not that Spiritualism and true apostolic Christianity, with its recorded signs, wonders and spiritual gifts, must stand or fall together, for spirit is the life and spring of the moral universe. And Paul, mentioning among the gifts, "the discerning of spirits," exhorted the Corinthian Spiritualists of his day, to "covet earnestly the best gifts," adding—"and yet; I show unto you a more excellent way." (Cor. 7:31.) Evidently, that "more excellent way" was a pure spiritual life.

The Words "Spiritism" and "Spiritualism."

No writer of eminence knowing the potency of prefixes or suffixes and understanding the genius of the English language, ever uses the above words interchangeably. As I have often said, they are not synonyms. Derivations and terminologies must be considered. Moral qualities are generally embodied in suffixes. For instance, a spiritual or spiritually-minded man is more, far more, qualitatively than a mere spirit man. All tribes, however rude and barbarous, are spirit men, that is, they are spirits now; but who in speaking of them, as conscious personalities would pronounce them intellectual and spiritual? Spiritual, therefore, is just as etimologically and legitimately related to spirit as is the word "intellectual," to intellect. No carping critic can write the word "spiritual" out of existence. An idiot is not all animal. The spirit germ is hidden within, though undeveloped in manifestation. But only a semi-idiot would pronounce such a human-shaped creature either intellectual or spiritual.

Spirit being divine, essential and immutable, Spiritualism relating to and derived therefrom, implies in its broadest sense a knowledge of everything pertaining to the moral and spiritual state of conscious beings, visible and invisible. It is cosmopolitan, eclectic and heaven-inspiring. Its spiritual gifts and clouds of witnesses above and below are God's present demonstrations of a future, conscious and progressive existence. And while Spiritualism does philosophically antagonize rude, iconoclastic materialism, it does not antagonize the Christianity of the living Christ, the inspiring Logos of the ages.

Notwithstanding the irregularities and disgraceful frauds hiding and sheltering under the wide-spreading branches of a cosmopolitan spiritism, it had and still has its uses. Tests, repeated tests, are helps to spiritual babes. Marvels, astounding marvels and phenomenal thunder-claps may be necessary to startle the flinty-minded materialist. Crutches are certainly useful for the lame; alphabets for children, and rude scaffoldings, too, are requisites during the construction of the temple.

The rudest raps may bring to some sorrowing heart the tender message of comfort. This is one of the higher aspects of spiritism. Phenomenal-hunting spiritists as well as thousands of sectarists, grow,—gradually grow up on to those loftier heights of that Spiritualism which gives rest—sweet rest and perfect trust to the soul.

Some of the most firm and clear-headed Spiritualists, however, that I ever met never attended a séance, never witnessed an alleged spirit phenomenon, nor heard a Spiritualist lecture. Listening to the "still, small voice of the spirit within," they grew up into Spiritualism just as naturally as daisies grow up from the rich soil, or as buds unfold when gently touched and warmed by springtime suns.

The Differentiation of Soul and Spirit.

There are intelligent spiritists in America who, in speaking of this modern movement, prefer the word "spiritism" to "Spiritualism," and this doubtless to get rid of the troublesome word "spiritual," which to them is an ever-piercing thorn. And yet, the leading scholars and philologists of the world define spirit as "Being," "Absolute Being," "Divine Substance," and spiritual, derived therefrom, is that which is characterized by self-consciousness, self-activity, moral force, and inner aspiration for the good and the pure. These definitions are sustained by Trench on "Words," and by Tuke on "Prefixes and Suffixes." "Spiritual" is a legitimate word, and is just as logically derived from and allied to the substantive "spirit," as "intellectual" refers to and is derived from "intellect." As well try to blot the word "mother" out of the English language as the word "spiritual."

When the disciples saw Jesus walking upon the sea, they said, "It is a spirit (phantasma)." In this phrase they expressed the common belief of those times in spirits, and the presence of the spirits of the so-called dead. Says Renan, "The group that pressed around Jesus upon the banks of the Lake of Tiberias, believed in specters and spirits. Great spiritual manifestations were frequent. All believed themselves to be inspired in different ways. Some were prophets, others teachers."

"Soul" and "spirit," remember, are not synonyms They should never be used interchangeably. Plato and the Nea-Platonian writers carefully marked this distinction. Paul spoke of the "dividing asunder of soul and spirit." The philologist Schubert considers soul the "inferior, varying part of the human being." Professor Porter notes that the "word 'soul' differs from 'spirit,' as the species differs from the genus." The soul (soul-body) may die. The phrase "immortal soul" occurs nowhere in the Biblical writings. But its destruction is spoken of several times in passages similar to this: "The soul that sinneth it shall die." This, remember, is never stated of the spirit.

In Job it is recorded that there is a spirit, not mere, unconscious wind or breath, but a spirit (rauch), "in man, and the inspiration of the Almighty giveth him understanding." This clear distinction between soul and spirit is distinctly kept up by the old Hebrews and by the better class of classic writers. Hence this Biblical passage: "In whose hand is the soul (nephesh) of every animal, and the spirit (rauch) of all flesh that is human."

"Spirit is God," exclaimed Jesus. The angels are called the "ministering spirits of God." Men are made in the image of God, and hence are spiritual beings. All angels were doubtless once men inhabiting this planet, or some of the others that stud the deepening depths, of heaven.

"It is the spirit that quickeneth," is the voice of ancient inspiration. "It is sown a natural body, it is raised a spiritual body." said the apostle.

"To be carnally (somatically) minded, is death; but to be spiritually (pneumatically) minded, is life and peace," said Paul. And in accordance with this teaching, Jesus cried out, "Father, into thy hands I command my spirit." Mark, he did not command his "soul" to the Father. God is not the father of bodies or of souls; but is, and is called the "God of the *spirits* of all flesh." And so, when the first martyr, Stephen, fell beneath the stones of infuriated murderers, his cry was, "Lord Jesus, receive my spirit." (Acts 7:59.) And then, mangled and bruised, the physical body of Stephen fell asleep, while his soul-body with his spirit—his immortal spirit—ascended into heaven—the higher spheres—to join the "spirits of just men made perfect."

CHAPTER XXXI.

The Supernatural—The Christ—Religious Spiritualists—Obsessions.

"NOW, concerning spiritual gifts, brethren, I would not have you ignorant. . . . But covet earnestly the best gifts; and yet show I unto you a more excellent way." (1 Cor. 12:1.)

Our fathers "did all eat the same spiritual meat, and did all drink the same spiritual drink, for they drank of that spiritual Rock that followed them, and that Rock was Christ." (1 Cor. 10:4.)

"Teaching them to observe all things, whatsoever I have commanded you and lo, I am with you always, even unto the end of the world." (Matt. 28:20.)

"And God wrought special miracles by the hand of Paul, so that from his body were brought unto the sick, handkerchiefs, and aprons, and the diseases departed, and the evil spirit went out of them." (Acts 19:11, 12.)

"For I long to see you that I may impart unto you some spiritual gift." (Rom. 1:11.)

Miracles are the heritage of the ages. The materialist denies their reality, sneers at their possibility. But how is it possible for him or any one to know whether a particular event, strange and marvelous, be a miracle or not? Who is competent to judge? Am I told that this wonderful occurrence, called a miracle, "is opposed to the laws of nature?" Aye—presumptious man; how do you know? Have you explored, discovered, measured and tabulated all the laws of *nature?* Are you absolutely omniscient? The boaster is never the philosopher. Many esteeming themselves great, have yet to learn the stupenduous lesson of spiritual humility.

If the word "Christ" be an exception, no word so frightens a materialistic spiritist, of moderate culture as the word miracle, or its virtual synonym, supernatural. And yet, we are literally enveloped in the enzoning realm of the supernatural. As a force it impinges upon and operates everywhere from seashore sands to stars, molding and manipulating the substances that scientists pronounce matter, or nature. Why, the saps that in springtime climb up from root and tree-trunk into buds and blossoms exhibits the supernatural by transcending the law of gravity,—that gravity which holds liquids as well as solids to the earth's surface. No encoffined corpse was ever known to lift itself from the casket and bury itself, but the conscious spiritual man in the human corpse-shaped body, lifts himself up into the proud air-ship and sails aloft among the clouds, singing the song of conquest over gravity. Who can, who dare, set bounds to spirit? —bounds to the supernatural? We are all unwittingly miracle-workers. In his "Analogy," Bishop Butler remarks, "God's miraculous interpositions may have been all along by the general laws of nature, above the comprehension of mortals. . . . There may be conscious beings to whom the whole Christian dispensation may appear as natural as the visible known course of things now appears to us." That is reasonable.

John Wesley, in writing his brother Charles, says, "I care not a rush for ordinary means, only that it is our duty to try them. All our lives, and all God's dealings with us have been extraordinary from the beginning. I have been preternaturally restored to health more than ten times." He further adds, "The real cause why the gifts of the Holy Spirit are no longer to be found in the Christian Church, is because Christians are turned heathen again, and have become so material that only the form of godliness is left." All too true!

Roman Catholics, unlike Protestants, have never denied the existence of modern miracles,—that is of spiritual manifestations. True, they pronounced the latter when actively manifesting on a low, vicious disorderly plane, "demoniacal;" and in this respect they were nearly right.

These modern spiritual phenomena are not miracles, however, in the sense that the seventeenth century schoolmen defined miracles. They are not violations of the immutable laws of nature, but the natural operations of higher laws, than the uncultured masses can comprehend. The supernatural is the natural upon the spiritual plane of existence. The philosopher and the adept readily understand this.

If Jesus, in his time, had telegraphed, with or without the wire, from Jericho to an apostolic friend temporarily residing at the foot of snowy Hermon; or if he had telephoned from Jerusalem over to the River Jordan, these methods of communication would have been pronounced astounding miracles.

Can He who made the eye not see? Can He who ordained law, whether in the sprouting of an acorn, or in the balancing of a starry constellation, not modify it, or bring into activity a higher spiritual law transcending it? In the measureless realms of absolute being, the Divine Personality reigns supreme. And so in the encircling lesser realms that belt, or enzone this planet, minor spirit personalities, reigning finitely as conscious individualities, produce spiritual manifestations, often made visible under proper conditions.

"All houses wherein men live," wrote Longfellow, "are haunted houses." And Mrs. Harriet Beecher Stowe, cherishing a similar belief, remarks: "I cannot get over the feeling that the souls of the dead do somehow connect themselves with the places of their former habitations, and that the hush and thrill of spirit, which we feel in them, may be owing to the overshadowing presence of the invisible." St. Paul says, "We are compassed about with a great cloud of witnesses;" but how could they be witness, if they cannot see and be cognizant of us?

Cultured Religious Spiritualists.

It yields me pleasure to here adduce the testimonies of some of the brightest and most illustrious Spiritualists that have written upon this momentous truth, conscious intercourse with the Spiritual world.

The eminent Robert Dale Owen, claimed by two continents, writing upon this subject said, in soul-stirring sincerity, "Spiritualism is the complement of Christianity." x x "Spiritual phenomena were the early witnesses of Christianity." "All thoughtful observers, when convinced of the genuineness of these phenomena, will be Christians as soon as they make sharp distinction between the simple grandeur of Christ's teachings, with their attending works and gifts as given in the synoptical gospels, and the Augustinian version of Paul's theology. I have sufficient evidence that these truths are gradually making their way. My friend, Dr. Crowell's well-timed work

'The Identity of Primitive Christianity and Modern Spiritualism,' has aided in bringing about this result—and I do not doubt their ultimate prevalence, for in essence and purpose they are one." In this marked passage the Hon. Mr. Owen was writing not of churchianity, not of creed or any theological confession of faith, but of Christianity, with its accompanying spiritual gifts, as it fell from the lips of the inspired Man of Nazareth.

The great seer Andrew Jackson Davis, wrote as follows, "Jesus instituted laws and customs above the popular conception of his time and country. And the people crucified him for what they considered sedition and conspiracy against the Roman government. But time and intelligence have developed the falseness of this act, and made it manifest that Jesus was misapprehended, and most ignobly treated. He was the model man, and a living example of what the race is destined to be."

Judge Edmonds of New York, distinguished alike for his legal ability and his admiration of Jesus, writing of Professor Hare, says, "Dr. Hare has all his life long been an honest, sincere and inveterate disbeliever in the Christian religion. But late in life Spiritualism comes to him, and in a short time works in his mind the conviction of the existence of a God, and his own conscious immortality. . . . The last time I ever saw him, he told me that he was at length a full believer in the Revelations through Jesus—that, in fine, he was now a Christian full in faith,—that but a few days before he had made a public proclamation of his belief at a meeting which he had addressed at Salem, Mass., and he read me a long article on that subject, which he had prepared for publication."

The learned Ex-Unitarian preacher and Spiritualist, Allen Putnam, of Boston, thus expressed his convictions.

The Supernatural—The Christ.

"The Child of Mary came into life pursuant to pre-arrangements made in spirit realms for his conception and training under spiritualized conditions. High, pure, and powerful spirits were his associates and helpers, while low spirits and spirit-forces were subject to his will. . . . We can and do offer our prayers of gratitude, put up our petitions, as the Apostles did, in the name of Jesus Christ, deeming him the most wise and efficient helper Godward; and yet, while a Galilean Rabbi a 'man approved of God' as the apostle Peter declared, he was the most affluent dispenser of heavenly gifts of any created being within our knowledge."

The eloquent Prof. S. B. Brittan, of New York, who for many years editorially graced the earlier pages of Spiritualism, thus expressed his estimation of Jesus of Nazareth whose humbler life and death were, he declares, "more glorious to humanity than the conquest of a thousand heroes.

"He was pre-eminent over all in devotion to his idea of the celestial life. Amid the noise of passion, and the jarring discords of the world, his soul was at peace. A spirit quickened by Divine fire; love that consumes the deepest resentment and forgiveness which co-existed with all human wrong, were conspicuous in the life of Jesus. When the world was faithless and disobedient, he stood alone—sublimely great —in his solemn trust and his immortal fidelity. That halcyon peace of the soul, that deathless love of humanity, and Godlike forgiveness of offenders, were incarnate in the revelations of Jesus. The church of the future must be built on the same foundation as the living church of the past. It is not the crucified Jesus but the risen Christ that saves. Other foundation can no man lay. But it is certain that we require a new, and, in many respects, a different superstructure. Sectarian creeds must perish. We must have a religious organization whose articles of faith shall be the moral precepts of Jesus—whose sacred books shall comprehend and unfold the discovered principles and the concentrated wisdom of all ages—all Bibles—and whose teachers shall be employed to illustrate the philosophy of the material and spiritual universe; and all, to instruct the people in the true science of pure and holy living."

When the above fathers in Spiritualism, Judge Edmonds, Robert Dale Owen, Dr. Crowell, Professor Brittan, William Fishbough, A. E. Newton, Joel Tiffany, Henry Kiddle, and other brave, unselfish workers were influencing exponents of Spiritualism, obsessions were virtually unknown. These earnest, unambitious writers and authors were, in the best sense of the word Spiritualists. They were religious too, in the broad-minded sense of the word. Who, aye, how few today are filling their places?

The learned E. D. Babbitt, M. D., LL. D., of the Institute of the Higher Sciences, Geneva, N. Y., writes in the following unmistakeable language, "We cannot grasp the true science of the universe without a conception of God. The word infinite, meaning without limit, may be applied to Him; for the bounds of the universe cannot compass Him. . . . Religion is aspiration for the good, the spiritual, the divine with an up-reaching toward the all-powerful One."

"Jesus was truly the Divine, the God incarnate, because every human soul is a spark of the Divinity incarnated, only humanity in general has far less of the Divine Life than had Jesus, the Christ. From childhood

He was inspired and though at times tempted by undeveloped spirits which in His age, were called demons and devils,—yet He was generally under the control of holy influences who filled His soul with such a divine efflatus, and kindled His magnetic power to such an extent that He felt that He was under the direct guidance of God himself,—that God was indeed His Father, and He so felt His unity of aim and spirit with God that He remarked, —'I and my Father are one' "—that is one in purpose. (Babbitt, on "Religion," p. 266.)

The Presence of the Nazarene.

In ecstacy, or worshipful fervor, Christians often exclaim "Come, oh come, Lord Jesus! Come into our presence! Come and abide with us." And some of these earnest souls declare in all sincerity that they feel His sweet divine presence. Far be it from us to dispute, or treat lightly, even by implication, what they so vigorously and strenuously affirm. But do they furnish any proof, any demonstrations to others that they are thus especially honored?

Clairvoyant Spiritualists and their guardians in the unseen world state most emphatically that they have seen in those higher angel realms Jesus, the central figure of the synoptic gospels.

Andrew Jackson Davis, the illustrious seer, declares unreservedly in one of his books that during one of those delegations of ancient spirits at High Rock, he clairvoyantly saw Jesus of Nazareth. And accordingly in all of his voluminous writings he speaks of Him only in words of profound reverence.

Twice have I had the great honor of conversing with the Man Christ Jesus. Once in Jerusalem just after a distinguished Rabbi had read for me several passages in the Talmud referring directly to Jesus, who it was there said practiced "the magic which he had learned in Egypt." The second time was in Glasgow, Scotland, through that very excellent instrumentality, David Duguid.

And now comes the recent testimony of the erudite Dr. Babbitt, of Geneva. (*Light of Truth,* May 28.) These are his pointed words:

"Two days after Christmas I began to receive the impresison that Jesus himself might come. I asked Dr. Elliotson if such a being as Jesus the Christ really had lived, notwithstanding the efforts of some writers to show that He never existed. The answer was "Yes." Then I perceived and was informed that the Sunday meeting was put off with the understanding that Jesus himself was to be with us. This, of course, was a great joy to me, for His was a name that had been glorified for so many centuries and among so many millions of the human race. That evening was quite an era in my life. The privilege of talking with so lofty a soul, one who had been developing for nearly nineteen hundred years, was very great. He signified that there were two points of historical experience in connection with His name that He regretted—first, the supposition that He was co-equal with God, although He had used the expression, "My Father is greater than I," and, secondly, the ideas of that day, into which He himself had fallen—namely, that there were really devils that entered into people, instead of undeveloped human beings as we now know them to have been, some of which he had cast out."

The Supernatural—The Christ.

Professor B. F. Austin, LL.D., known to the literati of Canada and America bore this striking testimony: "After years of candid investigation, under a great variety of circumstances, I dare affirm that the ethical system taught in these spiritual communications, in no wise at variance with the moral teachings of Christ, have never been surpassed in the lofty character of the duties it proclaims, or the power and variety of the motives it urges to secure obedience to law. I have seen again and again these phenomena, the high and the low produced under the most rigid conditions—have heard voices from heavenly worlds— have caught the living words of instruction and inspiration fresh from angel lips—have seen forms materialize and dematerialize like vanishing clouds, vanish as they did in Christ's time. Spiritualism is a revival of that Christianity which centered around and in that ideal Man of Palestine. It is a revival of the Spiritual, so alive and so potent, in Apostolic times. We only see in part and as yet, know in part, but eternity is before us. How sweet the lines of Whittier:

" 'I touched the garment hem of truth,
Yet saw not all its splendors.' "

Possibly, it may be proper to here express my own mature conception of Him who was styled "the Mediator between God and man." Referring in joyousness to Peter's definition, I see in Jesus of Nazareth "a man approved of God, among you by miracles, wonders and signs that God did by him." (Acts 11:22.) In moral grandeur and the tender spirit of self-sacrifice, His character rose almost beyond comparison with other seers and sages.

He worshiped in spirit. He never lost sight of the

spiritual world. God does not speak to Him from without. He feels that God is within Him. He needed no sound of thunder like Moses; no revealing tempest, like Job; nor familiar oracle like Grecian sage. He so consciously lived in the presence of the Father, and was continually overshadowed by the Christ, that he could truly say, "I and my Father are one." His pre-eminent greatness consisted mostly in His fine harmonial organization; in a constant communion with angels; in the depth of His sweet spirituality; in the keenness of His moral perceptions; in the expansiveness and warmth of His Divine sympathies; in His sincerity of heart; in His soul-pervading spirit of obedience to the mandates of right; in His devoted consecration to the highest interests of humanity; and in His complete and perfect trust in God.

Cherishing these sublime conceptions of the Christ, I can fervently exclaim, Behold "the Way, the Truth and the Life!" And, further, I can sincerely say that I believe in salvation, divine growth, through Christ—that is, through the Christ-principle of purity, aspiration, love, and truth,—believe in salvation, or soul-unfoldment through Christ, something as I believe in the opening buds and green fields through summer showers, something as I believe in ripening fruits and waving harvests, through autumn's golden sunshine! Christ, then, much like the Buddha, is the Sun of Righteousness and the Saviour of the world!

"Sweet Prophet of Nazareth, constant and tender,
   Whose truth, like a rainbow, embraces the world,—
The time is at hand when thy foes shall surrender,
   And war's crimson banners forever be furled:
When the throat of the lion no longer will utter
   Its roar of defiance in desert and glen,

When the lands will join hands, and the black cannon
    mutter
  Their discords no more to the children of men.

"The mist of the ocean, the spray of the fountain,
  The vine on the hillside, the moss on the shrine,
The rose of the valley, the pine of the mountain,
  All turn to a glory that symboleth thine;
So I yearn for Thy love, as the rarest and dearest
  That ever uplifted a spirit from woe,
And I turn to Thy life, as the truest and nearest
  To Infinite Goodness that mortals may know."
              —*James G. Clark.*

CHAPTER XXXII.

"Rescue Work on the Borderland of the Invisible World."

IT WILL be recollected by those who have carefully read the foregoing chapters, that while I have spoken of the ignorance and selfishness of the masses in China, India and darkest Africa; of crimson warfields in civilized nations; of selfishness, robbery, profanity, drunkenness, gambling, political frauds, dens of licentiousness, fashionable hypocrisies, murderous abortions, and the commission of million crimes unseen to mortal eyes, and these—the actors in all these scenes—thrust unrepentant, at each clock tick, into the unseen realms of spirits, have taken with them their identities, their depraved vindictive tendencies and their downward proclivities. Now, where are they? Their bodies are in dust and ashes; yet, *they* are here. Death is no savior—no ransoming redeemer. The murderous gallows is not the highway to glory. Those mentioned above took with them to the invisible world the hells they had made for themselves and others while in their mortal bodies. Now then, can they be reached? is the natural inquiry of the philanthropist. Aye, consider for a moment, that while the morally low and depraved have passed out of their physical vehicles to swell the countless multitudes of the dead, so also have teachers, reformers, philanthropists—those great loving souls of the ages who labored and lived for the moral education of humanity while encased in physical mortality. Workers, those grand toilers for human good here, become more *intensified workers* beyond the valley of death. Such blessed souls may be denominated, bands of rescuers, heavens divine helpers.

The Mission of H. Forbes Kiddle.

It cannot have been forgotten by reading Spiritualists that few, if any, more scholastic men, and certainly none more brave, upright and conscientious, ever graced the ranks of Spiritualism than Prof. Henry Kiddle, writer, author and for years Superintendent of the New York City schools. The son of this venerable Spiritualist, H. Forbes Kiddle, engaged in music and such literary pursuits as writing for magazines and book reviewing, has furnished the following pages under the heading, "Rescue Work in the Borderland of the Invisible World." This work is all the more interesting and suggestive, because the communications and visions occurred in his own city residence.

Rescue Work on the Borderland. 339

Such visions, such excursions into spirit lands as these described are exceedingly instructive, as well as vital inspiring forces for the bettering of humanity. This work of rescue must go on under the good providence of God, the Christs of God, the Buddhas of the ages, and ministering angels, until the last soul in darkness is touched with the fires of divine love, inclining the heart to say, "I will arise and go to my Father." He writes as follows:

"There is one phase of Spiritualism which has not received the attention its great importance merits, even from those who in other respects thoroughly appreciate the significance of the glorious spiritual illumination of these modern days. I refer to the work it is in the power of mortals to do, in conjunction with altruistic beings in the higher life, in aid of the helpless and often hopeless denizens of the dark and sad Borderland, which stretches out just beyond the valley of the shadow of death. It is a possibility fraught with inestimable opportunity for good to both the spiritual and material worlds. Nothing more retards the true progress of humanity than the clinging mass of ignorant and degraded "dwellers on the threshold."

Many human beings pass out of the physical body so lacking in spiritual development as to be insensitive to the inspirations or the magnetic influence of the higher realms. Their spiritual faculties are still in a mere rudimentary state, or, worse, are wretchedly atrophied. Spirits of this character are farther from the light of the true spiritual life than many still in the flesh. Their conditions are as diverse as the idiosyncrasies of human thought and impulse; but they cling naturally and instinctively to earth as the only resting place known to their consciousness, or are held to it through the operation of phychological forces which they are too feeble to resist. Not necessarily very wicked or malicious, are these poor groping creatures; on the contrary, in the majority of cases they probably are merely gross and ignorant. Often they are victims of some strange hallucination which has to be dispelled before they can make any progress. Whatsoever the condition of these dwellers in the "outer darkness," they are more easily reached through the coarse magnetism of earth than by the finer forces of the inner world. Indeed, the material plane is the common ground on which spirits of all grades can come in rapport, by means of mortal intermediaries; it is the center of life, the point at which the past and the future conjoin; the eternal now, perpetually absorbing the product of the ages for the unfoldment of that which is yet to be. Inhabitants of the boundless beyond, separated naturally by degrees of development, or held apart by radical diversity of thought, can be drawn together at the focal point of earthly mediumship. In this way mediums become instruments of upliftment in the hands of invisible beings engaged in the Christ work of drawing all souls up into the higher life. This peculiar function of mediumship was known to many of the early investigators, Judge Edmonds among the number, whose "Circle of Hope" was organized for the special purpose of assisting the invisibles who flocked to him in search of help. And Dr. G. A. Redman, a prominent medium of the early days, discussed the subject at considerable length in his autobiographical work, "Mystic Hours." It was his opinion that "too little attention is given to this class of our phenomena." "I am satisfied," he added, "that as we progress, we are able to bestow on spirits below us what we have received from those, whether spirit or mortal, in a more advanced stage of progression."

My Mission for Years.

For a number of years it has been my lot, a strange one, incredible to most people, to have many dealings with the numerous and diverse class of invisibles that haunt the shadows of the past. Through the instrumentality of two ladies who have devoted their mediumistic gifts to the work of spirit rescue and upliftment, all sorts and conditions of unfleshed human beings have come to our circles to be enlightened and aided in various ways. They have come singly and in groups; sometimes they have literally swarmed in upon us. More than once those who have come to scoff, have remained to give thanks.

Mr. Thomas Atwood, an English Spiritualist who is very earnest in this work, was requested at the outset of his mediumistic development to hold regular meetings, a sort of religious service, for the benefit of spirit-land wanderers. This he has been doing for several years. His clairvoyance enables him to see that his audience, though invisible to the outer sight, is often a large and attentive one; and he thus has the satisfaction of knowing that his labors are not in vain. Referring to his visitants in a recent article, he says of them, "Whatever form of body they assume after 'shoveling off the mortal soil,' they are *spirits,* just as much as they were in earth-life, no more; and in face of the fact that in very many cases they have no knowledge of having passed away from mortal life, and believe themselves still to be following their occupations as in former days. They seem to me to be, to all intents and purposes, men and women, and as such I always address them." He adds, "Some, moreover, of those brought to us are in so elementary a stage of development that it is difficult to realize that they were ever part and parcel of our great humanity. Thick darkness is the most appropriate word by which to describe the conditions they bring. That the human soul could be at so low a level, seems incredible, and yet, as we walk our streets, if we use our ordinary powers of observation, or recall some of our experiences in this life, surely the prototypes of these poor creatures will be easily recognizable by us. A step higher, and we get to men and women who have some dim perception of life. Many of these do not know who they are, what they are, or where they are. Gradually memory revives, and some incident in earth-life is called to mind. Another step higher, and we get a distinct desire expressed for help to be given, though in what direction this help is required seems to be quite unknown, for great difficulty is often experienced in making these people understand that they no longer are in the earthly body."

How Mortal Words Affect Spirits.

So, also, have I been urged to open our séances with an address. It seems that words spoken by mortals have the power of resounding in the spirit world, and that the voice literally *convokes* the invisibles. They are in that way aroused from their lethargy, or from the fixity of thought which so often holds them in bondage. If they are drifting waifs and strays,—the obsessing class,—the sound of the voice makes them pause. Viewed spiritually through the clairvoyant vision of our medium, I seem sometimes to be standing in the street as I speak, like an itinerant preacher. The spirits behave in like manner; some pass on in utter heedlessness, others pause in idle indifference, a number become interested. Occasionally, they will ask questions concerning the possibility of spirit progression—a novel idea, alas! to the vast majority of souls passing away from earth. Several have frankly told me they doubted the truth of what I said. One man remarked that he did not place much confidence in me because I was not a priest. "You talk like a Protestant," he added. At other times I appear to be in some kind of an auditorium, on one occasion in a very large building. It was crowded and the people seemed eager to hear what was said. At the ending of the address, the roof seemed to open, giving entrance to a bright light which flooded the place. Mr. Atwood speaks of finding himself in a great cathedral during one of his meetings.

We have learned through our experiences that persons upon entering the spirit world are prone to fall into a state of fantasy. This singular condition seems to be very prevalent in the after-life. It is the mental outcome of fixed earthly habits of life and thought. Though essentially ideal, the condition nevertheless, is absolutely real to those under the psychological spell which is its cause. Sometimes it might well be called a state of "collective hallucination." Mr. Atwood remarks, "I see before me frequently clairvoyant visions of men at work at their various trades; gas-workers at the coke ovens, blacksmiths at the forge, butchers selling meat, shoemakers repairing boots, and so on. I speak to them; apparently they do not hear me, for they still go on working. But suddenly the butcher loses his knife, next the joint he was cutting disappears, the block follows.

Where have they gone? He cannot understand this. And then for the first time he realizes that all was imaginary, and that he had only been dwelling in the past. What is he to do? Ask for help, I tell him. Pray for light, and guidance will be given to him."

Of like character have been many of the visions described at our séances, usually with the result that the fixed condition has been broken, thus opening the way for missionaries from the realms of light and altruism.

Self-Imprisoned Spirits.

Another numerous class of spirits comprise those that have become imprisoned within the narrow confines of their own ideas. Having passed out of the fleshly body with minds fixed upon some one idea, that idea takes complete possession of their consciousness, and they remain in a state of absolute isolation, from which they are aroused by some external means. This condition is a common fate of suicides and murderers. It is often caused, also, by a morbid dread of death. Then, too, it may be the consequence of any death by violence.

We have learned, furthermore, that strong-willed spirits have the power to hold their weaker brethren in psychological bondage. Thus the masterful ruler and the bigoted ecclesiastic are sometimes able to maintain their sway in the after-life. In his summary of Swedenborg's statements regarding conditions in the future state, William White remarks, "Hypocrites had for centuries made the world of spirits their home, and their organized imaginary heavens, or fools' paradises, repeating on a prodigious scale the civil and ecclesiastical impostures of earth, assisted by myriads of pious and well-meaning simpletons, who destitute of any inner sense of character, accepted for gold whatever glittered as gold."

It is to speak of these various classes, as well as to the hangers-on—who know full well their condition, but are too ignorant, or too indifferent to make any attempt to improve it—that earthly mediumship can be made of service. Nor is the work of value solely to the spirits. not a condition exists in spirit-life which may not be transmitted to earth by means of telepathy and thought-transferrence. Much of the tenacious adherence to old notions and customs, which constitutes so formidable an obstacle to mental and social betterment, might be traced to the involuntary influence of creed-bound conditions existing in the Borderland of the invisible world. The same might be said of the deplorable wicked tendencies—despondency, suicide and worse—whose contamination runs through society like the veritable serpent's trail.

The séances to which I have referred began about ten years ago with the medium whom I shall call Mrs. A. Only gradually did we come to understand that the spirit attendant desired her to confine her gift entirely to work on the spirit plane. When this point became clear in our minds, the proceedings took orderly shape and a systematic conduct of the séances was manifested. The sittings never were prolonged beyond an hour, and ended mostly with a benediction offered by the presiding spirit. Surrounding the circle, the medium saw clairvoyantly a band of spirits sitting with joined hands. We were bidden to "Go out into the waste places of life and have no fear."

Mediumistic Experiences.

After an unusually unpleasant experience, the medium often would be led into some cheerful region of the world of light and harmony, no doubt as a means of

counteracting the depressing effects of contact with the
darkened ones. On one occasion she found herself in the
bright abode of a community of progressed red men. It
seemed to nestle in the heart of a primeval forest. Gigantic trees loomed high into the invigorating air, and
a gentle stream of sparkling water rippled past the
snow-white, glistening tents. All this the medium described very clearly, remarking that she saw none of the
people. Immediately she heard a voice say, "One moment, little white squaw, and we shall be with you."
Then a noble Indian presented himself, followed by
others, all very large men. They said little,—taciturnity
is a strong peculiarity of their race,—but from them
emanated a magnetic force benign and cordial, and so
powerful that all the members of the circle felt its influence. In response to a question, they informed us that
it was their special spiritual mission to transmit a healing magnetism and a harmonizing influence to earth and
the lower planes of spirit-land. Deeply impressive was
the reverence they displayed for God the Great Spirit.
Hardly less so was the splendid manliness of their bearing and the spirit of kindly consideration which guided
them in all their actions. The medium was loath to depart from this pure and peaceful sphere, and when she
opened her eyes and her consciousness to the things of
the outer life, the shock was severe.

Mrs. A.'s phase of mediumship does not involve a
complete suspension of the outer consciousness; but she
often is so thoroughly overshadowed by the controlling
spirits as to assume all their peculiarities of manner and
expression.

The mediumship of Mrs. B. is of more recent development. She falls into a deep trance, and at the close of

the séance has not the slightest recollection of anything that has transpired. Her spirit, however, seems thoroughly awake, for she often converses with the invisibles, and displays great interest in all that occurs. The spirit of a French physician—not Dr. Phinuit, Mrs. Piper's associate—presides over the details of the work done through the instrumentality of this lady. He has told us, however, that he is subject to orders from those more advanced than himself. An earnest man of keen mind and strong character, his enthusiasm is most ardent. From him we have gained much suggestive information upon the subject of life on the lower levels of the invisible world. When first he presented himself, he informed us that he is "still the physician." "But, begone drugs," he added. Being questioned as to his present method of treatment, he answered, "Kindly thoughts, gentle guidance and the finer magnetic forces."

The Doctor is, indeed, still a scientist in the true sense of the term. His methods of treatment are purely scientific and might well be called applied psychology, —psychology in his world being the chief of sciences, science and religion there becoming one and the same thing. The character of his work must be extremely difficult, for the cases he introduces are certainly severe ones, —murderers, suicides, drunkards and all sorts of extreme cases of monomania. He has his assistants—assistants whom he has to select with great care and judgment. He states that it is his most difficult problem to find the spirit necessary to form the connecting link between the mortal medium and the particular case which he desires to reach. Indeed, this difficulty, so he has told us, constitutes the chief obstacle to the general work of spirit rescue and care. Well-meaning spirits of a certain grade of development are prone to become demoralized when they find themselves brought in connection with the material plane through attachment to the organism of the mortal medium. They succumb to the overpowering influence of the association of ideas, and in their fall, drag their medium with them. This danger, however, is not confined to any particular phase of mediumship, for intercourse between the two worlds invariably requires the conjunction of a medium at each end of the line of communication. This essential condition constitutes, so the Doctor states, the greatest peril of mediumship. And it looks very reasonable.

A Spirit's View of Obsession.

Regarding obsession, the Doctor has informed us that the danger is due to the presence of hordes of dazed, sluggish, undeveloped creatures swarming the psychical atmosphere of earth; especially are they attracted to the aura emanating from the haunts of the low, the vicious and the depraved. So feeble in will-power are these wretched victims of morbid, sinful conditions, and so nearly devoid of self-consciousness, that they are practically mere automata. When, therefore, they "flow into"—to make use of Swedenborg's expresison—the sphere of a mortal, the act is usually purely involuntary. The obsession, in fact, is mutual. Morbid mental tendencies and, especially a low state of physical health, furnish the conditions which open the way to spirit infestation.

Another sort of spirits to which the Doctor has referred, he tersely classifies as "rovers." The term is significant. Spirits of this class are thoroughly wide awake. There is no absence of self-consciousness, but they are so lacking in spirituality, the soul germ is so barren of vitality, that their inner nature can be unfolded only by sympathetic association with some person still undergoing the disciplinary process of existence in the flesh. Hence, until they are drawn to a mortal by the force of some subtle affinity, they are restless rovers, idle and indifferent, and often prankish. Occasionally, one of these roving spirits has paid us a visit. The slightest levity on the part of any member of the circle will often suffice to draw him to the medium. Mrs. B. does not welcome him with any too much cordiality; more than once she has upbraided the Doctor—a very real personage to her while entranced—for permitting him to intrude. When first he made his appearance, I asked him if he knew there were kind friends anxious for the opportunity to assist him. With coarse laughter, he responded, "Who cares for a crooked-faced old fellow like me?" To him, life seemed a miserable joke, a mockery. He simply refused to take seriously anything that was said to him. He did not remain long, being followed by the Doctor, who remarked, "Poor fellow, he has not yet found his friend." Then followed the statement concerning the class of spirits to which he belongs. Perhaps, however, this man's case may not be altogether hopeless, for during a more recent visit, he exclaimed, after I had admonished him to be gentle and considerate, "Why, that is what my mother used to say to me years and years ago." The Doctor seemed greatly encouraged by this remark; he said it indicated the beginning of soul activity.

The Destroyers of Innocents.

The lowest stratum of spirit-life, however, comprises souls "driven from earth before they have any separate existence as individuals." Having only a rudimentary individuality, they nevertheless, are alive, and form a clinging, net-like mass about the earth. During one of the séances, Mrs. B. was shown this condition. She seemed horrified at the sight, and exclaimed repeatedly, "If the world only knew!" A woman whose nefarious practices on earth had psychologically enmeshed her soul in this seething, suffering mass, then took possession. Weeping bitterly, she threw herself down on her knees, and uttered a most touching plea for release. After she had withdrawn, the medium saw many others in the same horrible plight, suffering in the hells.

We have been warned not to permit Mrs. B. to fall asleep while she is entranced. Therefore, whenever she shows any indication of drowsiness, while not under control, we admonish her to keep awake. One evening it appeared necessary to say to her quite sharply, "Don't fall asleep." Immediately, a spirit responded, "Why may I not sleep? If I slept, perchance I might dream of the bright lands of peace and light and purity." "Are you in darkness?" we asked. "In lowest hell," was the response. Soon we learned, however, that this soul's sojourn in the regions of darkness was entirely voluntary. He was a missionary from supernal Altruria. How sad appeared to him the conditions of those for whose good he had exiled himself; and how wearily he spoke of the difficulties attending the work in which he was engaged. He said he was trying to reach those held in bondage to "ungratified longings;" and the task was *so* severe, for the reason that they can be influenced "only through the senses." "You may be surprised, and shocked perhaps, to hear how these creatures, held so close to earth by enslaving passions, are dealt with after they have been aroused. They are placed in the company of little children, in whose atmosphere of perfect purity the stained souls are free from evil suggestion, while the contrast between themselves and their unsullied associates awakens within them a realization of their state."

It is not possible to describe the nobility of this soul's presence, the eloquence of his address, the inspiring spirit of self-abnegation he displayed. So deeply affected was the medium that, after he had withdrawn, she rose to her feet, impulsively held out her arms, and exclaimed, "Don't go, don't go! I love you!" When the Doctor presented himself just before the close of the séance, as he invariably does, he informed us, in response to our inquiry, that the noble visitor was "Acandar, a fine soul who stays from choice in the lands of darkness." We remarked that his experience on earth must have been extraordinary to fit him for present difficult occupation. The Doctor responded, "He passed through every degree. He was a priest; but long ago he broke from the thraldom of his church."

As I already have stated, the cases treated through the instrumentality of Mrs. B. are exceedingly severe. Indeed, the lady's courage sometimes falters, as she, in spirit, is confronted with her part of the work. Thus, on one occasion, she protested, "I don't want to go down there. Must I go there—must I go?" Then, reluctantly, she rose from her chair and walked slowly and cautiously across the room, stooping lower and lower as she proceeded, as if going down a steep incline, and repeating, "I will go; yes, I will go." At last she fell in a heap, as the wretched object of her quest took control. We led her back to her chair, the spirit all the while groaning and uttering disagreeable inarticulate sounds. He was speedily withdrawn. The Doctor, who immediately followed him, displayed unusual satisfaction, one might say, exaltation. "At last, at last," he exclaimed, "we have reached him." "What sort of a creature is it?" we inquired. "Monsieur," he answered, with characteristic demonstrativeness, "that man was completely absorbed in passional thought or reverie. The noxious emanations from his powerful mind were a thousand times more injurious and vile than the influence he exerted during his miserable life on earth. He sent forth vibrations in every direction. But now we have him; and at last he is face to face with himself."

One would naturally suppose that such an experience as this would work injury to the medium's physical health, or leave an unpleasant impress on her normal consciousness. Not so, however, on the contrary, more than once the headache of which she complained before the séance began, has vanished entirely at its close, while her mental condition usually is brighter and more cheerful.

With this lady, as with Mrs. A., the disagreeable, depressing experiences are followed by beautiful visions, or by visits to the regions of brightness. Several times she has visited the abode of her father in the spirit land; and it affords her great comfort to walk through the beauteous gardens and along the border of the shining river in his congenial company. Sometimes she complains of the dazzling light, and finds it necessary to shield her eyes with her hands. "Why, isn't that strange," she recently remarked, "I thought people heard music, but I *see* it. Why I am *in* music." One evening, she was in a boat drifting peacefully down a stream. Her lap was filled with flowers; and she in-

Rescue Work on the Borderland. 353

formed us in a whisper that a white-robed figure stood at the bow. Another time she described a great curtain of flowers, violet-hued and bell-shaped. From each flower there was pendant a little dove. The curtain parts, and through the opening streams a flood of light. Away in the distance she sees a group of figures clad in white garments. They stand at a table upon which is spread a large map or plan. It appears to be a conference; but the distance is so great that she is unable to learn anything regarding its object.

A Procession of Nuns.

Mrs. B. never has been present at any of Mrs. A.'s séances, yet there is a striking similarity in the general character of the conditions shown through both mediums. For example, some years ago Mrs. A. described a procession of nuns. She said they were passing "right through the circle." Their hands were shackled, and as they passed they implored us to release them. A curious condition, which I presume is best explained by Swedenborg's doctrine of correspondences, the chained hands being the outward representation of their spiritual state of bondage. Mrs. B. had no knowledge of this peculiar experience, but at one of her séances she also described a group of nuns standing near by. "How strange," she remarked, "they are all looking at their feet. I wonder what they are looking at? Why, their feet are chained! How curious!"

Unfortunate creatures that have met physical death in a state of intoxication, have been sadly numerous at both series of séances. They have not the slightest suspicion that they have passed out of the flesh. Some fancy they are still staggering through the streets; others are in a stupor. One man brought to Mrs. A. was still clinging to a lamp-post, so he imagined, and when he was spoken to, protested in characteristic drunken fashion that he was "all right." His skull had been fractured by a heavy fall, and death must have been instantaneous to have so rigidly fixed his mind upon the last conscious act of his life on earth. It was no easy matter to rouse this poor fellow. His overruling desire seemed to be to get home; but he wished that he was able to take care of himself. When at last the truth dawned upon him, his first thought was of his mother; a blessed thought,—it would prove his salvation, so we were informed.

One of the many striking cases that have been treated through Mrs. B. was that of the young man still wild with the excitement of a carousal. "His heart suddenly gave out," the Doctor afterward informed us; but he fancied himself to be still in the gay company, men and women, with whom his last moments were spent. Taking possession of the medium, he boisterously exclaimed, "Fill them up again!" and sings, "We won't go home till morning." His uplifted hand seems to grasp a drinking glass. He is eager to drink a toast, but is uncertain in whose honor it shall be offered. "Here's to," he cries out, and then hesitates. Again he repeats, "Here's to, Here's to —myself. Hurrah, hurrah!" It was very pathetic. The Doctor, however, assured us that his progress would not be slow, for he was good at heart, and, being young, his habits of thought were not fixed. "Merely a wretched victim of the spirit of revelry."

The Last Earthly Thoughts.

It appears that the state of the mind at the moment of death often becomes a most potent factor in determining the immediate condition of disembodied spirit. The literature of modern Spiritualism abounds in evidence of this fact. Cases of spirits engrossed—imprisoned, as it were— in the last thought that occupied their minds on earth, have been brought to our séances in great numbers. To describe them all would require a volume. One man with whose sphere Mrs. A. was connected, was eagerly scanning the stock list of his newspaper, and so intensely absorbed was he in his occupation that he impatiently resented our intrusion when we addressed him. Reading his thoughts, the medium could see that he was an embezzler. He had become deeply involved in speculation. Oh, how he feared exposure!

Mariners, their minds still filled with the panic of shipwreck, have been frequent visitors. One crew fancied they were still in the life-boat. So fully did Mrs. A. penetrate their sphere that the whole scene of the wreck became clear to her vision; and exceedingly graphic was her description of the gigantic mountains of water and the buffeted boat, perilously over-freighted. Occasionally, a glimpse of the sinking ship could be obtained.

How admirable has been the sturdy loyalty displayed by the sea-captains into whose sphere we have been introduced. With them there is not the slightest fear of death; simply the inflexible determination to be faithful to their charge. And when, sometimes only with great difficulty, we have succeeded in withdrawing their minds from the object of their devotion, the spirit of manly submission which governs their thought is most touching.

The Doctor has informed us that actors—especially *good* actors, he was careful to add—upon entering the spirit-world, often become so deeply involved in the characters they have portrayed on the stage that for the time being their own individuality is measurably if not entirely overshadowed. Spirits having fallen into this condition, are extremely difficult to reach. Sometimes, indeed, it is well-nigh impossible to extricate the real self-hood.

The Condition of Murderers.

Will my readers be shocked if I speak briefly of the conditions of murderers as they have been revealed to us? Naturallly, their state is one of painful horror. Sometimes it is the incident of the deed that occupies their mind to the obliteration of every other thought. Those that have been executed often carry into the beyond the overwhelming fear of death. Occasionally, they fancy themselves still on the gallows. Capital punishment is a sin against nature too cruel to contemplate. Others become absorbed in some hideous fancy derived from their crime; they are burying or concealing their victim, or fleeing from pursuit. Mrs. A. was led into the sphere of one man who imagined he was peering in through the window of a little cottage at a sight so terrifying that his hair stood on end from fright. It was the corpse of his victim upon which his gaze was riveted. Slowly would the horrible apparition rise from the floor, stare at him, and then gradually sink back again. How long this wretched soul had been in that state of agonizing torture, we could not learn, for the medium entered so intimately into his condition that she herself nearly swooned from fear and weakness, and we were compelled to bring the sitting to a close. Not, however, before we had succeeded in breaking the horrible spell. When the man discovered that he was free, he ran off with the speed of a hunted deer.

Another man, who had stabbed his victim during a bar-room brawl, imagined himself to be still in the midst of the scene. The medium perceived it all very clearly —the overturned chairs and tables, the flying glasses, the noise and general confusion. After having been aroused and brought to a realization of his true state, this unfortunate man begged us in a whisper not to let "the old mother" know anything about the affair.

On one occasion, after having liberated a spirit of this class, we inquired of the Doctor as to his present condition. He answered, "That man is now in a room; the door opens and a little child enters. She holds out her hands and says, 'Papa, we are all glad to have you come.' The man, however, covers his face with his hands and cries out, 'No, no, no!' Conscience had survived."

The Gambler's Destiny.

The gambler brought to Mrs. B. one evening afforded an impressive illustration of the fact that souls cannot always be judged rightly by external aspects and circumstances. Being controlled by this spirit, the medium, drawing her chair close to the table, acts as if absorbed in a game of cards. "Nine up," she exclaims, as she exultingly throws down on the table an imaginary card. At first the man is too intent upon the game to pay any heed to our words. Soon, however, he becomes interested, and when we suggest that he should now prepare himself for the new life, he cries out, "New life, 'new life,' did you say—is there a new life for me?" Gradually the medium sinks to her knees and clasps her hands in prayer. Then she stands upright with outstretched arms, in an attitude of ecstacy, and exclaims, "The light—the light!"

When conditions are favorable, as many as ten cases often are treated through Mrs. B. at a single sitting. The Doctor is untiring in the work to which he is devoting himself, arduous though it must be. "Their name is legion," he answered when asked whether conditions such as I have described in the foregoing pages are common. The rescue of one, however, usually opens the way to the release of others in a similar state. It is because this is so that he is hopeful that eventually the workers in the higher realms will be in a position promptly to reach each soul as it departs from earth. In the meantime, however, there is a vast work to be done; and he often expresses the wish that mediums might be brought to a realization of the fact that they are able to contribute most valuable aid in overcoming the consequences of humanity's age-long ignorance concerning nature's most delicate process, namely, the separation of the spirit from its fleshly tenement, and its adaptation to a spiritual state of existence.

The following discriptions are culled from the records of many séances with Mrs. A. as the medium:

A Black Abyss.

A spirit suddenly takes possession of the medium and begs to be told how he can be released from the darkness which surrounds him. Without warning, in an instant's time, he says he was hurled as if from a cannon into a black abyss. He cries out that he is suffocating, and implores our help. "Pray for me!" he exclaims repeatedly.

Entered Spirit Life Before Her Time.

A poor woman comes begging to be allowed to rest. She confesses that she forced herself into spirit life "before her time," and says she has been wandering without rest ever since. She has traversed a land dark and rough, filled with miry marshes, stones and brambles. Her feet are bruised, and she is weary, and oh, so lonely! In the far distance stretched green fields and bright woodlands; but though her journey had been a long and toilsome one, the bright country seemed no nearer. While speaking, she appeared to be standing in a swamp. the tall, coarse grass almost level with her head. She held up her hands and begged for help. Suddenly, the grass vanished, the ground became firm and dry, and a light streamed down upon her, making visible a narrow foot-path. The scene fades from the medium's vision while the woman is rejoicing that at last the way is made clear.

Still Acting His Part.

The scene is the stage of a theater. The auditorium is not in view, but the footlights are plainly visible. Upon the boards appears a man entirely absorbed in acting the part of Macbeth. He is the personification of earnestness. His gestures are almost laughably tragic. As he cries, "Lay on, Macduff," Macduff makes his appearance, and a fierce sword combat ensues. Suddenly Macbeth drops his sword and gazes at his opponent in amazement; for he recognizes in Macduff a dear friend and comrade whom he knows to be "dead." The truth seems instantly to dawn upon him; he grasps the dead man's hand, and they pass out of sight arm in arm. It is explained that the spirit who acted the part of Macduff, impelled by the ardor of his affection, had long been striving to enter the very positive sphere of his friend, and having asked the assistance of the band, was helped to introduce himself in the very natural way he adopted.

"Stage Struck."

The medium says she seems to be on the stage of a theater. Various scenes, the Forest of Arden, in " As You Like It," and others unlike any she ever saw, pass rapidly before her vision. A man stands before her posing theatrically. He wears an enormous slouch hat; a large black cloak is thrown across his shoulders. One of the circle remarks that the person probably is an actor. He answers, "Yes, and I *can* act too;" and speaks majestically of the "plaudits of the multitude." Strutting back and forth, he pompously speaks scraps of Shakespeare. "I am the melancholy Dane," he declares. The man has not the slightest idea that he is in another state of existence; and when he is asked if he is not weary of his life, answers "No, no, it is glorious." After a time, however, the medium sees that he begins to suspect that things are not exactly as he believes them to be. Then the stage glamour with which he has succeeded in surrounding himself gradually disappears. He dwindles miserably in size, while the stagey costume is transformed into rags. His appearance disgusts the medium, and his true character reveals itself. She exclaims, "Why, the man is a perfect hypocrite." He becomes angry, yet is in a panic of fear and clings to the medium with the desperation of a person clinging to the edge of a precipice. After he has been withdrawn, we are told that being now awakened to his real condition, he is within reach of his guardian spirit. Shams soon fade in the immortal realms.

A Fine Lady's Presence.

A large, dignified woman presents herself. She wears a black watered-silk dress over an enormous hoop-skirt. On her jeweled hands are lace mittens. Her hair is worn in the style of the middle period of the last century. Disdainful in manner, she seems to feel that she is not being treated with the deference due to her social station. We assure her we have no desire to be disrespectful, but suggest that in the spiritual world, of which she now is an inhabitant, the artificial social standards of earth no longer prevail. On the contrary, persons are measured in accordance with the intrinsic worth of character and achievement. She listens evidently as we expatiate upon this subject. Gradually, as her soul perceptions are awakened, the haughty bearing vanishes; and at last her large skirt collapses, she "shrivels all up." presenting a most wretched appearance. The medium perceives that she is accompanied by a number of associates. It seems these spirits for a long period had continued to be engrossed in the frivolous amusements and empty social observances that had occupied all their thoughts on earth. Long since, however, the condition had become intolerably monotonous. They yearned for something new, and it was this intense longing for a change that enabled the spirit workers to penetrate their sphere. Even now, however, not all are willing to face the sham reality of their condition.

A Gentleman of Leisure.

The scene is a city street. It is night, and a heavy fall of snow covers the ground. A man stands at the door of a large dwelling. He is striving to arouse the inmates, and appears to be very impatient. When the medium first sees him, he is clothed in tatters, and his form seems shrunken; as we address him, however, he is transformed into a fine-looking gentleman, wearing stylish clothes. We ask him whose house it is he seems so anxious to enter. He answers, "Why, it is my home, and I cannot understand why they do not open the door for me." After offering an apology for addressing him, we learn that he has been spending an evening with some friends. "My coachmen met with an accident," he states, "so I thought I would walk home; and now I cannot get in." Then the following dialogue ensues: "Have you not recently suffered from some severe fit of sickness?" "No, sir." "Not a sudden attack of any kind?" "Oh, yes, a slight dizziness, but that amounted to nothing." "Perhaps it was a more serious matter than you imagine?" "What do you mean, sir?" We inform him that he has left the physical body, but he absolutely refuses to accept the statement. "Why, sir, I am alive, and here's my house!" When it is suggested that his house is merely of such stuff as dreams are made of, he ejaculates, "Oh, dreams don't amount to anything!" Suddenly, he cries out, "Where's my house? I don't see it. It's gone. Where am I?" We repeat that he is in the spirit world, adding that good friends are anxious to prepare him for the new life. "But I do not want to die," he exclaims, "I am content to remain on earth." "Nature has decreed otherwise," we suggest, "and it will be wise to strive in a manly way to become reconciled to the changed conditions. Suppose some sudden financial disaster had swept away all your possessions." "That could not have happened," he answers, "and you cannot understand my position, or you would not talk to me in that manner. You cannot understand what it is to have all the comforts, that were mine, a fine home, servants to wait upon me, horses and carriages, and congenial friends." The unfortunate man is utterly crushed, and for a time is silent, when we inquire whether there is not some person "gone before" whose memory he cherishes and whom he should like to meet again. After a time, however, he answers, "Yes, there was one whom I dearly loved years ago; but she was taken from me. Oh! if she had not gone what a different man I might have been!" As he utters these words the medium sees a beautiful female figure away in the distance, " clothed in white raiment." When she describes the apparition, the man seems touched. "For some time after she left me," he soliloquizes, "I felt that she was near. Often I thought I saw her when I was alone in my room; but I cast it all from me as imagination." Words of comfort were addressed to him, and the spirit workers informed us that he being aroused, our part of the work was accomplished. The last glimpse the medium had of this wretched soul, he seemed to be "huddled up in a corner."

The Interrupted Mass.

The interior of a Roman Catholic Church is presented to the vision of the medium. A priest stands at the altar preparing the mass. The body of the church is well filled with attendants. The priest seems to be aware of our presence and looks upon us with annoyance as intruders. We ask him whether he is teaching his people that which will promote their growth as spiritual beings. He answers warmly that he teaches the doctrines of the true church. The congregation is now showing interest in the controversy. As the excitement increases, a number of priests rush into the place, among them a large noble-looking man who pushes his way to the front, despite the attempts of the others to hold him back. He addresses the people, imploring them to burst the chains that hold their souls in bondage, and, pointing to a door toward which he walks, invites all who will to join him in escaping from the thraldom which keeps them away from the true spiritual life. A number rise and follow him; they emerge from the building, and can be seen moving along through fresh green fields, everything becoming brighter as they proceed. Many, however, remain behind, seemingly in a state of utter indifference toward everything that occurred.

Rescued from Theological Bigotry.

A man, speaking through the medium, remarks, "I understand I can learn something about the law of progression by coming here." "Yes," we answer, "soul progression is a great and glorious fact." "If true," he responds, "it is indeed a stupendous fact." "And glorious," we suggest. But this he is not ready to grant, for he still is inclined to be faithful to the old theology. The medium now perceives that he is one of a number of persons. They are encompassed by a thick fog, no doubt representative of their bigotry. Just beyond the heavy cloud there stretches a bright and beautiful country. A man is seen coming down the mountain side. He approaches the cloud and delivers a poetical address on the subject of spiritual unfoldment, making use of the flower as an illustration. His head is shaven, and he is clad in the garb of a friar, a long gray gown with a corded belt at the waist. After he has finished his address, we ask him if he is a member of any ecclesiastical order. He answers, "The society of Jesus; but no longer." Adding, "Blame no one." Bidding us farewell, he places his arm over the shoulder of the man who first spoke, and they walk away together up the hillside, gradually vanishing from the medium's view.

Waiting for the Day of Judgment.

The medium says she is among the ruins of an old castle. Decay and desolation are apparent on all sides, while the high walls of the crumbling edifice appear to cast gloomy shadows upon the scene. In this dreary place a company of soldiers is encamped. Some of the men are lying listlessly on the ground, others pace back and forth among the fallen stones and decaying débris. We ask for the leader, and immediately a man presents himself. He stands with arms folded and head bent, manifesting great dejection. "What service are you now in," we inquire. "None whatsoever," he replies. "We are only waiting." "Waiting for what?" "For the sound of the last trump." "Are you quite certain that trump ever will sound?" "I have been taught so, and never have questioned the teaching." Gently we suggested to him that he was laboring under a sad error, and advise him to abandon the false notions which have been the means of holding him and his men away from the realities and activities of true spiritual life, which is one of continuous growth. "How am I to know what you say is true?" he inquires. We inform him that the knowledge has been transmitted from wise and good beings—angels of wisdom, who are anxious that all the dwellers in the darkness or ignorance and falsity should learn the truth and speedily take advantage of it. The man acted like one receiving some startling, almost incredible intelligence, and seemed dazed by it all. His language and manner indicated that he was a person of more than ordinary character and culture. He will now progress.

A Clergyman in Spirit Life.

The medium first saw a small table or reading desk, on which lay an opened book, resembling the Bible, being bound in pliable leather with gilt edges. Upon the book a man's hand rested negligently. The desk passed from her view, and then she saw a man sitting right in the midst of the circle. His legs were crossed, and he twirled a pair of eyeglasses around his fingers. His manner denoted *ennui* (probably assumed). The medium described him as being "dressed like a minister—an Episcopal minister." "Clergyman," he promptly suggested in correction, pronouncing the word with unctious precision. We intimated that we should be pleased to enter into conversation with him. After some hesitation, he informed us that he had come to learn something in regard to Spiritualism; his manner of making that declaration being supercilious, Spiritualism being pronounced with a sneer. Surmising that the man might not yet have discovered that he had passed through death, we expatiated upon the wondrous naturalness of the change, which for that reason often took place without the person becoming aware of it. But he stated, "Oh, I am very well aware of all that. The fact is, a number of my parishioners are here with me, and I find myself unable to instruct them how to proceed; for *surely there must be something more than this.*" The text, "Strait is the gate," etc., was quoted, the suggestion being offered that only through self-renunciation could spiritual advancement be achieved—only by the abandonment of the pride of self could the inner nature become sufficiently active to discern the light which shines to guide the pilgrim's footsteps to the portals of that gate opening into the true life. He seemed to feel that this was the truth, and appeared to realize its full significance. We advised him to cast aside his pride and go to his people with a frank confession of his ignorance. In that way he would gain spiritual strength sufficient to lead them all into the light. There was no longer anything like disdainfulness in his manner; and the word "lead" seemed very offensive to him. "No," he exclaimed bitterly, "I will *not* 'lead' them, but shall go only as one of them."

A Palace of Pleasure.

While I was making the usual preliminary remarks, addressed to the invisible auditors, the medium hears a man exclaim in an angry tone, "Don't you attempt to come in here. We have no time for any of your d—— nonsense." He stood at the entrance of a kind of "pleasure palace." It was a gorgeous affair, and being constructed largely of glass, the interior of the palace was clearly visible. In the glare of myriads of bright lights, the gay decorations, and the palms and other tropical plants made a most brilliant display. The medium having finished this description, "Sunset," a bright attendant spirit, manifested her presence, and urged us with unusual warmth to drive off the person barring the entrance to the place. "No longer shall that man be permitted to hold those unfortunate souls in subjection to his selfish will," she exclaimed. "Drive him away!" In the name of Infinite Goodness and Power, we commanded him to stand aside. His sense of guiltiness made a coward of him, his power vanished, and he fell to the ground, groveling in abject fear. The doors flew open, and the occupants of the place speedily rushed down the steps. Most of them were women, with painted faces and dressed in all sorts of gaudy costumes. One of them addressed us, expressing joy and gratitude that at last the hour of deliverance had arrived. Long had they been weary of their life, she said, but the influence the man exerted over them was so powerful they could not escape. Indeed, even if they had succeeded in breaking away, they hardly could have known how to proceed. And now, though they were all most eager for the opportunity to improve their condition, they felt that it would not be easy to break from slavery to their old habits of life. The structure had completely vanished before the medium was withdrawn from this peculiar sphere.

A Lake of Slime.

"It is very dark, and the atmosphere is heavy and oppressive," says the medium. She seems to be standing at the edge of a great black opening. Peering down into its depths, she discovers a mass of black slime.

"Why, there are people in it," she exclaims, in horror. "They are just wallowing in it." We quote for their benefit the scriptural saying, "The Light shineth in the darkness, but the darkness comprehendeth it not." Holding their hands up to their faces, they cry out, "No, no, not the light; we cannot stand the light!" We suggest that it is the light of wisdom and mercy; the light that discerns the goodness within the depths of every child of the Infinite. A faint light now shines down on the scene, while a rough footpath appears leading away from the slimy waters. Eagerly the people scramble on to this pathway, and as they move along, the medium sees that they have entered what looks like a dense forest. It is one step upward,—a gloomy place,—but they now have a firm foothold, and dull despair has surrendered to cheerful hope.

CHAPTER XXXIII.

Spiritualism as It Is, and the Message It Has for the World.

THE poetic and prophetic John of Patmos record, said when rapt in the ecstacy of vision, "I saw another angel fly in the midst of heaven having the everlasting gospel, to preach unto them that dwell upon the earth, and every nation, and kindred, and tongue, and people." (Rev. 14:6.)

God being Spirit, and consciousness, and love, and purpose, and will, this could have been no other angel than the angel messenger of a pure Spiritualism. Such angels are the heralds, the advance guards of new cycles, or new and nobler dispensations.

This angelic proclamation of the mystic revelator in vision, "the everlasting gospel," embodied, prophetically considered, the Father-motherhood of God, the brother-sisterhood of woman, the equality of all nations, races and tribes, the offering of opportunities to all, the enchanting messages of angels, the sweet inspiring ministries of spirits and the great energizing uplifting law of progress that infills and thrills with divine potency all those stars and suns that stud the ineffable immensities.

What then is the message of Spiritualism to the world? Has it a distinct and definite message? Emphatically it has—and the message is as cheering as it is momentous and mighty! Briefly stated it is this—*Immortality*—a future, conscious existence—*perfectly and satisfactorily demonstrated.*

Discarding blind faith, and fear, and fable and all dreamy emotionalism, it may be affirmed with emphasis that Spiritualists constitute the only body of thinkers in the wide world who make it a point to prove and present— and who actually *do present* the direct, the most irrefragible evidence of a conscious life beyond the grave. This, Spiritualists in all lands claim, and they strenuously, rigidly rivet their claims with the most positive proofs and demonstrations. This, then, is the *message,* the blessed message of all messages!

But this angel messenger of demonstration in planting the tree of life in Hydesville, the new Bethlehem, did not purpose to institute a new theological creed—to establish a new sect—to build up sectarian schools, or create a great church organization with such pharasaic accoutrements and ceremonies as baptisms, reverends, priests, robed bishops and tiara-crowned popes. Nothing of the kind! Its persistent voice was and is, "Walk in the spirit," "the spirit giveth life," "come unto me," "grow in the graces of faith, hope and charity," "eat of the tree of life, and so 'overcome' as to receive now the new name, the white stone, and that fadeless, brilliant, 'the morning star.'"

The message of Spiritualism then, is to you who doubt—you who meditate in the silence. Have no fear. The meteor cannot darken the sun.

The highly developed, harmonial man is immune from demon influences. When lived in moral purity, Spiritualism is the safeguard against—the happy preventive of obsessions, for it wards off and puts up electro-etheric bars against all low insiduous influences from the Tartarean spheres of darkness.

It teaches us that each should become a determined and purposeful conqueror of the discordant conditions of life about him, here and now.

It teaches us to assist others to rise and realize the fulness and wholeness of a true harmonial life here and now.

It teaches us to persist in the highest and noblest service, which service leads to moral success, here and now.

It teaches us to develop the spiritual, making life now and here larger, broader and grander in every way.

It teaches that there is one eternal omnipresent, omniscient, omnipotent, all-energizing *Force* at work, in an evolutionary and orderly way in cosmic dust, in the mineral, the vegetable, the animal, the man, the spirit, and all pointing unerringly to the upper regions of angelic and seraphic blessedness.

Oh, doubting agnostics, this spiritual message is for you—further investigate.

Denying materialists, this message is for you—think, seek, search deeper.

Hoping, fearing sectarists, this message is to you—reason, trust, believe, *know*.

New-thoughtists, this message is to you—look unto the rock from whence ye were hewn, demonstrate, be modest, be just.

Ambitious, mercenary worldlings, this mesage is to you—repent, reform and do it now.

Spiritists, this message is to you—unfold, enlarge, grow up into the higher spiritual life of love, seraphic harmony and transcendent peace.

Weeping, mourning mothers, the forms of whose dear ones are sleeping under the grasses and willows along the hill-sides, this message is to you—be reconciled, for angels are the tender care-takers and educators of your loved ones, in those higher, brighter spheres of innocence.

To the fearing, trembling at death's door, this message is to you—death is but transitional sleep, and to the really good is comparable to the flowering vine which clings, while climbing up the garden wall to bloom in fadeless beauty upon the other side,—prepare yourselves then oh, mortals! by just and holy living, to bravely, calmly and even smilingly face the inevitable.

This everlasting gospel sees in every cemetery an uprising harvest of souls, in every crystal stream a flowing Jordan, in every emerald-clad mountain a present Olivet, in every well-cultivated prairie a Caanan flowing with milk and honey and in every autumnal-ripening sun a benediction of infinite love.

Hearing of the dying or of one ready to die, from a

life's work well done, I say in my soul,—hasten the glad hour of deliverance, for a death spasm is but an uplift to a higher and better stage of existence. Dying is as enchanting as bird-music in leafy June,—golden as a sunset in a sapphire sea of evergreen isles. As my years lengthen, and I come nearer the translation, my heart sings like a wind-harp in calm, complacent joy.

Perfect rest, perfect peace is not obtainable in the body. Wandering in lands afar, and drinking from many fountains, I still sought for more crystal waters. Feasting at many luxuriant banquets, I still hungered for that inspirational bread that comes daily out of heaven. Listening to the solos and orchestras that cheer church and palace, I cried out all the more for those fascinating melodies that thrill with joy and ecstasy unspeakable, the blessed homes of the angels.

Earth's incompleteness saddens, tires me. Tarry not, O beautiful death angel, for under your mask is the majesty of immortality. Often the restful face of the corpse is wreathed in a subdued smile, caused by a rift in the cloud, a glimpse of loving, waiting spirit friends. This is the glorious victory of Spiritualism.

Bearing Testimony.

Hundreds of preachers in recent years have borne and are bearing testimony to the truth of a conscious converse between the worlds material and spiritual.

The Rev. H. W. Momerie, late professor of logic and metaphysics in King's College, London, exclaimed in a sermon:

"I say Christ's Christianity, for there are plenty of Christianities in the world. But Christ's consists in perfecting the individual character. His salvation is neither more nor less than self-development. Christ's plan was a very simple one; it is all summed up in a single word, love. He taught that men were to be saved by Divine love, and that as angels ministered in the past, so angels and spirits minister to men today. There are no walls of brass between the worlds visible and invisible. And if you look into the rationale of this, you will see that the plan of salvation is profoundly philosophical, perfectly in harmony with the best ethics and the highest metaphysics of today.''

The noted English author, Laurence Oliphant, whose name was, in the past so often used in Britain in connection with Spiritualism, summed up his religious convictions in the last years of his life upon one important matter, as follows (see *London Light*): ''As angels minister to mortals; as order is best preserved by having a sun in our solar system; a chief at the head of a nation; a father governing each family; a master controlling each business;—this being the universal law; so, considering the mightiest results with the least waste of energy, I believe in there being a holy personal ruler at the head of the whole moral universe, which Spiritual Ruler was the most potent figure in all accredited history, Jesus Christ.''

The distinguished Methodist, Bishop J. P. Newman, affirms this in a funeral sermon pamphlet before me.

''Christianity embodies all that is religiously good and true. That the spirits of the departed have returned to earth is a belief that is all but universal. Those eminent in the church for learning and piety have cherished this common faith. Two worlds met in Bible times; but does the communication between the two worlds continue to this day? It was the opinion of Wesley that Swedenborg was visited by the spirits of his departed friends. And it was Paul who asked, 'Are they not all ministering spirits?'"

That illustrious English Spiritualist, the late W. Stainton-Moses (M. A. Oxon), London, wrote with deep religious feeling these lines in an editorial in *Light*.

"There is nothing in the broad truths of that Christ-like Spiritualism, which we are taught, that is incompatible with what the true church requires us to believe. Indeed, there is nothing in what I have learned that conflicts with the simple teaching of the Christ, so far as it has been preserved to us. It is something to know that the whole fabric of religion, so far as it affects man, receives its sanction and stimulus from the doctrines of the higher Spiritualism with which so many of us have made acquaintance. And in days when it is the fashion to bring up time-honored truth for proof anew, when man has largely lost his hold on the ancient faith, when religion as a binding power is losing so much of its vitalizing influence, it is something to feel that by the mercy of that God who never fails to respond to the prayer of His creatures, we are being brought face to face with the reality of our spiritual existence by experimental evidence adapted to our understanding. I see in Spiritualism no contradiction to that which I know of the teaching of Christ."

The Continued Rescue of Souls.

Though obsessions prevail, though vast multitudes of earth's discarnate dwellers people the Cimmerian shadow-lands of Hades, the divine impulse changes not. The altruistic work of rescue goes on. Uplifting grace spans all worlds. The angel voice of good will to men is ever being rechanted. Its echoing words in all spheres are, "Return to thy Father's house."

Absolute annihilation is unthinkable. Nothing can be lost out of existence. God's roughest winds are utilized to stay the plague. The seemingly untimely rains that rust the wheat make autumn fields and forests more fresh and fair. Every winter has its balmy spring, and every ocean its glittering gems. Beneath the ice the crystal waters run. Under the compost the grass is green. Up from the mud the early flowers spring, and beyond the cross lies the crown. Under the roughest mortal exterior there lies the ego, the divine spark, the buried image of God, awaiting the resurrection word "Awake, come up higher!"

Self-Salvation Impossible.

Man, however egotistic and self-opinionated he may be, cannot save himself, cannot unaided fully perfect himself. He can no more do this than the egg can hatch itself without warmth,—no more than the winter-chilled bud can unfold and bloom without a vivifying influx from the spring-time sun. Visible and invisible helpers there must be. The saved man is harmonial, cultured, spiritually unfolded, and royal in thought and deed. He has pressed down the sensual under his feet. He has conquered the selfish. He has subdued all sensuous cognitions, and has attained such a lofty moral altitude of self-mastery through the Christ within, that he can say in all candor, "I am self-poised. I am a law unto myself. I am, in the highest sense of the word, a son of God."

When a depraved, wicked man dies, entering the underworld of conscious life, spirits who can discover the secrets of character, examine the spirit form, especially the brain, for therein was the source of thought and volition. Thus examined and understood, there is unrolled before him the panorama of his past life. Memory does not die with the body. Justice holds the scales. Each must thus come to the judgment. This judgment tribunal past, he is conducted to some disciplinary department of the planet's encircling zone for enlightenment and restoration. Jesus put to death in the flesh, "preached," said the apostle, "to the spirits in prison." Preaching implies opportunity. Gautama Buddha, the light of Asia, doubtless preached for centuries to Asiatic spirits in prison. The philosophers and reformers of all ages, when passing into the higher spheres, continue their work of teaching and preaching to spirits in prison. This spirit of love and charity thrills the souls of all the great moral heroes that graced the earth in agone ages. They are preaching to the morally dead to arouse them to life. Spiritual life is an active life, a social life, a constructive life, a redemptive life. Obsessing spirits are hearing, believing, and multitudes of them are moving up on to higher planes of existence where, after a time, they become divine helpers. Sometimes they bring these dazed, distressed spirits of the lower spheres into quiet, orderly séance rooms that they may the more fully cognize both their shadowy environment and their moral incompleteness. Seeing is knowing. Seeing is the first step to the awakening—seeing kindles the smoldering fires of religious aspiration and soul-unfoldment. Evolution is tireless. Leading, it shouts from every moral mountain top, *"come up higher."*

No Antagonism.

Truth stands upon its own foundation. It is invincible. Light does not antagonize darkness; it simply lifts the Eastern curtains and quietly lets in the morning radiance.

In no possible way does Spiritualism antagonize true and pure Christianity, the basic foundation of which is love to God, love to man and spiritual gifts. "By this," said the Christ, "shall all men know that ye are my disciples, if ye have love one for the other."

If our gospel abounding in spiritual communications be not morally uplifting, if it be not reverential, if it be not Christian in the broadest and highest sense of the word, if it does not touch the soul's depths with conviction, if it does not sweeten the emotions, if it does not quicken the spiritual consciousness and develop justice, freedom, reciprocity, fraternity and pentecostal consecration to the truth, it is of little avail. But Spiritualism—this "everlasting gospel" being of God and aflame with the divine spirit of love does this by arousing the spiritual nature, quickening the inmost self, thereby laying the foundation stones for the "new heaven and the new earth."

Consider, then, once for all that (I speak only for myself) Spiritualism, instead of opposing is the complement of Christ's Christianity. Adapted to this progressive period of time, it is the rounding up, the filling out, or the fulfilling of the Nazarene's prophetic words, "These signs shall follow them that believe," "and greater work than *these* shall *ye* do." And "lo, I am with you always," He exclaimed, "even unto the end of world."

Religious *school-men* and the solid University thinkers of Europe and everywhere, are constantly becoming more careful to draw the line between Petrine and Pauline churchianity and the Christianity of the living, illuminating Christ; and they should draw still more rigid lines of differentiation between a haphazard, fortune-telling, atheistic spiritism and a holy illumined Spiritualism, the one being largely from the lower spirit zones, the other angelic and morally elevating, teaching the reality of spirit helpers, the tremendous disclosure of a present soul-body and the pressing importance of purifying and harmonizing it so far as possible, before the transition, death which can only be accomplished by living the kind, unselfish and religious life. "Being reconciled," said the great gentile apostle, "we are saved by his life." It is not nationality nor color, nor atoning blood, nor confessions of faith that save; but in a word, *character*. It is right purpose, moral conquests and struggles to attain which saves and builds now for eternity.

Few comprehend the innate worth and dignity of humanity, or understand that all are of royal blood and interiorly a part of the Divine Essence, and that they should be so guided by the higher self as to produce moral resurrections and lofty characters here and now.

Earth's swarming races, on different planes of development, are on the way to enlightenment and completeness. They are learning by observations and journeyings through diverse experiences that there can be no permanent happiness, which is not based upon justice and holiness. No mortal, no nation is finished, but all are on the way to the uplands of the better and the higher.

This heaven-born all-inclusive Spiritualism, not only

strenuously affirms that men are spirits now, but that existing consciously hereafter they will be capable of loving converse with their friends still vestured in fleshly bodies, but it persistently affirms the necessity of soul-culture, of spiritual development now and here, by encouraging, pleading of each and all to listen whether sitting in the silence or engaged in the daily occupations of life, to the voice of the higher self. It is no paradox to say that the spirit speaks in the silence.

Though often so stated, Spiritualism is not a religion, is not *the* religion, but is *religion itself,* the tethering and cementing of the finite to the infinite—humanity to Divinity, and is destined to become the universally acknowledged religion of the world before the close of this wonderful century. Such is the prophecy which this moment inspirationally throbs in and thrills my being's depths.

"If you desire to investigate the spiritual, the divine mysteries of nature," wrote that great Spiritualist of Lasatia (born 1575), Jacob Bohme, "investigate your own mind, and ask yourself about the purity of your purpose. Do you desire to put the good teachings which you may receive into practice for the benefit of humanity? Are you ready to renounce all selfish desires, which cloud your mind and hinder you to see the clear light of eternal truth? Are you willing to become an instrument for the manifestation of divine wisdom? Do you know what it means to become united with your own higher self, to get rid of your lower self, to become one with the living, universal power of God, and come into sweet fellowship with angels, and so die to your own insignificant, terrestrial personality? Or do you merely desire to obtain great knowledge, ever evanescent, so that your curiosity may be gratified, and that you may be proud of your science, and believe yourself to be superior to the rest of mankind. Consider, that the depths of divinity can only be searched by the divine spirit itself which is latent or active in you. Real knowledge must come from your own divine interiors, not merely from externals; and they who seek for the essence of things merely in externals may find the artificial color of a thing, but not the true spiritual thing itself."

O Searchers after truth! O students of psychic science! "Try the spirits," watch them closely, test them by their teachings, study rigidly the influences they exert upon their mediumistic subjects. Figs do not grow upon thistles, nor does virtue spring into dazzling brightness from the cesspools of night! Shun, then, the hells; be deaf to the siren songs of demons; pray to the angels, those masters of destiny; love the Christs of the cycling ages; be just to all men, and humbly reverence God.

> Oh, yet we trust that, somehow, good
>   Shall be the final goal of ill;
>   To pangs of nature, sins of will,
> Defects of doubt, and taints of blood.
>
> That nothing walks with aimless feet,
>   That not one life shall be destroyed,
>   Or cast as rubbish to the void
> When God has made his pile complete.
> —*"In Memoriam."*

When Spiritualism, the handmaid of science, of reason, and of Christ's Christianity, with its divine Fatherhood, its motherhood, its brotherhood, its present heavenly ministries, its disciplinary retributions for wrongdoing, its open-heartedness toward all reforms, its self-mastery of the passions; its ideals in the distance unattained, its sweet charities for human misfortunes; its parlor séances and altars of worship; its sacred home influences; its inspiring aid to true religion; its consecrated temples where youth and age may blend in reverential communion; its encouraging words to the sick; its comforting voice to the weeping mourner; its tender messages from the loved ones that have crossed death's silent river into those calmer seas, those holier realms of immortality, where loving hearts ne'er grow cold, sacred friendships never wane and celestial suns never set; when *this* Spiritualism, I repeat, becomes a living knowledge and a practical power the wide world over, as prophesied of and promised by the hosts and the potent hierarchies above us, then will the will of God truly be done upon earth as it is in heaven.

"Peace I leave with you! From days departed
    Floats down the blessing, simple and serene,
Which to his followers, few and fearful hearted,
    With yearning love, thus spake the Nazarene!"

THE END.

www.ingramcontent.com/pod-product-compliance
Lightning Source LLC
Chambersburg PA
CBHW031419150426
43191CB00006B/328